1-2 THESSALONIANS

NCCS | New Covenant Commentary Series

The New Covenant Commentary Series (NCCS) is designed for ministers and students who require a commentary that interacts with the text and context of each New Testament book and pays specific attention to the impact of the text upon the faith and praxis of contemporary faith communities.

The NCCS has a number of distinguishing features. First, the contributors come from a diverse array of backgrounds in regards to their Christian denominations and countries of origin. Unlike many commentary series that tout themselves as international the NCCS can truly boast of a genuinely international cast of contributors with authors drawn from every continent of the world (except Antarctica) including countries such as the United States, Puerto Rico, Australia, the United Kingdom, Kenya, India, Singapore, and Korea. We intend the NCCS to engage in the task of biblical interpretation and theological reflection from the perspective of the global church. Second, the volumes in this series are not verse-by-verse commentaries, but they focus on larger units of text in order to explicate and interpret the story in the text as opposed to some often atomistic approaches. Third, a further aim of these volumes is to provide an occasion for authors to reflect on how the New Testament impacts the life, faith, ministry, and witness of the New Covenant Community today. This occurs periodically under the heading of "Fusing the Horizons and Forming the Community." Here authors provide windows into community formation (how the text shapes the mission and character of the believing community) and ministerial formation (how the text shapes the ministry of Christian leaders).

It is our hope that these volumes will represent serious engagements with the New Testament writings, done in the context of faith, in service of the church, and for the glorification of God.

Series Editors:
Michael F. Bird (Ridley College, Melbourne, Australia)
Craig Keener (Asbury Theological Seminary, Wilmore, KY, USA)

Titles in this series:
Romans Craig Keener
Ephesians Lynn Cohick
Colossians and Philemon Michael F. Bird
Revelation Gordon Fee
John Jey Kanagaraj
1 Timothy Aída Besançon Spencer
2 Timothy and Titus Aída Besançon Spencer
Mark Kim Huat Tan
2 Peter and Jude Andrew Mbuvi

Forthcoming titles:
James Pablo Jimenez
1–3 John Sam Ngewa
Acts Youngmo Cho and Hyung Dae Park
Luke Diane Chen
Matthew Jason Hood
1 Peter Eric Greaux
Philippians Linda Belleville
Hebrews Cynthia Westfall
Galatians Brian Vickers
1 Corinthians B. J. Oropeza
2 Corinthians David deSilva

1-2 THESSALONIANS
A New Covenant Commentary

Nijay K. Gupta

CASCADE Books • Eugene, Oregon

1–2 THESSALONIANS
A New Covenant Commentary

New Covenant Commentary Series

Copyright © 2016 Nijay K. Gupta. All rights reserved. Except for brief quotations in critical publications or reviews, no part of this book may be reproduced in any manner without prior written permission from the publisher. Write: Permissions, Wipf and Stock Publishers, 199 W. 8th Ave., Suite 3, Eugene, OR 97401.

Cascade Books
An Imprint of Wipf and Stock Publishers
199 W. 8th Ave., Suite 3
Eugene, OR 97401

www.wipfandstock.com

PAPERBACK ISBN: 978-1-62564-448-0
HARDCOVER ISBN: 978-1-4982-8653-4
EBOOK ISBN: 978-1-5326-0101-9

Cataloguing-in-Publication data:

Names: Gupta, Nijay K.

Title: 1–2 Thessalonians / Nijay K. Gupta.

Description: Eugene, OR: Cascade Books, 2016 | Series: New Covenant Commentary Series | Includes bibliographical references.

Identifiers: ISBN 978-1-62564-448-0 (paperback) | ISBN 978-1-4982-8653-4 (hardcover) | ISBN 978-1-5326-0101-9 (ebook)

Subjects: LCSH: 1. Bible. Thessalonians—Commentaries. | I. Title. | II. Series.

Classification: BS2725.3 G89 2016 (print) | BS2725.3 (ebook)

Manufactured in the U.S.A.   JULY 8, 2016

Table of Contents

Preface vii
Abbreviations List ix

Introduction 1
   Excursus: Was the Church of the Thessalonians a Male-Only Guild? 8
   Excursus: Gentile Believers Incorporated into Israel's Story through Jesus 12
   Excursus: Hypothesizing a Clandestine Attack 14

Thanksgiving for the Thessalonians (1 Thess 1:1–10) 38
   Fusing the Horizons: Blood-Blind in the New Covenant Community 42
   Fusing the Horizons: Metamorphosis 45

Paul's Blameless Ministry (1 Thess 2:1–12) 50
   Excursus: Gentle or Infants? (2:7b) 55
   Fusing the Horizons: Integrity and Transparency in New Covenant Leadership 59

Praiseworthy Endurance Amidst Persecution (1 Thess 2:13–16) 61
   Excursus: Could Paul Have Written 1 Thess 2:14–16? 62
   Fusing the Horizons: A Hospitable Community for All People 64

Paul's Love, Pride, and Concern (1 Thess 2:17—3:13) 66
   Fusing the Horizons: Life Together 74

Exhortation to Persevere and Grow in Holiness, Love, and Integrity (1 Thess 4:1–12) 77
   Excursus: Sexual Immorality in the Greco-Roman World 79
   Excursus: "Sibling Love" (philadelphia) 84
   Fusing the Horizons: A New Covenant Community of Love 86
   Excursus: Work and Quietness 88
   Fusing the Horizons: Living Quiet Lives in a Noisy World 90

The Hopeful Fate of the Christian Dead (1 Thess 4:13–18) 92
   Fusing the Horizons: The New Covenant People of Hope 100

The Day of the Lord: Preparedness and Perseverance,
Not Prediction (1 Thess 5:1–11) 102
   Excursus: Whose Peace and Security? 105
   Fusing the Horizons: War and Peace: The New Covenant Community in Action 108

Final Instruction (1 Thess 5:12–28) 111
   Fusing the Horizons: The New Covenant Community, A People of Prayer 119

Thanksgiving and Hope (2 Thess 1:1–12) 120
   Excursus: Eternal Destruction (2 Thess 1:9)? 126
   Fusing the Horizons: Can Suffering for the Kingdom Be a Blessing? 128

Perseverance and Hope (2 Thess 2:1–17) 131
   Fusing the Horizons: Living beyond Fear 144

Mission and Community (2 Thess 3:1–18) 145
   Fusing the Horizons: Leadership and Work 153

Bibliography 155

Subject Index 163

Scripture Index 183

Preface

To say that researching for and writing this commentary was a delight would be an understatement. It was an act of joyful sanctification to bathe myself in the Greek and English texts of 1–2 Thessalonians on nearly a daily basis for a couple of years. Sometimes it is questioned whether yet another commentary is needed, not least on 1–2 Thessalonians where there are already a number of good works on the shelves. My perspective is that it is an ongoing exercise of hearing the Word of God afresh. I was eager to write this commentary for the joy of my own learning, and doing "theological reasoning" about what these letters mean for us today. As I have had opportunities to share some of my research and findings with students, I have become more and more convinced that 1–2 Thessalonians are too-often-overlooked gems in Scripture. We glimpse some of the most striking moments of Paul as vulnerable, humble pastor and friend. We get a sense for how Paul calls believers to respond to suffering. We learn about the dignity and worth of good, honest labor as productive work as well as public witness to the gospel. First and Second Thessalonians have a unique ability to speak to us, not in spite of the fact that they do not instruct in a general and generic manner, but because they are so heavily contextualized. We are privileged to catch a glimpse of Paul's "real life," "real relationships," and "real struggles." And we see an Apostle, his apostolic companions, and his fellow believers come together as a household of faith under God the Father and through the unique Son, Messiah Jesus, to encourage one another. It is a beautiful display of the church.

My thanks go to the series editors, Michael Bird and Craig Keener, for the invitation to be involved in this series. I am especially grateful for their vision to acquire a globally diverse set of authors, and for their being mindful about including voices of women and ethnic minorities. There were a number of scholars who were kind enough to share with me unpublished materials on the Thessalonian Correspondence; my gratitude goes to them: Karl Donfried, Gene Boring, Todd Still, John Byron, Andy Johnson, Steve Walton, and Michael Gorman.

I presented some of my research findings to the Biblical Ethics group of the Society of Biblical Literature, and my appreciation goes to them for creating an opportunity for helpful feedback. Also, two students at George Fox Seminary—Evan Simmons and Daniel Bela—journeyed with me through the Greek text of 1–2 Thessalonians over the course of the 2014–15 year contributing many insights into these texts and stimulating my own curiosity. I would also like to thank the George Fox University and Seminary Faculty Development Committee for awarding me a period of research leave to complete this book (Grant GFU2015L05).

This commentary is dedicated to my family: my wife, Amy, for her patience when I was working intensely on this book, and her Christian model as "loyalty that works . . . love that labors . . . and endurance driven by hope in our Lord Messiah Jesus" (1 Thess 1:3); for my children (Simryn, Aidan, and Libby) for the play-filled delight they bring to my life. They are my "glory and joy" (1 Thess 2:20)!

(NB: In the commentary, we have preferred to use "Messiah" instead of "Christ." Secondly, all biblical quotations are from the NRSV except for 1-2 Thessalonians where I have supplied my own translation. When there are any exceptions, they are marked.)

Abbreviations List

AB	Anchor Bible Commentary
ACCS	Ancient Christian Commentary on Scripture
AJPS	*Asian Journal of Pentecostal Studies*
ANTC	Abingdon New Testament Commentary
BBR	*Bulletin for Biblical Research*
BECNT	Baker Exegetical Commentary on the New Testament
BNTC	Black's New Testament Commentary
BTB	*Biblical Theology Bulletin*
BZNW	*Beihefte zur Zeitschrift für die neutestamentliche Wissenschaft*
CBQ	*Catholic Biblical Quarterly*
CBR	*Currents in Biblical Research*
CTJ	*Calvin Theological Journal*
DPL	Dictionary of Paul and His Letters
EBC	Expositor's Bible Commentary
EKKNT	Evangelisch-Katholischer Kommentar zum Neuen Testament
ExpTim	*Expository Times*
HTR Pearson	*Harvard Theological Review*
HTS	*Hervormde Teologiese Studies*
ICC	International Critical Commentary
JBL	*Journal of Biblical Literature*
IVPNTC	InterVarsity Press New Testament Commentary

JSNT	*Journal for the Study of the New Testament*
JSNTSup	Journal for the Study of the New Testament Supplement Series
JTI	*Journal of Theological Interpretation*
L-N	Louw-Nida, *Greek-English Lexicon of the New Testament*
LNTS	Library of New Testament Studies
NCB	New Century Bible
NIB	New Interpreter's Bible
NICNT	New International Commentary on the New Testament
NIDB	New Interpreter's Dictionary of the Bible
NIGTC	New International Greek Testament Commentary
NIVAC	New International Version Application Commentary
NTL	New Testament Library
NTR	New Testament Readings
NTS	*New Testament Studies*
NTT	New Testament Theology
PAST	Pauline Studies
PNTC	Pillar New Testament Commentary
RHPR	*Revue d'Histoire et de Philosophie Religieuses*
SBLDS	Society of Biblical Literature Dissertation Series
SoGBC	Story of God Biblical Commentary
SHBC	Smyth & Helwys Bible Commentary
SNTSMS	Society of New Testament Studies Monograph Series
SP	Sacra Pagina
TLZ	*Theologische Literaturzeitung*
WBC	Word Biblical Commentary

WUNT	Wissenschaftliche Untersuchungen zum Neuen Testament
ZECNT	Zondervan Exegetical Commentary on the New Testament
ZTK	*Zeitschrift für Theologie und Kirche*

Introduction

"Everything that is done in the world is done by hope" —LUTHER

"Hope means hoping when everything seems hopeless"
—G.K. CHESTERTON

"Faith goes up the stairs that love has built and looks out the windows which hope has opened." —CHARLES SPURGEON

Paul's message to the Thessalonian church in 1 Thessalonians can be summarized in one word—"hope." Hope, for Paul, was not a word representative of mere longings or wishful thinking. It was, not unlike we see in Hebrews, something certain, but invisible. Hope was the word Paul used to talk about the invisible (but real) future promised by the invisible (but real) God who gave the most certain assurances of the fulfillment of his promises in the death and resurrection of Messiah Jesus as well as the "deposit" of the Holy Spirit.

The word "hope" only appears a handful of times in these letters (1 Thess 1:3; 2:19; 4:13; 5:8; 2 Thess 2:16), but it represents well Paul's central emphasis: *in the tumult, chaos, confusion, and rough-and-tumble of life, you must trust God and God's future by moving forward in faith and faithfulness.* Hope is his word for a *targeted* faith, anticipatory faith, quite similar to what we see in Heb 11:13. According to Hebrews, the Old Testament people of faith did not live in the world of the final fulfillment of God's promises, but "saw it all from a distance and welcomed it" (NLT). Another translation says they "greeted it from afar" (RSV). While they obviously never reached it, they mapped their journey towards it, as it were, and ran with outstretched arms. Their job, in their time, was not to get to the destination, but to live their present life in the light of that hope, to navigate their vessel (to change the metaphor) according to that beacon.

Hope, in the Christian vocabulary, is a worldview word. If "faith" represents the reliance on an alternative reality based on the revelation of God according to his work and words vis-à-vis *the past and present*, then "hope" involves the sustaining of a present alternative view of reality based on what God has promised to do *in the future*. Christians do not look ahead simply in order to be done with life and float away to eternal bliss in heaven. They lean on hope to survive, live, and even *thrive* in the present by seeing through God's eyes, and particularly God's promises about what he is going to do.

We might better understand what Paul says in 1 Thessalonians, and why he says it the way he does, by thinking through the social nature of how we understand reality. Social anthropologist Clifford Geertz explains that all humans develop "webs of significance" that sustain a larger world around us. It is that intertexture of symbols, relationships, and frameworks that give us stability and comfort in life.[1] However, there are always threats and challenges to our world-structure. The question that remains is whether or not one's symbolic world-system can accommodate and maintain its integrity in light of perplexities. Geertz goes on to argue that religious systems are particularly designed to secure and stabilize the human and community under just such circumstances if they are fit for the task.

What does this have to do with Paul? It is easily recognized that Paul writes 1 Thessalonians to a community that is beginning to lose its confidence and foundation of its faith. There are problems, questions, and perplexities on many levels and in a variety of areas. This triggers a kind of "fight or flight" reaction that could cause serious problems in the future. Paul, though he was not a modern social anthropologist, knew that he had to help them re-establish *terra firma* beneath their feet and their weak knees. He did so by anchoring their faith to the past (and their exemplary reception of the gospel), to the present (as they have shown ongoing resilience and love in recent times), and especially their future (as their hope is in a coming Lord Jesus).

This letter, 1 Thessalonians, is Paul's work as a master-builder who shapes a distinctly Christian worldview that profoundly brings together heaven and earth. Christians live in "waiting" (1:10), as they have one eye on the sky and anticipate the descending rider-of-the-clouds (4:17). They do this, not to abandon the physical earth, but to await the Sovereign and Judge who will finally bring justice to an unjust and cruel world. However,

---

1. See Geertz 1973.

if one eye looks up and forward towards the future return of the Lord, the other eye is fixed on the earthly work of *today*. Paul uses the language of *work* throughout the letter—the Thessalonians' work (1:3), Paul's unending manual labor (2:9), the ministry of the apostles (3:5), and the expectation that all Christians will live daily lives of honest and fruitful productivity (4:11; 5:13). Christian hope is not star-gazing. Christian hope is not lazy— Paul made sure of it. Martin Luther echoes a Pauline conviction when he writes that "Everything that is done in the world is done by hope," but that hope is seen *in the doing of life*.[2]

Christians live in hope, an idea captured remarkably well by Aristotle's pithy saying, "Hope is the dream of a waking man."[3] I think Paul would have adjusted this a bit to say, "Hope in Jesus is the vision that drives believers who work and witness in a dark world as they dream of a redeemed tomorrow" (1 Thess 5:8; 2 Cor 5:7).

Thessalonica and the Thessalonian Church

The City of Thessalonica

In 316 BC, Thessalonica was built on the site of Therme below the Hortiates mountains. Macedonian military leader (and later king) Cassander named this city he founded after his wife, the daughter of Philip II and half-sister of Alexander. Thanks in no small part to Thessalonica's port, it became a prominent city.[4] In 187 BC, King Philip V (221–179) permitted Thessalonica to issue its own coinage, further boosting its economy.

When Rome took control of Macedonia (168 BC), it was divided into four republics and Thessalonica became capital of the second district. In the following years Thessalonica made several important political moves; firstly, it refused to support a revolt against Rome among Macedonian cities led by Andriscus (149 BC). Instead, it hailed Roman praetor Metellus,

---

2. Later in the commentary we will demonstrate that Paul was likely influenced in his thinking on this matter by the story that Jesus tells in Mark 13:34–37. Even though 1 Thessalonians was undoubtedly written before Mark, Paul probably knew of this kind of Jesus tradition. For a case made that Paul was especially drawing from the Jesus tradition linked to Matthew 24 (more specifically), see Shogren 2012: 31–37; cf. Rigaux 1956: 98–101.

3. See Diogenes 1853: 18.

4. Nigdelis 2015: 2.

suppressor of the revolt, as "savior."[5] A few years later, Thessalonica was named the capital of the province of Macedonia. The Romans took special interest in this city largely for its size and location.[6] They built the Via Egnatia, a roadway that ran east-west from Dyrrhachium on the Adriatic Sea to Thessalonica. It was intended, in the first place, for military use, but became a major thoroughfare for trade and travel more broadly.

About a century later, after Julius Caesar was murdered, Thessalonica again shrewdly supported Octavian and Mark Antony over and against Brutus and Cassius. In return for this loyalty, Antony bestowed upon Thessalonica the status of *civitas libera* (free city). This special privilege meant that Thessalonians could operate with considerable autonomy while also receiving support from Rome.[7] Additionally it received tax concessions. It is no exaggeration to say, then, that this status "ushered in a prosperous new era for Thessalonica."[8] By the time of Paul, Thessalonica was a large, cosmopolitan city; Antipater of Thessalonica referred to it at the "mother of all Macedonia."[9] The largest ethnic population in Thessalonica at that time was Greeks, but there is evidence for the presence of other groups including Italians, Thracians, and Jews.

Religion in Thessalonica

The religious atmosphere in Roman Thessalonica was diverse. While traditional Greek deities were widely honored, including Zeus, Asclepius, Aphrodite, and Demeter, the city also dedicated worship to Egyptian gods such as Serapis and Isis. In 1917, an ancient temple was discovered in Thessalonica that is now called the Serapeion. This temple probably dates to the third century BC. Thessalonians also had an interest in the myth of Cabirus. We learn from Clement of Alexandria the legend of two brothers who killed a third sibling and buried him at the foot of Mount Olympus. Cabirus is depicted in worship as a young man with no beard. Devotees worshipped the murdered Cabirus as a savior who would return and bless the people, especially the poor.[10]

5. See Smith 2004: 57.
6. Nigdelis 2015: 4.
7. See Harris 2013: 270.
8. Donfried 2002: 35.
9. *Palatine Anthology* 4.228.
10. While it was once common for scholars to assume the prominence of this cult in Paul's time, this is now questioned; see Pillar 2013: 103–5.

We should also add that Thessalonica established a cult in honor of the goddess Roma. Furthermore, they built a temple for Caesar. The Thessalonians, as noted above, understood the significance of showing loyalty and respect to Rome. Coins have been discovered that identify Caesar as divine. To challenge the divinity of Caesar would be a threat against Rome itself. This may offer important background for understanding the seriousness of the threats against Paul and his ministry when he was brought before the city officials (the politarchs) on the accusation that he was supporting a rival king named Jesus (Acts 17:5–6).

Paul in Thessalonica

While Paul mentions his coming to Thessalonica in 1 Thessalonians, the book of Acts contains a number of details about his experience there.[11] While in Troas (Asia Minor), Paul received a vision of a "man of Macedonia" begging him to cross over into Macedonia to help his people (Acts 16:9). Paul and Silas wasted no time setting sail into Samothrace and Neapolis to bring the gospel to the Macedonians. He eventually went to Philippi where his ministry caused a stir and locals accused them before the authorities. They were beaten and imprisoned, but the Lord miraculously delivered them. Before departing from Philippi, Paul and Silas encouraged the new believers there including Lydia, the first convert of Europe.

Paul and Silas travelled through Amphipolis and Apollonia to Thessalonica. They went to the Thessalonian Jewish synagogue and Paul preached about Messiah Jesus on three Sabbath days (17:1–2). Luke recounts that "Some of them were persuaded and joined Paul and Silas, as did a great many of the devout Greeks and not a few of the leading women" (17:4).

Some jealous Jews incited "ruffians" (F. F. Bruce refers to them as a "rent-a-mob"!) to turn the city against Paul and Silas. Unable to locate the two strangers, the mob attacked Paul's host Jason and other new believers in Jesus. They were brought before the city authorities under this accusation: "These people who have been turning the world upside down have come here also, and Jason has entertained them as guests. They are all

---

11. Some scholars question the historicity of Acts and, thus, its relevance for reconstructing Paul's experience there. However, this commentary follows the lead of a number of scholars who accept the general accounts of Luke's narrative understanding that, while he had his own theological interests, he was still intending to convey the history of the earliest church. See Keener 2012.

acting contrary to the decrees of the emperor, saying that there is another king named Jesus" (Acts 17:6–7).

While Jason and the others were released when they posted bail, still the city was perturbed by this matter. Paul and Silas took their leave under the cover of darkness, making their way to Beroea (17:10). Luke makes it a point to say that the Jews there were more receptive to the gospel than in Thessalonica (17:11). Still, Paul's Thessalonian troubles were far from over. Some Jews from Thessalonica heard about Paul's successful ministry in Beroea and travelled there to turn those people against him as well (17:13). Thus, Paul was forced on to Athens. After Acts 17, Luke offers no more clues regarding the situation in Thessalonica.[12] What we surmise about the situation that led to Paul's writing of the Thessalonian letters must come primarily from historical reconstruction and guesswork based on information from the letters themselves.

The Church of the Thessalonians

Before considering the exigencies that gave rise to 1–2 Thessalonians, it behooves us to consider the nature of the church of the Thessalonians. According to Luke, *some* Jews responded positively to his preaching, a *great number* of "devout Greeks" and "not a few leading women" (Acts 17:4). As for the first group, Luke's *some* is probably a small number, given how he represents the overall offense of Paul's gospel to the Jews in Thessalonica (e.g., versus Beroea). Who are these "devout Greeks"? They are Gentile "god-fearers," non-Jews who attached themselves in some way to the Jewish synagogue. Perhaps they were attracted to Jewish morality, worship of this one particular god, or the Jewish festivals.[13] Some scholars have expressed doubts about the historical reliability of Luke's account, especially because Paul characterizes the Thessalonian believers as those who turned away from idols to the one God and to Jesus (1 Thess 1:9–10).[14] This appears to some to mean that the church was comprised almost exclusively of Gentile idol-worshippers who would have had no association with Judaism.[15] How-

12. Luke does mention certain Thessalonian believers who cross paths with Paul, namely, Aristarchus and Secundus (20:4; cf. 27:2).

13. See Dunn 2009: 560–61; Runesson et al. 2008: 121.

14. See especially Ascough 2003: 202–3.

15. See Gaventa 1998: 20; Ascough 2015: 9. Richard Ascough argues that Luke's account in Acts 17 about the first converts to Christianity in Thessalonica being Jews and god-fearers cannot be harmonized with the impression from 1 Thessalonians. He

ever, as Todd Still notes, if Paul had attracted Jews and god-fearing Gentiles away from the synagogue towards faith in Jesus, this would explain Jewish hostility against Paul that is attested in both Acts and 1 Thessalonians (see 1 Thess 2:15).

> If Paul did have some success in luring God-fearing and well-off Gentiles away from the synagogue by his preaching and continued to poach on Jewish preserves even after he had been cut off from the synagogue, then it is reasonable to think that he would have provoked a negative Jewish response. Not only would the Jewish community have viewed Gentile adherents as potential proselytes, but they would also have valued their financial and social support. While Jewish jealousy or zeal incited by Paul's missionary activity among synagogue adherents only partially explains Paul's conflict with Thessalonian Jews, it may well have been a primary reason that Paul encountered Jewish opposition in Thessalonica (and elsewhere).[16]

The third category of people Luke mentions in Acts 17:4 is "leading women," women of wealth and influence (i.e., elite). It is possible that these women were benefactors to the Jewish community in Thessalonica. Lynn Cohick offers the example of Capitolina, a Gentile woman who gave money to the synagogue at Tralles (Asia Minor).[17] This aligns with other examples in the New Testament of women of means attracted to the gospel of Messiah Jesus (such as Phoebe, Romans 16). Although the church must have had a few wealthy believers, the majority of the church would have been relatively poor, the kind of people who work with their hands (1 Thess 2:9; 4:11; 5:14).[18] How large was the church in Thessalonica? Narrowing this number down is impossible, but Eugene Boring is probably correct that we are talking about dozens, not hundreds.[19]

---

explains: "The natural understanding of this text is that these initial adherents in Thessalonike were not Jewish or even Jewish sympathizers. They were, in fact, non-Jews who worshiped one or more of the many deities in the Greek and Roman pantheon, if not also a few local gods alongside them. The Thessalonian Christ group is thus a Gentile group at its core" (9).

16. Still 1999: 70–71.

17. See Cohick 2009: 187. Bruce Winter also notes a mid-first century AD inscription in honor of the civic patroness Junia Theodora of Corinth; see Winter 1994: 46.

18. See Nestor 2012: 64–65; cf. Witherington 2006: 43.

19. Boring 2012: 210.

Excursus : Was the Church of the Thessalonians a Male-Only Guild?

Richard Ascough has made the argument that the church in Thessalonica may have started as an artisan guild or association that, as a group, embraced Paul's good news about Messiah Jesus.[20] Firstly, he notes that Thessalonica had many guilds of various kinds. Secondly, Paul himself refers to *working with hands* (4:11), which may identify his readers as co-members of an artisan association. For Ascough, this would align with what appears to be a sole focus of the letter on *men* (see 1 Thess 4:4), thus he proposes that the church would have been nearly male-only, as some guilds were gender-exclusive in Antiquity.[21] He notes, on this matter, how apt Paul was in this letter to refer to this church as "brothers." Ascough also appeals to 1 Thess 1:9, how the Thessalonians *turned* (plural) away from idols to *serve* (plural) the living and true God, as evidence for the collective nature of their conversion.

This theory has piqued the interest of several scholars.[22] However, we must be careful not to turn possibilities into probabilities. After all, as Lindsey Trozzo notes in her critique of Ascough's theory, Paul is not necessarily using the language of working with hands in 4:11 in a technical sense.[23] Also, Trozzo argues that there is insufficient evidence to assume that artisan guilds were gender exclusive.[24]

Furthermore, what would stop Paul from encouraging them to include women in their believing community?[25] As M. Johnson-DeBraufre also urges, even if it were true that this church was guild-like and was male-only, does that imply the complete absence of women?[26] As early churches often met in houses, Johnson-DeBraufre wonders where believing women might have heard Paul's letter in these spaces, as assistants, slaves, relatives, and other-

---

20. See Ascough 2000: 311–28; 2003: 186-90; 2010: 53.

21. See Ascough 2003: 186.

22. One commentator of which I am aware, Linda M. Bridges, has taken up Ascough's proposal and integrated this theory into her commentary; see Bridges 2008.

23. Trozzo 2012: 41.

24. Trozzo points out that Paul's associate Priscilla herself was a *female* tent-maker (p. 42), perhaps even co-participant in a guild with her husband Aquila; see Keller 2010: 3; see also Johnson 1992: 322.

25. Trozzo 2012: 43.

26. Johnson-DeBaufre 2010: 99.

wise.²⁷ We ought to be careful not to narrow Paul's language of siblingship to men only. There is ample evidence from Paul's letters that the term *adelphoi* (lit. "brothers") is inclusive of women as well (hence NRSV: "brothers and sisters").²⁸ Just because specific women are not *named* does not mean they are not *there*.

Why Did Paul Write 1 Thessalonians?

Paul was not a "writer" in the sense that he did it as a hobby, or even vocationally. He *wrote* to communicate, but he much preferred being face to face (1 Thess 2:17; 3:10). In that sense, he echoes the sentiment of 2 John 1:12: "Although I have much to write to you, I would rather not use paper and ink; instead I hope to come to you and talk with you face to face, so that our joy may be complete." He was an apostle with a mission and message, but clearly he was like a *pastor*, wanting to guide his own flock; or like a mother wanting to care for her children (1 Thess 2:7). Paul did not typically write letters to update his churches on his situation or simply to check in on them. His tendency was to write as a form of problem-solving, whether to correct, pacify, comfort, encourage, etc. It behooves us to ask, then, *why did Paul write 1 Thessalonians*?

Again, the challenge in answering this question is that the only real evidence we have (aside from some of the information listed above related to Acts 16–17) must come from guesswork based on the letter of 1 Thessalonians itself. Howard Marshall underscores the difficulty with this illustration: "It is rather like the problem of trying to form a picture of a modern church simply on the basis of the official minutes of its business meeting; we should know very little about what actually happened in its services and other activities or about the kind of people who made up the congregation."²⁹ Nevertheless, we ought to learn what we can and be able to distinguish what is certain from what is probable, and then also consider what is plausible.³⁰

---

27. Johnson-DeBaufre 2010: 100.
28. See Trebilco 2012: 24–25; Horrell 2001: 299–303; Horrell 2005a: 406.
29. Marshall 1984: 4; in relation especially to gleaning from Acts 17:1–10a.
30. For methodology on historical reconstruction, see Barclay 1987; Gupta 2012.

Persecution and *Pistis*

The first thing that is clear in Paul's letter is that the Thessalonians experienced persecution from the beginning (1:6; 2:14). This would not have been a state-enforced persecution, but rather harassment from community members who were troubled by their newfound religion and practices (again, note the scenario in Thessalonica in Acts 17:1–10a). Thessalonian believers in Jesus would have been taught by Paul to devote themselves exclusively to the one God, thus they would have withdrawn from local pagan rites, festivities that typically had important political dimensions. They would have been charged with "atheism"; as Philip Esler explains, "To be respectable and decent meant taking part in the [local, religious] cult; old was good and new was bad; Thus, religion served to strengthen the existing social order. To deny the reality of the gods was absolutely unacceptable—one would be ostracized for that, even stoned in the streets."[31]

With this kind of context in mind, most scholars presume that the persecutors were Gentiles, not Jews. Such a view, though, would discount Luke's information in Acts 17 where it would seem *Jews* played a major role in the hostility against Paul's ministry and local allies. Again, the scholarly tendency is to put doubt on Luke's account for two reasons. Firstly, some argue that Luke has certain theological and narrative habits that shape how he presents Paul's ministry, in this case leading to doubts regarding the historicity of his version of the situation in Thessalonica. Secondly, such a view *seems* to contradict what Paul writes in 1 Thess 2:14, that the Thessalonian believers "suffered the same things from *your own compatriots* as they [the Judean churches] did from the Jews." The implication here seems to be that the Thessalonians were persecuted by *Gentile Thessalonians* while the Judean believers were persecuted by *Jewish* neighbors. However, the meaning of the word for *compatriots* here (*symphyletēs*) is contested.[32] Again, many scholars *assume* that Paul is referring to Gentile Thessalonian "compatriots,"[33] but when Paul proclaims that the Jews "drove us out" (1 Thess 2:15), why could not the same Jews that drove Paul out of Thessalonica also persecute the Thessalonians believers?[34] First Thessalonians

---

31. Esler 2001: 1200; see also Barclay 1993: 512–30.
32. See Johnson 1999: 282.
33. So Barclay 1993: 514; cf. Witherington 2006: 37
34. On the meaning of *symphyletēs* in Paul's time, see Taylor 2002: 784–801. Taylor explains that, while *symphyletēs* once carried the meaning of blood relation (i.e., ethnic association), it eventually expanded in meaning to cover administrative, military, and

2:14–16 makes good sense in Paul's argument if Paul is connecting Jewish persecution in Judea to Jewish persecution in Thessalonica.[35]

My inclination is to find a way to bring Acts 17:1–10a together with what Paul writes in 1 Thessalonians. While the implication of 1 Thess 1:9–10 is that the Thessalonian believers were largely Gentiles (forsaking idol worship), it very well may be that they were Gentile god-fearers prior to meeting Paul (see above, *The Church in Thessalonica*, 6–7). Again, some scholars consider it incredible that Paul might assert this about Gentiles who had already turned to the God of Israel.[36] However, this assumption is misguided. Paula Fredriksen explains that Gentiles who chose to "visit with" Jews and their God felt "free to observe as much or as little of Jewish custom as they chose—free, indeed, to continue worshiping their own gods."[37] Shaye Cohen makes the same case about the possibility of god-fearers as polytheists, and seeks to help moderns understand how ancient Greeks and Romans thought.

> Those who see Judaism and Hellenism as discrete entities are perplexed by the phenomenon of the God-fearers. Some have even questioned their existence. After all, how can gentiles become a "little bit Jewish"? And why would they want to? The explanation is to be sought in the other conception of Hellenism discussed above. Many Greek and Romans adopted the gods (e.g., Isis, Cybele, Mithras, Jupiter Dolichenus) and practices of various "barbarian" nations without converting or losing their identity. Similarly, thinking that the God of the Jews was like the god of other nations, they added him to their pantheon.[38]

The theory that I find most plausible related to the Thessalonian church is this: a group of Gentiles were attracted to Jewish life and became

---

political connections. Those who work with a narrower (ethnic) meaning for *symphyletēs*, Taylor urges, are drawing from a very limited pool of occurrences.

35. See Donfried 2002: 200–206.

36. So Wanamaker: "Such a remark [in 1 Thess 1:9] would seem inappropriate if the majority of his Gentile converts had already turned their backs on pagan religious practices by affiliating with the Jewish synagogue" (1990: 7).

37. Fredriksen 2015: 183–84. Furthermore, Fredriksen notes: "this shifting synagogue population of interested outsiders would have provided Paul with the bulk of his target audience: active pagans who were nonetheless interested to some degree in the Jewish god, and who had some sort of familiarity, through listening, with the Bible" (again 184–85); see also Dunn 2009: 563.

38. Cohen 2006: 47; see also Cohen 1999: 171.

associated with a synagogue (hence Acts 17:4). They maintained an interest in multiple gods, but also honored the god of Israel. Perhaps it was not too long after this interest that Paul introduced them to Messiah Jesus and many of them came to believe Paul's gospel. This situation would, indeed, anger certain Jews in just such a way as we see in Acts 17 and also in 1 Thess 2:14–16, if *symphyletēs* refers to Jewish Thessalonian compatriots. Paul could write that they had turned from idols to serve God because they had *not* done so as god-fearers despite their prior interest in Israel's god.

Excursus: Gentile Believers Incorporated into Israel's Story through Jesus

It is often pointed out that Paul does not quote the Old Testament (LXX) in 1 Thessalonians, and that this fact probably means that the Thessalonian believers were Gentiles who did not know the Jewish Scriptures.[39] That they were mostly Gentiles is almost certain, but the assumption that Paul consciously avoided quoting Scripture for that reason is hasty. First Thessalonians is *saturated* with Old Testament imagery, motifs, expressions, and ideas. Paul clearly crafts their identity in such a way as to draw them into the story and even the identity of Israel. They are *ekklēsia* as the people of God (1:1). They are *beloved of God* (1:4), as Israel is; they have been made precious to God (1:4). They are recipients of Israel's *good news* (1:5), the "word of the Lord" sounded forth from them (1:8), they will be rescued from Yahweh's wrath (1:10). They are taught how to "walk" with God (4:1), to obey his will regarding holy consecration (4:3, 7). They are identified as those separate from "the Gentiles who do not know God" (4:5). They are true light (5:5), those destined for salvation (5:9). If Paul was trying to communicate in a non-Jewish style, he failed.[40] While Paul did not feel the need to make explicit *arguments* from Scripture, he was clearly drawing these Gentiles into the story and identity of Israel through Messiah Jesus.[41]

It is possible that Jews from the synagogue where these Gentiles once worshiped (as god-fearers) tried to maintain an ongoing relationship with them, hoping to "win them back," so to speak, even if through fear. Perhaps they

39. E.g., Witherington 2006: 49; cf. Wanamaker 1990: 7.

40. See E. Johnson 2012: 144–45.

41. F. Matera argues much the same for how Paul identifies the Philippian church; see Matera 1999: 122; cf. Cambell 2006: 59–60; cf. Richardson 1969: 200.

urged, "We cannot ensure you will survive the wrath of God if you continue on following this Jesus." The fear of wrath may have scared the Thessalonians enough they lost some security in their identity in Jesus. Paul, then, wrote 1 Thessalonians as a form of *subversive rhetoric*, trying to undo any of the damage done by fear-inducing words from opponents. His clear message to them in 1 Thessalonians is that their hope is found in Jesus alone; through him they are secure as God's beloved, his chosen people. Paul would not have been saying this *over and against* Jews, but rather in affirmation of Gentiles incorporated into the people of God through Messiah Jesus. Thus, Paul can argue that he *wants* Gentiles saved, while the Jews (particularly those hostile to believers in Jesus) displease God by preventing this (1 Thess 2:15).

Knowing of the Thessalonians' persecution (1 Thess 3:1–6), Paul and his apostolic associates were concerned about the Thessalonians' *pistis*. Typically this word is translated "faith" (1:3, 8; 3:2, 5–7, 10; 5:8). However, *pistis* is a polyvalent Greek noun and can cover a range of meanings from belief to trust to faithfulness and loyalty. The way that Paul talks about the strength of the Thessalonians' *pistis* he is almost certainly not referring to their *beliefs* as such. Rather, *pistis* was a term used in the Greco-Roman world especially in relation to loyalty.[42] Also, around the time of Paul, Jews in particular were using *pistis* as a way of referring to pledges of loyalty within a covenantal relationship.[43] Particularly in chapter 3 of 1 Thessalonians, Paul refers to his concern for their *pistis* in the context of affliction. Timothy was dispatched to see about their *pistis* lest the tempter overwhelm them (3:5). Paul was not worried about their *belief* per se, but the "whole package" of their commitment to the Messiah and their complete trust in him. The best terms to translate *pistis*, then, are probably "trust," "loyalty," or "faithfulness."[44]

---

42. See Malina 2003: 359.

43. See esp LXX Neh 10:1; also Josephus *Ant. Passim.*

44. I believe the translation "faith" is best justified when Paul clearly appears to be using *pistis* in reference to trust that goes against natural senses, "believing the unbelievable," so to speak; see 2 Cor 5:7. For similar argumentation regarding the best translation of *pistis* in 1–2 Thessalonians, see Andy Johnson 2016, forthcoming on *pistis* in 1:3.

Sexual Purity

A second matter that Paul addresses in the letter relates to sexual purity. Paul calls for control over the body, lest they succumb to heathen lust (4:3–4). The Greco-Roman lifestyle was highly permissive when it came to male sexuality. Men often had sex with multiple people, though it was considered especially inappropriate to commit adultery by sleeping with another man's wife. Paul called for a strict kind of holiness and purity that sought to honor one another and God (4:6).

The Dead in the Messiah

A third problem in Thessalonica apparently pertained to the death of some members of the church (4:13–18). Paul felt the need to comfort them by urging that the recently-deceased believers would be especially honored at the return of the Lord. Many scholars believe that the Thessalonians naively thought that everyone would remain alive until the return of the Messiah, so the death of church members was perplexing and even traumatizing. This is possible, but it does not account for the unusual emphasis Paul places on the dead in the Messiah being lifted up *first*, before the living at the return of the Messiah (4:15). Why would they receive this honor of priority? A minority of scholars (including myself) hypothesize that those who died may have been *martyred*, killed by persecutors.[45] This view accords well with how it could be possible that several people died in the same small believing community around the same time a short while after Paul left. Furthermore, it explains why Paul focuses on their position of honor—those who died for their allegiance to Messiah deserve such a special role.

Excursus: Hypothesizing a Clandestine Attack

One scenario that could bring several issues together in 1 Thessalonians is the consideration that the opponents of the believing Thessalonians planned some kind of clandestine attack. Let's say certain upset Jews, (former) friends of these god-fearers-turned-Jesus-followers, secretly attacked their workshop or apartment building. Let's say they set it on fire at night. This could explain

---

45. See Pobee 1985: 114; Donfried 1997: 221–23; Witherington 2006: 139; L. T. Johnson 1999: 285, Donfried and Marshall 1993: 28, and Gorman 2004: 150 are open to this possibility as well; see also Gorman 2015.

how some people died at once. It could also explain why some are "weak" (injured?) and others are "faint hearted" (5:14). Furthermore, what if these same Jews blamed this fire on "the wrath of God" because these god-fearers began to follow Paul and worship Messiah Jesus (whom these Jews would have considered a false messiah)? What if these Jews tried to convince the Thessalonian believers that they could reclaim "peace and security" if they forsook Jesus and returned to the synagogue (5:3)? What if Jewish prophets "prophesied" further doom if they did not (see 5:20–21)? Paul's wider message would be clear in response to this: Jesus is Lord, he is judge, salvation and hope are centered on him.

Coming of the Lord

The last major concern that Paul raises relates to the timing of the coming of the Lord (5:1–11). Paul is unwilling to say more than that it will be unexpected (5:2–3). He turns their attention away from timetable theories towards faithfulness and upright behavior *today*. The *timing* doesn't matter if, in waiting for the master, you are *always* at work in your duties (see Luke 12:41–48). Somewhere along the way, a fear struck them that they might not be ready. Paul comforts them by reminding them of their firmly-anchored identity in the Messiah (5:9), but challenges them to live faithfully in light of that identity.

Minor Concerns?

The above issues (persecution, sexual purity, the dead in the Messiah, the coming of the Lord) are Paul's main concerns in 1 Thessalonians, but potentially he was also addressing other, minor matters. For example, there is some evidence that the church may have had internal divisions and communal problems; Paul seems to briefly address these (see 4:9–11; 5:12–15). Also, Paul may have had a small concern for those he calls *ataktoi* ("the idle troublemakers"), but his mention of them is brief enough that it is not significant at this point for him (5:14; it becomes a major problem by the time he writes 2 Thessalonians). Also, is it possible that the Thessalonian believers had been thrown into confusion by (false?) prophecies (5:20–21)? Again, this is plausible, but the brief mention offers little information.

Paul on Trial?

A final matter worth considering as a reason for 1 Thessalonians pertains to whether Paul felt the need to defend himself (especially in order to maintain the integrity of the gospel he preached). Many scholars, including myself, detect a defensive tone in Paul's self-description in 2:1–12. Paul felt the need to say that he was not deceitful, nor did he resort to trickery. He was not a flatterer, nor motivated by greed or popularity. He did not want their money and tried to remain blameless before them. In chapter three, he communicates his relief when he heard the report from Timothy that the Thessalonians remembered him fondly and wanted to see him (3:6).[46]

But why would Paul feel the need to defend his integrity? Perhaps, when he had to flee spontaneously at night (see Acts 17:10a), suspicions arose about Paul's sudden disappearance. As Michael Holmes explains, Paul was concerned

> that his behavior and that of his companions might be misunderstood—or, more likely, misrepresented—in a way that would call into question the validity and integrity of the gospel itself. Religious charlatans and frauds were a dime a dozen in the ancient world, and the way Paul and Silas slipped out of town in the middle of the night would have made it only too easy to pigeonhole them as just one more pair of rip-off artists out to scam people. From there it was only a short step to the conclusion that their message was no more truthful than they were, and thus the people might reject it along with them.[47]

Images and Themes in 1 Thessalonians

There is no denying that Paul loved using metaphors and images to help his churches understand their identity in God through Messiah.[48] He loved to use word pictures to capture what it means to serve Messiah Jesus. His letters are peppered with dozens of metaphors, but we can easily identify three key "images" that dominate 1 Thessalonians in particular: family, cult, and military.[49]

---

46. For a discussion of the scholarly debate related to whether Paul was being defensive or not in 2:1–12, see 50–52.

47. Holmes 1998: 22.

48. See Williams 1999; Collins 2008; Gupta 2010.

49. It should go without saying that Paul used the rich imagery of the identity of

Family

There is no more powerful and comprehensive metaphor used in 1 Thessalonians than that of the church as *family*. It is easily recognized, even from the first verse, that God is called *Father* (1:1; cf. 1:3; 3:11, 13). More striking than that, though, is the frequency with which Paul calls the Thessalonian believers *brothers and sisters (adelphoi).*[50] The community of Messiah Jesus is more than a club of like-minded religious people. They belong together in the most intimate kind of relationship that can be conceived.[51] So well-known did this image become of early Christianity that in the second century outsiders accused Christians of being incestuous because some were married who called each other brother and sister.[52]

Paul does not explain *why* he calls the Thessalonians "brothers and sisters," but undoubtedly this would have been explained when he first taught them about their faith. Paul would have preached about the unique sonship of Messiah Jesus, Son of God, and that all may *also* become children of the one God *through* Jesus, Gentiles receiving the blessing of being included in the unique adoption of Israel (Rom 8:29; Gal 4:5; cf. Rom 9:4; Col 1:13; Eph 1:5).

For Paul, to be "brothers and sisters" through the Messiah is not merely a term of endearment, nor simply a theological construct; Paul expected the *reality* of this theological truth to create an intimate community. Beginning in 4:9, Paul addresses the matter of *philadelphia*—sibling-love. It was encoded into their corporate life to express this kind of kinship love and Paul commends them for this. He expected—and found—deep affection within this group.

As for Paul's own relationship with the Thessalonians, part of his purpose in writing the letter, no doubt, is to underscore his love and affection

---

Israel (beloved, chosen, etc.) to describe these Thessalonian Gentile believers; see above 12–13.

50. The Greek word *adelphos* (brother) appears almost twenty times in this one short letter (1:4; 2:1, 9, 14, 17; 2:14, 17; 3:2, 7; 4:1, 6, 10 [x2], 13; 5:1, 4, 12, 14, 25–27). Compare this to Galatians where *adelphos* appears only four times (Gal 5:11, 13; 6:1, 18, 21, 23).

51. Note how Joseph Hellerman explains that in the Roman world the sibling relationship was the strongest relationship in existence, even stronger than husband-wife or parent-child. Hellerman argues that one entailment of making this theological sibling-ship association would be that fellow believers would not fight for honor against each other, because siblings do not compete with each other for honor (see Hellerman 2009: 15–25).

52. Beattie 2005: 118.

for these suffering fellow-believers. Thus, when he calls them "brothers and sisters," not only does this remind them that they are siblings *to each other*, but also that *he is their brother through Jesus*. Yet, he is not unwilling to mix metaphors, even familial ones! He also portrays himself in comparison to a *mother tenderly nourishing her beloved* (2:7) and also a *father encouraging his children* (2:11–12).[53] When Paul writes about the pain he felt having to leave them prematurely, he says that "we were made orphans by being separated from you" (2:17). Only such a profound word-picture could convey the heartbreak he felt at being removed from their presence.[54] For Paul, again, the church was not *like* a family, it *was* family.[55]

Cult

In 1 Thessalonians, the second key image from which Paul draws comes from the Jewish cult, particularly Jewish notions of holiness, purity, and sacrifice.[56] The foundation for how Jews understood holiness comes from their idea of a holy God, a God who is all-powerful, perfect in all righteousness, and yet also perfect in love and mercy.[57] When God brought Israel out of Egypt, he called them to be a holy nation (Exod 19:6), a people set apart for himself. Their way of life was meant to be *in contrast* to that of the sinful world, and also they were intended to *display* the true nature of their God.[58] Holiness and purity were also important when it came to temple service and sacrifice. Priests must be consecrated, and part of their priestly service was to "distinguish between the holy and the common, and between the unclean and the clean" (Lev 10:10). Very specific protocols existed for how things were to be done. Atoning animals offered in sacrifice must be

---

53. On the motherly image of Paul in his letters, see Gaventa 2007: 3–78; specifically on 1 Thessalonians 2:7, see McNeel 2014: 123–74.

54. See Collins 2008: 18–19; cf. Burke 2003: 135.

55. See Banks 1994: 47–57.

56. See Gupta 2010: 40–42.

57. See Psalm 77.

58. See Goheen 2011: 193: "The lives of the people of Israel look *backward* to creation; they embody God's original creational design for the whole of human life. Their lives look *forward* to the consummation: they are a sign of the goal to which God is taking redemptive history.... Their lives are to face *outward* to the nations; they are to be a contrast community, leading lives that differ from those of the peoples around them. Israel is to challenge the cultural idolatry of the surrounding nations while embracing the cultural gifts God has given it." This is a nice vision of the fullness of what it meant for the people to be "holy" as a covenantal obligation.

without blemish (see Lev 1–9; Num 28–29). The same is used in the New Testament of Jesus, a lamb "without defect or blemish" (1 Peter 1:18); and, again, the same is used to characterize believers (Eph 5:27).

One of Paul's favorite ways to refer to believers is "saints" or "holy people"—typically he begins his letters addressing his churches with this label (so 1 Cor 1:1–2). Though he does not use this title in 1 Thessalonians, he does refer several times to the importance of their becoming holy in view of the return of the Messiah (see 3:13; 5:23). In 4:3, he summarizes God's will for them as *hagiasmos*, "consecration" (often translated "sanctification"). As James Thomson notes, while it would not have seemed strange to Gentiles to relate religion to purity or holiness, "Paul extends the sphere of holiness from the cult to include aspects of daily life, including sexual relationships."[59]

Both of the two wish-prayers in 1 Thessalonians (3:13; 5:23) use holiness language in relation to the presentation of the Thessalonians before God at the return of Jesus, such that it is almost as if they will be offered as a living sacrifice then. Paul sees it as his pastoral duty to prepare this eschatological offering, and he is particularly anxious that this sacrifice is perfect. This would make sense in light of Rom 15:16 where Paul portrays himself as an apostle-priest responsible for the offering of the Gentiles such that they may be "acceptable, sanctified by the Holy Spirit."[60] Ultimately, Paul's use of cult language (holiness, purity, sacrifice) has to do with his understanding that believers owe their whole life in dedication and service to the redeeming God. Paul's emphasis on the day of reckoning in this letter is not meant as a threat (which would stand at cross-purposes with his desire to comfort them), but as an indicator of the will of the One who truly matters.

Military

Though it explicitly appears only briefly, mention should also be made of Paul's use of a military image: "Since we belong to the day, let us be sober, and put on the breastplate of faith and love, and for a helmet the hope of salvation" (5:8). Paul was clearly encouraging them to close ranks, as it were, and be vigilant in the face of opposition. Occasionally in his letters Paul did use war metaphors (Rom 13:12; 2 Cor 6:7; 10:4; cf. Eph 6:11–17). He wished to represent the present time as one of opposition against evil—hence his

---

59. Thompson 2011: 72; see also Harrington 2001: 197.
60. See Gupta 2010: 130–32, cf. 155–71.

appeal to the Thessalonians needing to continue to live as people of day and light, not darkness and night. Roman soldiers were known for resoluteness and bravery, and their unswerving allegiance to the sovereign. So too the Thessalonians were called to be intrepid in the face of persecution and to war against darkness in service of the Lord Jesus. It should be emphasized, though, that while Paul may have drawn from Greco-Roman language of warfare,[61] he did not endorse Rome's way of bringing peace (i.e., through bloodshed). The "armor" he summons them to don is that of loyalty, love, and hope (5:8). Their "warfare" should not be characterized by *violence*, but nevertheless they should be on the *offense* in the mission of the gospel, and not simply on the *defense*. Their faith should carry the marks of resoluteness and fearlessness as God goes before them and empowers them. The Messiah has called them, no doubt, to a peace-keeping and peace-making mission, but it ought to be anything but *passive*.

Perhaps today some balk at the use of warfare language in relation to Christian theology and life, but Paul was not an especially macho or aggressive person. Rather, he was attuned to the reality of a cosmic war being waged against the forces of evil. When he writes to the Romans, he warns them about "what time it is." It is almost time for the day to dawn, for the Messiah to return. However, that does not mean that it is time to sit back and wait for him to descend. Quite the opposite: "Let us then lay aside the works of darkness and put on the armor of light" (Rom 13:12). Waiting for the Parousia involves "active waiting," readiness such that we are found doing the work of the kingdom when the Lord visits us unexpectedly. If we really believe we have a battle to win against evil, we will be all-the-more serious about making every moment count. That was a message Paul wanted the Thessalonians to learn well.

Along with the above key *images* in 1 Thessalonians, we can add a number of important *themes*: wrath and salvation, trust and work, hope and endurance, thanksgiving and joy, and—last but not least—love.

"Wrath" and Salvation

For some reason, the Thessalonians were particularly concerned with the end of the world. Certainly Paul taught them about things yet to come, but he would have wanted neither to instill fear nor paranoia. Still, in his first letter he did not shy away from talking about divine wrath. For Paul,

---

61. See Krentz 2003: 344–83.

wrath (*orgē*) was not about an unbridled divine fury that might break out at any time for any reason. Rather, the divine *orgē* was about God's anger for justice, his disgust at a world spun out of control, and his passion for recalibrating the world he created so that it lived according to the standards of equality and peace for which he originally made it.

Paul warned the Thessalonians of this impending judgment day, and instead of them fearing it, they could take heart that Jesus was the Rescuer and that they were not going to face the judgment of God's justice-anger (1:10). They had the hope of a sure salvation (5:8) because God has made their position secure through Messiah Jesus (5:9). Instead, those who seek to do evil, to hinder the reconciling and redeeming gospel, will face wrath because they do not wish for all to know God's salvation in Jesus.

Loyalty and Work

Another important theme in 1 Thessalonians involves *pistis* and *ergon*—"loyalty" and "work." There has been an unfortunate tendency in Christian history in the past few centuries to make "faith" something opposed to "work," but in 1 Thessalonians these words make a happy pair: "work of trust" (1 Thess 1:3). "Work" is the outworking of "trust." Paul commends both. Their "trust" is known throughout Macedonia as they follow Jesus despite great opposition (1:8), and Paul was comforted by Timothy's "good news" of their ongoing allegiance to the Messiah (3:6).[62]

First Thessalonians is most well-known by Christians, and even in scholarship, for Paul's teaching about eschatological events. No doubt Paul gave attention to what is penultimate and ultimate. However, it is unfortunate that his Thessalonian letters are not equally known for Paul's teaching on the importance—and even the goodness—of work. Paul reminds the Thessalonians of his *work and toil* as he made his own living while in town so as to prevent being a financial burden on any of them (2:9). We learn from 1 Corinthians that Paul knew the privileges extended to apostles to be free from manual labor so as to devote his full attention to preaching the gospel and equipping churches (see 1 Cor 9:6–7). Paul even goes so far as to say that the Lord Jesus *commanded* the apostles to take gifts from believers to support their daily needs—*and Paul sometimes chose to "disobey" that command!* But why? Why did Paul work? From his ministry in Thessalonica we learn that he wanted to stay above reproach when it came

---

62. On the meaning of *pistis* in 1 Thessalonians, see above 10–13.

to money. So many con men paraded through town and took money from gullible locals. Paul wanted to protect the integrity of the gospel.

Another key point that Paul underscores is the importance of daily work in order to continue to be productive in the community and to care for any needs. Some lagged on their work, perhaps even began leeching off of wealthy, sympathetic fellow-believers. As generous as this might be, Paul wanted to encourage each person to be responsible and productive as they are able. Paul tells the Thessalonians to put their hands to good use, to focus on being a contributor to the community "so that you may command the respect of outsiders, and be dependent on nobody" (4:11–12). Raymond Collins offers a salutary reminder that Paul teaches us what it means to be human in his work.

> How we work is a matter of imitating the example of the apostle Paul and his companions. Working is a way of being a responsible co-citizen within society. How we work is also a matter of responsible participation in the ongoing creation of God, whose own tale of creation is cast in the form of a story about someone at work (Gen 1).[63]

Hope and Endurance

This introduction began with a reflection on "hope" (*elpis*) as a central theme for 1–2 Thessalonians. I will only briefly touch upon this again. Paul mentions that he gives thanks for their "endurance of hope"—the perseverance and tenacious forward-march that is produced by a hunger to embrace God's promised future. Interestingly, Paul says that *his hope is the Thessalonians* (2:19). How can he say this? Because he sees the power of God at work in *their* trust in God and believing allegiance to the Messiah, and he foresees God's validation of his ministry work as God judges their lives. Paul's hope wasn't "blind." He could see it in the lives of his children.

Paul was a bit fearful that they might lose their hope, having lost loved ones and beginning to lose their focus (4:13). Paul does not tell them to stop grieving. He does not tell them to "put on a happy face." Grieve, yes. But grieve with hope. Grief with hope is lament without despair.

I am reminded of Hosea 6:1–3.

---

63. Collins 1996: 96.

> Come, let us return to the Lord; for it is he who has torn, and he will heal us; he has struck down, and he will bind us up. After two days he will revive us, on the third day he will raise us up, that we may live before him. Let us know, let us press on to know the Lord, his appealing is as sure as the dawn; he will come to us like the showers, like the spring rains that water the earth.

His appearing is a sure as the dawn. He will heal us. He will raise us up. Paul may have even been thinking about such verses when it came to the death of some beloved Thessalonians. Hope is walking in the light of the future dawn. Christian hope is *anticipatory imagination.* Christian hope is the capacity to actualize and embrace the power of God's promised (and, thus, certain) future in the present through Jesus. Hope is less a wish and more a muscle that must be exercised (see Rom 5:3–5). And we exercise hope by enduring trust and hard work.

Thanksgiving and Joy

In light of the perilous ministry life that Paul endured, it is striking that his letters, not least 1 Thessalonians, are characterized by thanksgiving: he is thankful for his Thessalonians brothers and sisters who accepted the gospel with joy and faith (1:6; 2:13) and who show great resilience in affliction (1:2–3). Paul himself rejoiced in their life (2:19–20). They became a source of deep happiness for him (3:9). He passed on a ministry of thanksgiving to them as well (5:18).

Thanksgiving and joy require faith and hope. It is easy to wallow. It is convenient to complain. It is a discipline to release oneself from worldly comparison, from "keeping up with the Joneses," and to learn to live a quiet life (4:11). Paul tells the Philippians, writing to them from prison, that he has learned how to be content; sometimes you have a little and sometimes you have more (Phil 4:11–12). He trained himself *not to* wager his joy on *stuff* so that he could *always* be thankful.

Love

I would be remiss not to include love (*agapē*) in the list of themes for 1 Thessalonians. This completes our discussion of the faith-hope-love triad, and it also represents well the emphasis Paul places on love as the deepest expression of true discipleship. Love, for Paul, is not mere sentimentality, nor a fleeting or occasional emotion. He basically commences the letter by reference to how love can inspire labor—we are most motivated to work hard on behalf of what we love (1:3). Reference to their steadfast love appears in 3:12. But I wish to focus on 4:9–10. Here Paul reminds them of how they should love one another like family (*philadelphia*—"sibling love"). David deSilva offers a nice, succinct illustration of what this kind of sibling love looks like: "Rather than insisting on having one's own way at the cost of a brother or sister's well-being, the loving sibling will forgo his or her rights in order to safeguard the well-being of the other."[64]

At the end of 1 Thessalonians, Paul offers a few instructions to the Thessalonians, one of which especially captures his understanding of love—*dedicate yourself to caring for the weak* (5:14). In the competitive Greco-Roman world it only paid off to help those who can help you. Paul radically cuts through this *quid pro quo* mentality to focus on cruciform love, a kind of pure generosity that places an interest and care on the other. The Messiah would, of course, have served for Paul as the prime model (see Rom 15:3)—just as Matthew points to the fulfillment of Isa 53:4, "He took our weaknesses and carried our diseases" (Matt 8:17 NET). To care for the weak (1 Thess 5:14) is to live out the ministry of love demonstrated by Jesus.

2 Thessalonians: The Story Continues[65]

First and Second Thessalonians is not the only example of a set of texts written to the same church. We have two letters that Paul wrote to the Corinthians, for example. However, those Corinthian letters are quite different, dealing with a separate (though not unrelated) set of problems. The challenge we face with 2 Thessalonians, in relationship to 1 Thessalonians, is that these two letters are very similar. Also, we do not have *further* information (e.g., from Acts) to fill the modern reader in on what happened after 1 Thessalonians. Again, we are left to read 2 Thessalonians and try to guess how the story continued after the first letter. At the very least we can say confidently that things did not get better for the Thessalonians after Paul's first letter; rather, they worsened.[66] It appears that they are experienc-

---

64. deSilva 2001: 83.

65. Some scholars doubt that Paul wrote 2 Thessalonians. Here we operate under the assumption that Paul *did* write 2 Thessalonians, and a discussion of authorship issues appears at the end of the introduction under the title: "Who Wrote 2 Thessalonians?" (pp. 30–37).

66. Most scholars who hold that Paul wrote 2 Thessalonians argue that the second

ing even *more* persecution. Furthermore, they appear to need teaching on how things will happen and turn out at the Lord's impending intervention. David deSilva summarizes aptly the probable situation that gave rise to this second letter to the Thessalonians.

> The believers had made some positive progress in the direction that 1 Thessalonians has urged them, as Paul affirms their growing mutual love and the steadfastness of their faith. Relationships with the community are sufficiently strong and have become sufficiently primary for most members that Paul believes the Christians can now use shaming and shunning within the group to reinforce certain believers (2 Thess 3:14–15). Nevertheless, the pressures from outside the group continue to demand Paul's attention—he continues to encourage the Christians to resist that pressure.
>
> A second issue revolves around a misunderstanding of Christian eschatology, thinking that "the Day of the Lord has arrived" (2 Thess 2:2). Indeed, it is possible that such a misunderstanding arose from the discussion of 1 Thess 5:1–11 and perhaps from some glossing of the copy or copies of that letter circulating among the other house churches in Thessalonica. Finally, the "idle" or "disorderly" (*ataktoi*) of 1 Thess 5:14 emerge here as a more evident problem requiring the believers' direct intervention (2 Thess 3:6–15).[67]

Persecution

In the first letter, Paul takes the role of comforter and encourager to those Thessalonians who face opposition. In the second letter, Paul's tone is more serious, and he emphasizes not only future relief for these beleaguered believers, but also inevitable judgment upon the persecutors.[68]

Eschatology

The second chapter of 2 Thessalonians appears to comprise the main teaching that Paul wanted to pass on. Apparently somehow the Thessalonians came to believe that the "Day of the Lord" arrived.

---

letter must have been written not long after the first; it must have been written before Paul's visit narrated in Acts 20; see Morris 1975: 30.

67. deSilva 2001: 543.
68. See Marshall 1984: 23; Fee 2009: 241.

> As to the coming of our Lord Jesus Christ and our being gathered together to him, we beg you, brothers and sisters, not to be quickly shaken in mind or alarmed, either by spirit or by word or by letter, as though from us, to the effect that the Day of the Lord is already here. (2 Thess 2:1–2)

Paul's reference here to being *taught* (spirit/word/letter) about the arrival of the Day of the Lord appears to imply that some group was impressing this notion on them—further evidenced by his next warning that they be deceived by no one (2:3). Who would have taught them this is unclear.

Traditionally, scholars have assumed that Paul wrote 2 Thessalonians to correct a misunderstanding of his earlier instruction that the Day of the Lord will come suddenly (cf. 1 Thess 5:2). Here in 2 Thessalonians, according to this view, the Thessalonians "can relax because the apocalyptic signs that must precede the coming of that day have not yet occurred, namely, the apostasy, the appearance of the lawless one or son of perdition who is anti-God, and the activity of Satan with portended signs and wonders."[69] However, 2 Thessalonians does not offer a point-by-point timeline of eschatological events. There is a bigger concern at work in this text.

My own hunch is that the same Jews that persecuted the Thessalonians somehow convinced them that the "Day of the Lord" has dawned—not completely, but insofar as the traumatic events experienced in their community (e.g., deaths) are evidence of divine displeasure.[70] Perhaps their message to the Thessalonian believers was this: *We are beginning to see the wrath of God, repent and return to our community. It may not be too late.* If this is the case, Paul's letter carries the urgent task of re-establishing their identity in the community of Jesus and that the Thessalonians are safe and secure in Messiah Jesus alone.

In the central section of 2 Thess 2:1–12, Paul's main points about eschatological events are these:

- Things will get much worse before they will get better—expect a great "rebellion" among those who claim to know God (2:3)

---

69. Brown 1997: 590.

70. John Barclay points to the years 51–52, according to Tacitus, as "particularly ill omened, with prodigies such as repeated earthquakes and a famine." This may have led the Thessalonians to believe that the Day of the Lord had dawned. But Barclay adds this caveat: "it is not necessary to rely on this precarious, though tantalizing, connection. A fevered apocalyptic imagination can interpret almost any unusual event as an eschatological moment, and divine wrath can explain many types of calamities." See Barclay 1993: 527–28.

- There will be a great enemy that is characterized by disobedience to God (the Lawless One) (2:3–4); he serves under Satan and will deceive others through miracles (2:9–10)
- God has allowed there to be a "restrainer" to hold back the Lawless One (2:6–8)
- Despite how harrowing these happenings will be, the Lord Jesus will destroy the Lawless One effortlessly when he returns (2:8)

There are some similarities between Paul's teaching here and Jesus' eschatological discourse in Matthew 24. Jesus explains that deceivers will come (24:4–5), wars and disasters will multiply (24:6–8), persecution will intensify (24:9), apostasy and betrayal will mar the church (24:10), false prophets will mislead (24:11), *lawlessness* will corrupt love (24:12)—*but the one who endures to the end will be saved (24:13)*.

So also Paul says: *We are thankful for you, beloved Thessalonians, because you are the "first-fruits" of Thessalonica, and you have held fast to the truth. Glory will come. Stand firm (2:13–15)*. Paul narrates the future, not to assuage curiosities, nor even to diffuse panic, but to *demonstrate* the losing side is going to lose—not because it is weaker *per se*, but because ultimately it is lawless and wicked. If the Thessalonians have become *confused* about which side to stand on to survive the coming wrath, Paul offers an important clue—follow the obedient and righteous ones.

(No) Work

A third important issue that Paul handles is that of a group he calls the "idle troublemakers" (3:6–12). Already in 1 Thessalonians he warns the idle (1 Thess 5:14), but in this letter the problem with them seems to have worsened such that his rebuke is stern. It is possible that, in a state of emergency and discernment in the church in light of what seems like apocalyptic signs, some local leaders "dubbed" themselves spiritual leaders (perhaps imitating the authority of Paul). They are *rebellious* insofar as they undermine the community life by being mere "busybodies"—people who meddle and pontificate, but get nothing done (2 Thess 3:11). They disrupt the productive, daily life of the community and they ignore the teachings Paul passed on to the Thessalonians.

Paul seeks to distance himself and the church from these troublemakers by first pointing out his own habit of *working for a living*. Paul did not expect the church to feed him, so these idle men should not. Paul toiled day and night, even though he had the "right" to receive material benefits from them (3:9). Still, he wanted to model the principle, "Those unwilling to work will not get to eat" (3:10 NLT). Paul wanted to underscore the value of good, honest work, self-reliability. It is not that people should ignore the needs of others—after all, he wrote in his earlier letter that they should devote themselves to the weak, no doubt feeding them if need be (1 Thess 5:14). The focus here is on those who *refuse* to work, not those who *cannot* work.

Ultimately, though, even though some believers were acting in a rebellious manner, Paul makes it a point to say that, though they ought to be "shamed" (3:14), they should *not* be treated as enemies, but rather as erring brothers (3:15).

Themes of 2 Thessalonians

Many of the themes that appear in 1 Thessalonians also can be found in 2 Thessalonians (e.g., faith/trust, love, salvation), but here we will focus on two key themes particularly distinctive to 2 Thessalonians.

Dignity and Honor[71]

At some point and for some reason, the Thessalonians were doubting their sense worth and dignity. In the Greco-Roman world, the social value of honor was the most important capital. Paul spends ample time in 2 Thessalonians reminding them that, despite all the goings-on in their community in recent days, they are people of worth and value before God. Paul can give thanks for their faith and love *because it is right to do so* (1:3). He can boast in them, they are acting with honor before God (1:4). Their suffering is not a sign of *shame*—quite the contrary. In fact, through this suffering, paradoxically, they are being made *worthy* of the kingdom of God (1:5). They can look forward, not to rejection and destruction, but rather to *glorification* when the Messiah returns (1:12; 2:14).

It is all too easy to seek out self-value from society, and when the going gets rough, it's more comfortable to go with the grain of culture. The Thessalonians struggled with the pressures coming from those around them, unhappy with resistance to their new faith. Paul was trying to enlarge their

---

71. See Carter 2010: 282–99, esp. 292–93.

vision to see how what they are doing—in loving and caring for one another and others despite this opposition—was adding to their future glory and that they would be vindicated and honored in the end.

Justice and Peace

Related to the concern about dignity, Paul also seeks to handle the inevitable question that comes to those who suffer—*is God fair* (theodicy)? Can God be trusted to do what it right? Why does he keep silent and invisible? What have I done such that he won't rescue me?

Paul responds to the Thessalonians' suffering by pointing to a future hope—God will rebalance the world at the right time. While it is difficult to wait for that right time, it is sure and he can be trusted to work it all out.[72] Suffering and wrath are not ultimate things, they are *penultimate* things. I would like to echo here the point Michael Gorman makes in relation to judgment language in the book of Revelation:

> Revelation's visions of judgment symbolize God's *penultimate* (next-to-last) rather than *ultimate* (final) activity in human history. That is, judgment is a means to an end; the goal being eschatological salvation, the creation of a new heaven and new earth in which humanity realizes its true *raison d'etre* as reconciled peoples flourishing together in the presence of God and the Lamb.[73]

Much the same could be said of 2 Thessalonians. All the apocalyptic turmoil that Paul prescribes is far from the end-vision of salvation and God's redeeming justice. Despite what looks like eschatological *chaos*, the *ultimate* hope is harmony. Thus, Justice in 2 Thessalonians should be joined by his brother Peace.[74] Paul's ultimate interest in peace (*eirēnē*) is demonstrated in how he ends this letter: "Now may the Lord of peace himself give you peace at all times in all ways. The Lord be with all of you." Peace is not only what will exist in the end, when the apocalyptic dust has settled. Believers can embody and live out lives of peace-making and peace-keeping now.[75]

---

72. See Johnson 1999: 289; also Krentz 1991: 54.
73. Gorman 2011: 138–39.
74. Bassler 1991: 71–85; see also Swartley; Gorman 2015: 142–211.
75. Again, see especially Gorman 2015: 142–211.

Who Wrote 2 Thessalonians?

In the above examination of 2 Thessalonians, we have taken for granted that Paul wrote 2 Thessalonians. However, especially since the early twentieth century, scholars have wondered whether Paul wrote it, or it was written by someone else in his name (i.e., pseudonymous).[76] For most of the twentieth century, more and more scholars accepted the arguments for 2 Thessalonians being pseudonymous. The reasons for this are many and vary somewhat from one scholar to the next, but these features tend to be raised when 2 Thessalonians' authenticity is questioned: *copycat, style, historical implausibility, tone, pseudonymous "tells," and theological differences.*[77]

Against Pauline Authorship

COPYCAT

A first, and perhaps the most decisive, reason that some scholars believe 2 Thessalonians is pseudonymous is its relationship to 1 Thessalonians, in particular how similar it is.[78] Edgar Krentz points to several identical (or nearly-identical) features: identical salutations (1 Thess 1:1; 2 Thess 1:1), both have long thanksgivings, both include a second thanksgiving in the middle of the letter (1 Thess 2:13; 2 Thess 2:13), both have letter bodies which close with "a request to God expressed by a volitive optative."[79] Both letters also ask the "God/Lord of peace" to do something (1 Thess 5:23–24;

---

76. In 1798, J. E. C. Schmidt argued that, while 2 Thessalonians was probably written by Paul, the section 2:1–12 was a later insertion into the text by a separate writer. In 1903, W. Wrede made a more comprehensive case for 2 Thessalonians being pseudonymous; for an insightful, though brief, discussion of the history of scholarship on the authorship of 2 Thessalonians, see Thiselton 2011: 11–15.

77. It is sometimes noted that 2 Thessalonians includes vocabulary unusual for Paul, but this kind of argument has largely been debunked for two reasons; firstly, each extant letter of Paul contains its own set of distinctive vocabulary based on the specific subjects of that letter in its context; second, we are simply dealing with too small of a sample of Paul's writings to decide what kind of words count as "unpauline." Even those who are certain that Paul did not write 2 Thessalonians admit that the study of the vocabulary of this text contributes little to the debate; see Krentz 2009: 444; Menken 1994: 32: "There is a more or less general agreement that, from the point of vocabulary, 2 Thessalonians is no less Pauline than the recognized letters."

78. So Menken 1994: "This literary dependence is the decisive argument against Pauline authorship of 2 Thessalonians" (40); see also Boring 2015: 212.

79. Krentz 1992: 6.518.

2 Thess 3:16). Additionally, both letters use the same rare word *kateuthynai*, although in different contexts (1 Thess 3:11; 2 Thess 3:16). Krentz's point here is not to show *similarities*, but rather what seems like *copying* or a conscious *dependence* on the first letter. This leads to the natural question, "Why would Paul copy himself in this almost mechanical way?"[80] The implication is that Paul would have no need to copy himself, but this is the kind of thing that a pseudonymous writer would do, having 1 Thessalonians in his possession and wanting to create another letter that *appears* Pauline.[81]

STYLE

Every writer has his or her own writing personality or style. One person (today) says "you know?" at the end of a sentence, while another says "you know what I mean?" Some scholars, examining the "styles" of 1 and 2 Thessalonians, note a difference.[82] Second Thessalonians employs certain turns of phrases (such as "good hope" and "eternal comfort") that don't resonate with the style of Paul's other undisputed letters (like 1 Thessalonians, but also Galatians, Romans, 1–2 Corinthians, Philippians, and Philemon).[83] Another possible difference in style is the author of 2 Thessalonians' preference for longer and more complex sentences.[84] Christina Kreinecker has argued recently that 2 Thessalonians diverges from 1 Thessalonians in the way that the author makes requests (using the verbs *erōtaō* and *parangelō*).[85]

HISTORICAL IMPLAUSIBILITY

A third matter involves the discovery of features of a text that simply do not fit into the timeline of a historical Paul. For example, some scholars have noted the two appeals to "tradition" in 2 Thessalonians (2:15; 3:6)—is

---

80. The question is raised by Raymond Brown, 1997: 592. Other scholars who point to this phenomenon as an indicator of pseudonymous dependence include Richard 1995: 21; Esler 2001: 1213.

81. So Bailey reasons: "it is impossible to conceive of a man as creative as Paul drawing upon his own previous letter in such an unimaginative way" (1978–1979: 136); as cited in Still 1999: 51.

82. See Boring 2015: 215–17.

83. See Richard 1995: 22.

84. See Brown 1997: 493.

85. See Kreinecker 2013: 197–220.

this not language that is indicative of a more developed age of Christianity, rather than something Paul would have appealed to in AD 51–52?[86]

Another issue that has raised questions about historical plausibility is the way that the Lawless One is portrayed in 2 Thessalonians 2:1–12 as what appears to be Nero back from the dead (hence, Nero *redivivus*). Some scholars argue that if this Lawless One is a return of Nero, then the author of 2 Thessalonians must have already thought Nero was dead—and he died in AD 68, a time too late to fit into Paul's ministry to the Thessalonians.

Tone

Several scholars have raised the issue of the difference in *tone* between 1 and 2 Thessalonians. It appears that the tone of 2 Thessalonians is impersonal and formal, while that of 1 Thessalonians is more affectionate and intimate.[87] The difference is so stark that it seems to some that this is probably not the same Paul.

Pseudonymous "Tells"

Perhaps one of the most important arguments made by those who do not think Paul wrote 2 Thessalonians is that the text features elements that seem like a pseudonymous "tells" or giveaways. The best example of this is 2 Thess 3:17 where the author directly states: "I, Paul, write this greeting with my own hand. This is the mark in every letter of mine; it is the way I write." Could this be a pseudonymous writer trying *too hard* to present himself as Paul? As Krentz facetiously comments: "The author of 2 Thessalonians doth protest too much, methinks."[88]

Theological Differences

A final matter in this debate specifically relates to theological divergences in 2 Thessalonians compared to 1 Thessalonians. As this argument goes, in 1 Thessalonians, Paul's eschatological emphasis is on the soon-coming

---

86. See Brown 1997: 594.

87. See Furnish 2007: 132; Bridges 2008: 195.

88. Krentz 2009: 469; cf. Collins 1988: 223. Some scholars also think we see an undermining of 1 Thessalonians itself by the so-called pseudonymous author of 2 Thessalonians when he refers to a false letter "as though from us"—some surmise that in this case 2 Thessalonians was possibly written to reject 1 Thessalonians.

return of Jesus. However, in 2 Thessalonians the point is the opposite. Linda McKinnish Bridges offers this summary of how 2 Thessalonians is different: "The motion slows; the action shifts into low gear. The author of 2 Thessalonians states that a series of selected events must first take place before the end. The list is long, systematic, and highly descriptive, using stock imagery from the world of apocalyptic language." She summarizes, "In 1 Thessalonians the end is near. In 2 Thessalonians, however, the end is way out of sight!"[89]

To be fair, among those Pauline letters that scholars consider pseudonymous or deutero-pauline (Ephesians, Colossians, 2 Thessalonians, 1–2 Timothy, Titus), it is harder to make the case for 2 Thessalonians than, for example, 1 Timothy.[90] The case made against the authenticity of 2 Thessalonians does not rely on any silver bullet, but rather on cumulative evidence. Now we turn to responses to the above arguments for pseudonymity as well as other factors that offer support for authenticity.

Defending Pauline Authorship

What can we say in response to the *copycat* or mimicking dynamics of 2 Thessalonians in comparison to 1 Thessalonians? Leon Morris sees the dependence as a point in favor of authenticity—it is as equally likely that 2 Thessalonians is "Paul being Paul" (so to speak) as it is that it was someone else copying him.[91] Howard Marshall adds that the high level of structural similarity between the two letters could be explained by the short time between Paul's writing.[92] Gordon Fee offers his own point that, though some structural elements are the same, the way that structure is filled is different. The pseudepigrapher would have been simultaneously working in a dependent way (borrowing skeletal features of 1 Thessalonians) and a creative way (introducing his own ideas and arguments).[93] While the "copycat" nature of 2 Thessalonians is admittedly noticeable, it is very difficult to determine

89. Bridges 2008: 196.

90. Roose, though, explains that "German scholars almost unanimously view 2 Thessalonians as a pseudepigraph"; see 2006: 109n6.

91. Morris 1975: 23.

92. Marshall 1984: 30–31. G. Beale goes one step further by suggesting that Paul drew heavily from 1 Thessalonians as a conscious strategy: "Could this not be the case especially if he were trying to get them to recall the content of the first letter?" See Beale 2003: 31.

93. Fee 2009: 239.

what this means for the nature of its authenticity. The arguments based on *style* fall prey to the same methodological criticism.[94] Analysis of the style of 2 Thessalonians is simply inconclusive. Andrew Pitts has recently investigated its style based on insights from linguistics and especially in light of "register influences."[95]

The matter of historical implausibility is potentially more significant, but the two issues often raised (appeal to "tradition" and the Lawless One as Nero) can be otherwise explained within Paul's ministry to the Thessalonians. Paul does mention what he previously taught them several times in 1 Thessalonians (3:4; 5:1–2), and he uses the specific language of "tradition" in 1 Cor 11:2 (cf. Rom 6:17; 16:17). On the matter of Nero *redivivus*, if a pseudepigrapher were writing after AD 70, Marshall believes it unlikely that the author would refer to this Lawless One setting himself up in the *temple* (since the Jewish temple was destroyed in 70; see 2 Thess 2:4).[96]

What about the *tone* of 2 Thessalonians (as more cold and authoritarian)? Abraham Malherbe defuses this concern aptly:

> [I]t needs to be stated that it is fundamentally wrong to compare the language of the two letters in this way. The investigation is shaped by the question of pseudonymity, which means that differences are concentrated on and their significance is exaggerated. There is either no, or at the most insufficient, attention given to how the changes in the situation in Thessalonica may have caused Paul to consciously adopt a different style at points to achieve his present goal, into the one he had when he wrote 1 Thessalonians. All Paul's letters, after all, have their peculiarities.[97]

As for 2 Thess 3:17 as a pseudonymous "tell," the possible scenarios that would give rise for a pseudepigrapher to make such a statement are hard to imagine. The pseudepigrapher would have to be relying on 1 Corinthians

---

94. See Marshall 1984: 32.

95. Andrew Pitts defines "register" as "contexts for language varieties ranging from literary genres to social situations" (including, e.g., audience design); see 117. He notes that using basic statistics (vocabulary, "style") to settle the matter of authorship is methodological dubious given the range of possible options for how Paul might respond to all the variables; see Pitts 2013: 151–52.

96. Marshall 1984: 191.

97. Malherbe 2000: 367; see also Witherington 2006: 29. Although Menken agrees that an author can change tone from one letter to the next, he imagines this less likely if Paul himself wrote both letters in so short of a timespan (Menken 1994: 30–31). Perhaps, but this would imply his "tone" is determined by his mood (alone?) rather than his rhetorical strategy.

16:21 where Paul also announces, "I, Paul, write this greeting with my own hand." How did the pseudepigrapher come to have 1 Corinthians in his possession, and then what would possess him to write a pseudonymous letter to the *Thessalonians?* If he had a collection of Pauline letters, he would be writing in the second century or later. Aside from the question about why he would write a letter with such specific details to Thessalonica (dealing with issues that would have related to the community in the middle of the first century), there is also the matter of why the pseudepigrapher would make the claim that this is how Paul writes in *all* his letters (2 Thess 3:17), when knowledge of a wider collection would *not* demonstrate this.[98]

The last area of "theological differences" is also not a serious obstacle in view of authenticity. Only a simplistic view of Paul's theology *and* how he engages in nuanced ways with churches dealing with various problems can eliminate Paul from the equation of the authorship of 2 Thessalonians. Leon Morris points out that it is rather common for writers with an apocalyptic worldview to "hold to the two ideas of suddenness and the appearance of preparatory signs."[99] John Barclay perhaps says it best:

> Apocalypticists are notoriously slippery characters. Many apocalyptic works present conflicting scenarios of the end and inconsistent theses concerning signs of its imminence. That Paul should write both of these apocalyptic passages, and do so within a short space of time, is by no means impossible; why should his apocalyptic statements be any more consistent than his varied remarks about the law?[100]

---

98. Paul mentions writing by hand in Gal 6:11, 1 Cor 16:21, Col 4:18, and Phlm 19. Otherwise, in letters like Romans and 2 Corinthians he says no such thing (nor in 1 Thessalonians). It could be that he wrote in final words in his own handwriting in the original documents – and the first readers would be able to notice this. But by the time a pseudepigrapher got a handle on a set of Pauline texts, they would have been copies, thus he would not have knowledge of this practice of Paul if it was typical of his letter writing. See Foster 2012: 13–14.

99. Morris 1975: 21. Furthermore, F. F. Bruce urges that the same soon/not-yet dynamic is indicative of Jesus' eschatological teaching in the Synoptics (Bruce 1982: xlii–xliii).

100. Barclay 1993: 525.

Conclusion on Authorship

Despite the surge of popularity in favor of the vote for pseudonymity in the early and middle twentieth century, confidence in this decision has largely waned in the UK and North America.[101] Probably many are like me: *agnostic*.[102] I have lost confidence that we have the tools and the samples sufficient to render a judgment of "not written by Paul" on texts like 2 Thessalonians and Colossians. My assumption of authenticity is not borne out of 100 percent confidence, but rather in a *lack* of persuasive evidence to the contrary. I follow the guidance of Markus Barth in his evaluation of the authenticity of Colossians: *in dubio pro reo*—"when in doubt, side with the accused" (or as we sometimes say, "innocent until proven guilty"). Those who argue from pseudonymity may have "rescued" Paul from inconsistencies, but they insufficiently explain why someone would write such a letter, in Paul's name, to one specific church, about issues that relate to 1 Thessalonians

---

101. See Foster 2012: 154; thus this proclamation by Eugene Boring is probably untrue: "This [pseudonymous conclusion] is now probably the majority view among critical scholars" (Boring Intro 362). However, Fee's statement towards the opposite is also exaggerated: "the writing of a commentary on this letter in and of itself tends to push one towards authenticity regarding authorship, so that there has been only one significant commentary in English [Earl Richard] over the past century and a half that has tried to make sense of this letter as a forger" (Fee 2009: 237). Fee may be right if we only include technical (advanced) commentaries, but if we broaden the outlook to academic commentaries since 1995 (the last twenty years), this seems to be the result:

2 Thessalonians as Authentic: Weima (2014), Shogren (2012), Thiselton (2010), Fee (2009), Witherington (2006), Green (2002), Malherbe (2000), Holmes (1998)

2 Thessalonians as Pseudonymous: Thurston (2013), Bridges (2008), Furnish (2007), Richard (2007), Smith (2000), Gaventa (1998) [and we ought to include Menken 1994]

This represents, probably, the real state of the debate that the question about the authorship of 2 Thessalonians is far from closed, and scholars are nearly evenly divided on the issue at present. Paul Foster offers results from an informal poll regarding authorship he conducted at an academic conference. Of the 111 New Testament scholars polled, Foster reports that 63 percent said "yes" in respect to the question asking whether Paul was the author in the case of 2 Thessalonians. Only 13 percent said "no." And another 35 percent claimed they were "uncertain."

102. Bonnie Thurston prefers to interpret 2 Thessalonians assuming pseudonymity and she notes the typical concerns with authenticity. Interestingly, though, she mentions that, despite the lack of any conclusive evidence, she chooses to follow "the weight of scholarly opinion" (which she assumes is a consensus against authenticity). Also, she admits that assuming pseudonymity requires a *Sitz im Leben* (life setting) for a later pseudepigrapher, the determination of which "has proved to be a difficult task." See Thurston 1995: 160.

and very particular problems there, repeating the first letter quite closely in some ways, and yet obviously wanting to say something new.[103] Unless these issues can be resolved, it seems to me to be the most sensible option to attempt to understand the letter as it is written, Paul to the Thessalonians.

---

103. So, in a forthcoming commentary, Andy Johnson asks (calling into question the plausibility of pseudonymity): "If someone knew 1 Thessalonians as part of a corpus of Pauline letters that had begun circulating in the late first or early second century and if the theology of 2 Thessalonians really is so different from that of 1 Thessalonians and the rest of Paul's letters, how would the person have hoped to persuade anyone—at least anyone familiar enough with Paul or this corpus to care about a writing in the name of Paul—that 2 Thessalonians was from him?" See Johnson 2016.

Thanksgiving for the Thessalonians (1 Thess 1:1–10)

Prescript (1:1)

> **1:1** Paul, Silvanus, and Timothy, to the church of the Thessalonians in God the Father and the Lord Messiah Jesus—grace and peace to you.

Ancient letters of Paul's time began much like what we see in 1 Thessalonians: sender—recipient—greeting. In this case, while Paul uses "I" several times throughout the letter (2:18; 3:5; 5:27), he lists his co-workers Silvanus and Timothy. It is probably not the case that they served as co-writers in a formal sense, but rather Paul wanted to express that he functioned as part of a larger group (and Timothy and Silvanus were people whom they already knew; 3:2). While we think of Paul as *the* apostle to the Gentiles, we must remember that, even in the account of Paul's acceptance by the "pillar apostles" in Galatians, it is Paul and *Barnabas* who receive the right hand of fellowship (Gal 2:9). He often demonstrated a hearty spirit of community and collaboration—as 2 Cor 1:19 reminds us, Paul, Silvanus, and Timothy proclaimed the gospel *as a team*.

In most of his letters, Paul identifies himself as apostle or slave, but here he is simply "Paul." The most likely reason for this unadorned appellation is that he was not determined to reinforce his authority, and he wished to write a simple letter of encouragement and teaching for a church that he loved and cared about deeply.[1]

Paul writes to the church of the Thessalonians *in* God the Father and the Lord Messiah Jesus. Perhaps, in our familiarity with this kind of language in Paul's letters we might miss its potency. Paul was marking the identity of this community as primarily determined by their relationship with God and Jesus the Messiah, and in particular that they now have life and security and wholeness of their being within the ambit of that realm.

---

1. See Best 1986: 60.

Paul explains in Colossians that the Father "rescued us from the power of darkness and transferred us into the kingdom of his beloved Son" (1:13 AT). This is precisely the sentiment carried by the statement in 1 Thess 1:1—*this is who you are, this is where you are, you belong with God and Jesus and they have made a home for you.*[2] It becomes clear very early on in the letter that the Thessalonians are facing many burdens, worries, and afflictions, and Paul's reminder to them that they have been relocated, as it were, into the realm or domain of God and Jesus supplies a kind of identity-anchor on the stormy sea of life.

Here he adds too his wish for God's "grace and peace" to them. This is a typical kind of well-wish for a letter of his time, but these are two very important words for Paul theologically. It is not simply a nice sentiment from Paul, but a mark of the ongoing, out-flowing work of the gospel of Jesus the Messiah where he ever has more favor[3] to bestow. Keep in mind that in chapter five he warns them not to be naïve, embracing cheap offers of "peace and security" from the world (5:3). When Paul conveys words of peace, it is a deeper kind than the world can offer, just as Jesus said, "Peace I leave with you; my peace I give to you. I do not give to you as the world gives. Do not let your hearts be troubled, and do not let them be afraid" (John 14:27). As Jesus comforted his disciples, so Paul his converts—Jesus "released" his peace and left it for his followers; Paul offers it to the Thessalonians.

Thanksgiving for the Thessalonians' Praise-Worthy Trust (1:2–10)

> **2**We always thank God for all of you whenever we remember you in our prayers. **3**In particular we continually remember in prayer before our God and Father your loyalty that works, your love that labors, and your endurance driven by hope in our Lord Messiah Jesus. **4**And we know, my dear brothers and sisters, who are loved by God, that God chose you, **5**because our good news did not come to you as a message only, but it also came in a powerful way through the Holy Spirit and deep conviction, just as you know what kind of people we became when we were with you for your

---

2. The collocation of "God the Father" and "the Lord Messiah Jesus" is critical for Paul's Christology. As F. F. Bruce explains, this demonstrates "the exalted place which the risen Christ occupies in the thoughts of Paul and his colleagues"; see Bruce 1982: 7.

3. "Favor," or generosity, is another way to translate the Greek word *charis*; see Barclay 2015.

sake. **6**And, as for you, you became people who imitated us and the Lord when, in the midst of great affliction, you accepted the message with the joy of the Holy Spirit. **7**So then you became a model for all those who believe in Macedonia and Achaia. **8**The message of the Lord trumpeted forth from you, echoing not only throughout Macedonia and Achaia, but your loyalty towards God went out into every place, even to the extent that we didn't need to tell anyone. **9**For they themselves report about us the kind of welcome we had with you, and how you turned towards God, rejecting idols in order to serve a new master, the living and true God. **10**And you wait eagerly for his Son to come from heaven, the one whom God raised from the realm of the dead, Jesus who will rescue us from God's coming anger for justice.

As far as we can tell from the Pauline letters in the New Testament collection, his opening greeting was typically followed by a word of thanksgiving (Galatians being the obvious exception). He was moved to prayer and thanks to God because of something special about God's work in and through his people (here the Thessalonians' exemplary reception of, and reaction to, the good news of Messiah Jesus). Of special note, in 1 Thess 1:2, is the constancy and passion of Paul's prayer-life (see also 5:17). The catalyst for his thanksgiving-prayer here was his *memories*. For Paul, remembering was a kind of spiritual discipline (Rom 1:9). Looking to God's work among his people (and both God's faithfulness and theirs) was critical for survival in a world full of uncertainties and pressures. The same word that Paul uses for memory in 1:2 is found in the Septuagint in Deut 7:18. There Moses enjoined the Israelites, at a time when they were afraid to step out in covenantal trust into an unknown future, to *remember* God's power over and against Egypt when he led them out. Israel was regularly called to establish a memorial whenever they saw God's faithful work (see, e.g., Joshua 4:7).

The Thessalonians are enjoined to remember their own record of trust. Paul introduces here his familiar triad of trust, hope, and love (see 1 Thess 5:8; cf. 1 Cor 13:13). Traditionally, *pistis* is translated "faith" in the New Testament, but here it takes on the more common Hellenistic meaning of "loyalty" or "trust."[4] Paul is not really commending them for what they believe *per se*, but rather for their firm commitment to God from the start.[5]

---

4. See Best 1986: 68, 81. See also extended discussion in the Introduction to this commentary, 10–13.

5. So deSilva 1996: 73: "'faith' in that context clearly refers to the believers' perseverance in their commitment to the new social reality called the [church of God] in the face

Pistis here is a word marking the orientation of the will—it is an active word for Paul in the same way love (*agapē*) is an active word. In ancient Greek literature, *pistis* was regularly used with the meaning of "pledge" or "bond." This reflects aptly Paul's concern: the Thessalonians were known for their bold and active *loyalty and obedience* that are seen in real-life action or work. Similarly, he commends them for their love that is marked by labor. With these two statements about faith/love and work/labor, Paul is not trying to make a strong and clear differentiation between the two ("work" and "labor"), but rather desires to look at their lives from several angles (loyalty, hope, love). In 1:3, the "love" for which Paul gives thanks is possibly their love for God, laboring and working out of affection for him. However, it is probably a more comprehensive kind of love that is directed towards God (vertically) *and* others (horizontally). In 3:6, after Timothy is sent by Paul to check on the Thessalonians, he brings back report of their "trust and love" and that they wanted to see Paul as he did them.

The last element in 1:3 that Paul mentions is their track record of "endurance driven by hope in our Lord Messiah Jesus." Sometimes *hypomonē* ("endurance") is translated as "patience," but this word should be understood here as more of an active term (moving forward in spite of resistance), rather than a passive one (holding your ground).[6] We have a perfect image of this word in Hebrews 12:1 where the author presses the readers to "run with *endurance* the race set out for us." We know that the Thessalonians were struggling with persecution as well (see introduction, 10–13).

I think a military analogy is also fitting to portray this endurance. Imagine a soldier training and preparing for war. He goes out into the battle and, despite his extensive education, real war is simply a chaotic mess. It is frenetic and long and exhausting. *Endurance* and courage are his allies. The thought of giving up (in retreat or surrender) is natural, but that is no way to win a war! Not to mention what the commander, let alone the emperor, would say to a deserter! In the apocryphal text Sirach (written not long before the time of Paul), Ben Sira wrote this to his readers: "Woe to you who have lost your endurance! What will you do when the Lord's reckoning comes" (2:14)? The Thessalonians are not in this kind of trouble, but they seem to be just at the place where they need some motivation to press on in trust and faithfulness (see 1 Thess 3:10). Paul's advice is more consonant with Ben Sira's word a bit later on: "[God] encourages those who

---

of the dominant culture's resistance and disapproval."

6. Morris 1975: 42; Beale 2003: 47.

are running low on endurance" (17:24). Paul prays the same kind of hope continues to push them that is seen in the Ephesian church of Revelation 2:2–3: "I know your deeds, your hard work and your endurance . . . I also know you are enduring patiently and bearing up for the sake of my name, and that you have not grown weary."

The main purpose of this introductory discussion (1:2–10) is encouragement and comfort. He does this in 1:3 by appealing to *their* history of trust in God, but in 1:4 he also underscores *God's* relationship with them. Three descriptors are used here. First, they are "my dear brothers and sisters." This is probably Paul's most central image used in 1 Thessalonians to help re-describe their special identity in Messiah Jesus—he refers to them as Christian siblings almost two dozen times across the five chapters. They have been adopted into a single family and household under God the Father (1:1) through Jesus the Son (1:10), so that Jesus could become "the firstborn among many brothers and sisters" (Rom 8:29).

What does it *mean* to be brothers and sisters in the Messiah? In the Greco-Roman world, there were few relationships more intimate and important than that of siblings—not only were they close through spending time together growing up, but there was an almost instinctual desire to protect and seek out the welfare of one's brother or sister. When someone was in times of trouble, siblings could be counted on for aid and encouragement. While Paul himself writes to them as a brother in the Messiah, someone with deep concern, he also strongly exhorts them to take care of one another (4:9, 18; 5:11, 15) in a way that was really only true of family members in the wider world.[7]

Fusing the Horizons: Blood-Blind in the New Covenant Community

A letter like Galatians reminds us that Christians are "color-blind," not privileging Jews over Gentiles as fellow-heirs of the kingdom of God. In 1 Thessalonians we are reminded that Christians are "blood-blind," we are meant to treat fellow believers like family. In Paul's world, as in ours, people tended to care for their family in a way not true of outsiders (the proverb "blood is thicker than water" makes good sense in just about any culture). What happens when Paul links perfect strangers by the bond of siblingship? They are not kin biologically, but the sheer frequency of use of this language from Paul

---

7. See further Trebilco 2012: 16–66.

demonstrates that, for him, this was more than a rhetorical device or banal label. Perhaps, even, the Thessalonians would have felt a bit of a shock when Paul started talking about "love between siblings" (*philadelphia*)—the kind of endearment and care that related to real family members (1 Thess 4:9).

In most churches that I visit, rarely have I seen this kind of "blood-blindness" of which Paul writes. But I have seen it once. In the late 1990s I did some missionary work in Eastern Europe. In Macedonia, ethnic Albanians (about 20 percent of the population) and ethnic Macedonians have a history of conflict. On the streets, everyone is conscious of the cultural dividing lines between Albanians and ethnic Macedonians and the hostility is palpable. But in our college ministry communities we saw something amazing—Albanians and Macedonians, not only sitting together and singing, but hugging and sharing and loving one another without hatred or prejudice. St. Paul would have felt proud that his siblingship theology took root in that community and blossomed.

How do we view the people around us in our own churches? Are they strangers with whom we exchange friendly greetings? When needs are raised, do we feel responsible to take care of one another? Has the gospel properly "blinded" us to blood?

The second descriptor Paul uses for the Thessalonians is that they are "loved by God," or "God's beloved" (1 Thess 1:4). No doubt, Paul was applying to the Thessalonians a description that characterized the Lord's intimate love for Israel: "When Israel was a child, I loved him, and out of Egypt I called my son" (Hos 11:1; cf. Isa 5:1; 57:8; Jer 12:7; Mal 1:2). Often, in the Old Testament, the Lord's affirmations of his love came at a time when Israel felt abandoned. Perhaps this too applies to Paul's use. That is, in spite of all the Thessalonians were going through, God's own relationship and attitude towards them was secure (cf. Rom 8:38–39). They are not part of a nameless, faceless mass down below while God sits at a far distance in heaven. The ones called "beloved" are truly *known* by God and he cares for them deeply.

The third descriptor follows quite closely from the second: God *chose* them (1 Thess 1:4). The focus here (*eklogē*) is not a kind of one-sided election (i.e. "predestination"), but more a testimony to how *precious* they are in God's eyes. Imagine a couple passing by an alley and noticing a poor, homeless child lying on the ground half-dead. Their heart goes out to the child and they rush over and carefully scoop her up and find her care, later adopting her into their family. They were not forced to shelter her, but they went out of their way to rescue her and she becomes *precious, one-of-a-kind, an object selected through persistent attention and interest.* No doubt, in the midst of their trials and tribulations, the Thessalonians felt ignored by God. Perhaps they felt rejected. Paul responds tenderly: he chose you then, he loves you now.

We see a parallel in Isaiah 44 in view of Yahweh's care for Israel. In the prior chapter, Yahweh reminded Israel that her exilic state was not an accident, but the result of a heritage of rebellion against God's commands and counsel. However, rejection on God's part was not to be the last word.

> But now listen, Jacob my servant; and Israel whom I have *chosen*: this is what the Lord God who made you says, the one who formed you in the womb; your rescue is yet to come, do not be afraid, my servant Jacob, my *beloved* Israel, the one I have *chosen*. (Isa 44:1–2)

How does Paul know that the Thessalonians should be confident and secure in their identity in God (especially as beloved and precious)? In 1:5 he reminds them of their reception of the message of the good news. It was not merely an exchange of words, but the presence and power of God was profoundly felt. Paul refers to the gospel coming, literally, "in power and in the Holy Spirit." This is probably a hendiadys best translated "in a powerful way through the Holy Spirit." Paul, here, is repeating his remembrance motif, prompting the Thessalonians to look back to the memorable happenings of their initial conversion. Probably Paul is referring to the manifestation of "signs and wonders" (miracles) at that time (see Rom 15:13, 19), but he may also have in mind their positive reaction to the good news.[8] Apparently that was enough to give them "deep conviction" that the gospel message was reliable and trustworthy.[9] They also had the example of Paul and his associates as additional testimony to the reliability of the good news.

---

8. See Twelftree 2013: 180–87.

9. The early Christian letter called 1 Clement uses this same language of "deep conviction" in reference to the proof supplied by the resurrection of Jesus that supported them along with the presence and power of the Holy Spirit (42.3). There is some debate over whether the "deep conviction" was on the part of the Thessalonians (in their acceptance of the good-news message) or on the part of the apostles (who preached with boldness and assurance from God). My own inclination is to see it as the former, in agreement with Bruce 1982: 14.

The last clause of 1:5 mentions that the Thessalonians ought to remember "what kind of people we became when we were with you for your sake." Even if the Thessalonians knew what this broad statement means, it is difficult for us, uninformed readers to discern. It could means that they acted honestly and with integrity, as these matters are taken up in 2:1–12. However, the way Paul phrases this clause, it seems that he and Silas somehow went out of their way to be something or act in a way that proved better for the Thessalonians. Two possibilities are worth considering. First, he could be making reference to how he became like an infant among them (2:7), someone vulnerable and without status. He makes it clear enough that he and Silas had every right to assert their authority as "apostles," but they chose not to. A second option is a reference here to Paul's work-policy with them. He chose to work "night and day" so as not to burden them with his financial needs (2:9). I have a slight preference for the second option because it is a bit more tangible and, thus, would be easy to recall for the Thessalonians at Paul's mention, but in either case the point is clear: the Thessalonians, at that time, had a crystal clear picture of God at work among them in the ministry of the apostles and the work of the Spirit. How easy it is to leave a mountaintop experience and begin to doubt the power and truth that was so present and lucid in that moment.

Fusing the Horizons: Metamorphosis

It is hard to tell in English, but Paul repeats an important keyword in 1 Thessalonians: *ginomai*. This verb can be translated "to come" or "to become" based on context. Paul uses this verb twelve times in this letter, four times in 1:5–7. The Thessalonians *became* imitators of the apostles and the Lord Jesus (1:6; 2:14). And they *became* an example for the Macedonians and Achaians (1:7). The apostles *became* holy and blameless among them (2:10). This can make it sound like believers are always transforming into something better, something more glorious. Certainly this is true in the sense that Paul discusses in 2 Cor 3:18: "And all of us, with unveiled faces, seeing the glory of the Lord as though reflected in a mirror, are being transformed into the same image from one degree of glory to another, for this comes from the Lord, the Spirit." As we are gravitationally pulled into the orbit of God's grace and power, we are reshaped into the "the image of [God's] Son" (Rom 8:29).

But that can make it seem like the Christian life is simply one of glorious transformation, like an unassuming caterpillar becoming a beautiful butterfly. However, a glorious transformation is not the *only* kind of change that believers must undergo. In a sinful, hostile world, there is another kind of "becoming"—believers sometimes must *become* something less glorious in the eyes of the world. When writing to the Corinthians, he told them that he had to suffer becoming (*ginomai*) like garbage in the world's eyes in order to bring them the gospel (1 Cor 4:13). Sometimes the calling of a Christian is to transform into something ignoble, shameful; this is the only way Paul can say: "death is at work in us, but life is at work in you" (2 Cor 4:12). We see this clearly modeled by Jesus in Phil 2:5–11 where he took upon himself the humble station of a human who had to face the shame of death on a cross (2:8). Christ's own *"becoming"* was to become a reject (John 1:11).

This may be what Paul means when he says that he *became* an infant (see below 54–56) with them (2:7). In this context, it means something that would not come naturally to Paul. For the sake of the Thessalonians, Paul had to undergo a change, a metamorphosis, but not always into something more attractive from a worldly perspective. Yet this *becoming* is inspired by the Messiah and empowered by the Spirit.

We would do well to remember, then, that God intends to change us. Obviously he wants to cause us to grow in holiness. But we must also consider other ways we might need to go through a metamorphosis in order to bring goodness and blessing to someone else. Perhaps that change will not seem "glorious," but if it benefits and blesses the other, it will bespeak Christlikeness.

In 1:6 we learn for the first time in the letter that the Thessalonians faced bitter persecution when they accepted the good news. They did not shrink from faith, nor did they retaliate against any trouble-makers, but met the occasion with joy, the same kind of godly reaction that was seen in the suffering apostles, the prophets, and even the Lord Jesus himself (1 Thess 2:14–15). The Thessalonians became the poster-children of what Paul would commend years later to the Romans: those who "Rejoice in hope, endure in suffering, persist in prayer" (12:12 NET). So noteworthy was their surrender and commitment to Jesus and his kingdom that their fame spread throughout Macedonia and Achaia and beyond, and they became a model and example of gracious perseverance (1:7–8).

So admirable and even unexpected was their bold loyalty to Jesus that the message about him spread quickly, moving even faster than the apostles could travel to share this news. One is reminded of the Israelite spies who encountered Rahab. The Canaanite prostitute did not need to be told about the fame of Israel and the power of Yahweh because she had already heard and she revered the God who "dried up the water of the Red Sea" (Joshua 2:9–11)!

Apparently, distant Achaians and Macedonians came to know the story of the work of God amongst the Thessalonians, in particular how they "turned towards God, rejecting idols in order to serve a new master, the living and true God" (1 Thess 1:9). Paul helpfully clues us into the probability that the Thessalonians are mostly Gentile believers, since Jews abhorred idols (Rom 2:22) and considered worshipping with cult statues a mark of reprobation (1 Cor 5:10–11; 6:9; Gal 5:20; cf. 1 Pet 4:3).[10] Idols were known to be, according to Jewish thought, dead and inefficacious (cf. Acts 14:15).[11] Given that the early Christians represent pagan worship as a kind of ignorance and slavery (Heb 9:14), it takes the intervening work of God to bring illumination, wisdom, and freedom to know and worship the true God.

If we look at a Jewish text like Bel and the Dragon, we learn that Jews (like Paul) were educated with stories that reminded them that idols are not real gods, but objects made with human hands. This is distinctly *not* true of the living God who created all things and rules over all creatures (see Bel 1:5). Idols reflect the imagination of their artisan (a mere human) and, thus, they are as corrupted as human sinners. Thus, Jews and Christians could associate idolatry with sexual perversion and greed (see Col 3:5). When the Thessalonians rejected their idols, then, they also turned away from a pagan, godless way of life. As Beverly Gaventa explains, this required a whole new way of life:

> Paul's words about turning *from* idols to serve God imply that faith in the God of Israel who is the Father of Jesus Christ is not an

---

10. Note, though, that in the Introduction I consider the possibility, even likelihood, that this church was comprised of many "god-fearers," Gentile pagans at once time associated with the Jewish synagogue and later became believers in Messiah Jesus. See 6–13.

11. For a discussion of Jewish anti-idol polemic and Gentile cult statue worship in the era of the New Testament, see Gupta 2014.

optional practice to be added on to previous values and commitments. One cannot serve this God alongside idols; they must be put away. The claims of Christian faith are all-encompassing.[12]

When they turned towards the one God, they committed themselves to "serve a new master" (*douleuō*). To call this slave-service was not to imagine this as cruel, de-humanizing slavery, but more like the joy a trained soldier experiences under a professional, if demanding, senior officer who knows what it takes to carry out a mission successfully. Howard Marshall notes that this kind of service is life-giving because its focus is on the doing of what is good and right, rather than "being in bondage to sin."[13]

To become a slave of Yahweh is to be written into the story that Scripture tells, which involves the covenant with Israel and which reaches a climax with the appearance of Messiah Jesus. While Jesus' (first) coming launched a new phase in salvation history, he ascended into heaven and promised to return again.

We read in 1 Thess 1:10 that Paul commends these believers who turned to God as they "wait eagerly for his Son to come from heaven, the one God raised from the realm of the dead, Jesus who will rescue us from God's coming anger for justice." There is a kind of passive dimension of the word "wait" (*anamenō*) here (as in "to stay put"; Judith 7.12), but Paul probably uses it in a more transformative manner. They live their lives in eager anticipation of Jesus' return; they have re-oriented their lives around this arrival.[14] The kingdom of God is a kind of invisible reality because Jesus is in heaven and it appears like the worldly powers are in control. To wait for, or anticipate, Jesus' return means living according to an alternative vision of power and value that is unseen, but is surely to come. The Thessalonians have shown signs of aligning with this not-yet kingdom even under pressure and affliction. The tables will turn, so to speak, when Jesus returns because God is coming with wrath ("anger for justice"; 1:10b). God's wrath, or anger, is not borne out of an unbridled temper, but the justice-orientation of God towards a rebellious world.[15] Paul preached an impending assize that would call the world to account for its hedonism, bloodlust, oppression of the weak and poor, and rejection of the authority and wisdom of God. Those who received "the good news" of Messiah Jesus in this life might not

---

12. Gaventa 1998: 20.
13. Marshall 1984: 58; see further Harris 1999.
14. See Marshall 1984: 58.
15. Ibid., 59.

be many, and they would face opposition for their commitment, but Jesus would recognize them at his coming and rescue them as his own people.[16]

---

16. See Wanamaker 1990: 88.

Paul's Blameless Ministry (1 Thess 2:1–12)

¹For you know for yourselves, my dear brothers and sisters, that our coming to you was not useless. ²On the contrary, even though we had suffered before and were mistreated in Philippi, as you know, yet we were given courage by our God to speak God's good news to you despite fierce opposition. ³For our appeal did not come from an error, or impure motives, or trickery. ⁴Rather, as we have been approved by God to be entrusted with the good news, so we speak, not to please mortals, but to please the God who tests our hearts. ⁵For we never appeared with flattering words, as you know, nor by trying to be fake to hide greed—God serves as our witness!—⁶nor chasing after glory from mortals—not from you, nor anyone else. ⁷We could have done this, imposing our weight as "apostles of the Messiah." But, instead, we became infants among you. Like a nursing mother tenderly caring for her children, ⁸so we felt about you. It pleased us to share with you, not only the good news of God, but also the depths of our souls, because you became beloved to us.

⁹For you remember, my dear brothers and sisters, our labor and toil; night and day we were working to prevent burdening any of you when we preached the good news of God to you. ¹⁰You yourselves stand witness, along with God, how holy and just and blameless we were before you who believe.¹¹As you know, towards each one of you as a father to his children, ¹²we were encouraging you, comforting you, and insisting that you live your lives in a manner worthy of the God who is calling you into his own glorious kingdom.

While Paul focuses in the first chapter on the Thessalonians' own faithful reception of the good news and their trust in God through Messiah Jesus, he then turns to his own ministry (2:1–12) with special concern to demonstrate his blameless and exemplary apostolic behavior.[1] Scholars have wondered whether Paul is being defensive (as if his own behavior and

---

1. Though I refer in this section to "Paul," this is simply a shorthand way of referring to the Pauline apostolic team, as he repeatedly refers to "we" and "our" implying inclusion of others in his leadership cohort.

motives have been questioned by the Thessalonians), or if his *apologia* is more instructive (directing his readers to his model behavior in the face of difficulty and temptation). Perhaps it is best to think of this section as serving both interests. Given Paul mentions his premature separation from them (2:17; cf. Acts 17:14), it very well could have been that one day Paul was with the Thessalonians preaching and ministering to them, and the next day he was just gone. This may have shocked many Thessalonian believers and Paul may have fell under suspicion of being a kind of con man. While he is very clear that he did not force them to pay him money (2:9), he probably would not have refused gifts from generous believers (see Phil 4:15). If rumors spread that Paul was a fraud, his tone and insistence in this section would be sensible (not unlike the tone of 2 Corinthians; see below).

Jeffrey Weima has offered what is probably the strongest rationale for the view that Paul was, in fact, defending his character and ministry in view of criticisms, potential or real. Three pieces of "evidence" from 1 Thess 2:1–12 lead Weima to this conclusion. Firstly, we have, twice stated, appeal to God as witness (2:5, 10)—a relatively rare phenomenon in the Pauline corpus (Rom 1:9; 2 Cor 1:23; Phil 1:8). Secondly, Paul refers to his having been examined and approved by God for his ministry (2:4). Thirdly, Weima appeals to the string of antithetical statement in 2:1–12. I would register my own pieces of evidence in addition to Weima's. The possibility that Paul takes on a defensive tone in 1 Thess 2:1–12 is strengthened significantly by the appearance of remarkably similar language in 2 Cor 12:11–19, a text where it is certain that Paul's rhetoric is defensive.

> Look, for the third time I am ready to come to you, and I will not be a burden (*katanarkoō*) to you, because I do not want your possessions, but you. For children should not have to save up for their parents, but parents for their children. Now I will most gladly spend and be spent for your lives! If I love you more, am I to be loved less? But be that as it may, I have not burdened (*katabareō*) you. Yet because I was a crafty person (*panourgos*), I took you in by deceit (*dolos*)! I have not taken advantage of you through anyone I have sent to you, have I? I urged Titus to visit you and I sent our brother along with him. Titus did not take advantage of you, did he? Did we not conduct ourselves in the same spirit? Did we not behave in the same way. Have you been thinking all this time that we have been defending ourselves to you? We are speaking in Christ before God, and everything we do, dear friends, is to build you up. (2 Cor 12:14–19 NET)

First Thessalonians 2:1–12 bears more than a few similarities to what Paul writes above. Notice the use of *dolos* (deceit) in both places (1 Thess 2:3; 2 Cor 12:16), as well as the language of burdening (*epibareō* 1 Thess 2:9; *katabareō* 2 Cor 12:16).[2] If there is a question as to whether or not Paul's self-descriptive language in 1 Thess 2:1–12 has a genuinely defensive purpose (to put to rest any concerns or criticisms from the Thessalonians about his motives or intentions), the connections between this passage and 2 Cor 12:14–19 (where a real defensive concern is explicit in chapters 10–13) convince me that Paul is doing more than offering himself as a model of good behavior.

The above notwithstanding, it is a mistake to think that 1 Thess 2:1–12 is *only* apologetic or self-defensive. Paul did not write 1 Thessalonians as his deposition in view of an apostolic trial. The letter is, ultimately, a letter of encouragement and instruction *for the sake of the Thessalonians*. Thus, the idea that Paul had a self-defensive interest should not cancel out his concern to be a model for the Thessalonians and to enjoin them to good-news obedience. As Michael Holmes aptly puts it, "The heavy concentration of direct appeals in the last part of the passage (2:9–12), in which Paul reminds the Thessalonians of how he exhorted them to holy living, confirms that the primary function of this section is not defense or apologetics but exhortation."[3]

If we link 2:1–12 to the larger concerns of the letter and the situation of the Thessalonians, it makes good sense to see this passage as positioning Paul as the model of one who works and labors and endures in the face of opposition and problems. This seems to be the more important contribution of this section. Paul draws attention, in particular, to three areas: his courage (2:1–2), his integrity (2:3–7a), and his tender-care (2:7b-12).

Paul's Courage (2:1–2)

Paul, beginning again with appeal to the Thessalonians as his Christian siblings (see 17–18), calls them to remember. In the first chapter he urged them to recall *their* conversion and *their* commitment to Jesus. Now, in chapter two, he prompts them to call to mind a viewpoint of *his* part of the story, where Paul, Timothy, and Silvanus did not forsake their vocation even in

---

2. *Epibareō* and *katabareō* are cognates that share the same root in Greek (*bar**); according to standard Greek lexicons, their meanings are indistinguishable.

3. Holmes 1998: 60.

the midst of intense suffering and mistreatment. To get a sense for what this mistreatment may have looked like, we could turn to Acts 14:5 where the same term *hybrizō* ("mistreated") also appears. There Luke recounts that Gentiles and Jews *harassed* Paul and Barnabas at Iconium, a situation that escalated to the level of their nearly being stoned to death. The term *hybrizō* was also used by Luke in respect to Jesus when, at his trial, he was derided and spat upon (Luke 18:32). In view of such provocation, it was admirable for Paul and his companions to be courageous and continue to preach the good news openly.[4] When Paul writes about being "given courage," this term (*parrēsiazomai*) carries the idea of public, confident testimony. There is a kind of "devil-may-care" stubbornness here. Paul is shaping a particular vision that carves out a safe space for Christian identity that can withstand the storms and winds of unfavorable public opinion.

Paul's Integrity (2:3–7a)

Paul goes on to talk about his ministry, especially that he behaved in their presence in an upright and blameless manner—he showed unassailable integrity. His main concern is to be an example for the Thessalonians regarding how to respond to pressure and conflict with integrity and how to maintain an irreproachable reputation.

In 2:3, when he refers to the introduction of his message or appeal, he urges that it did not come from error, meaning that it was not a distortion of the truth. Nor from impure motives, as if aligned with wickedness. And far be it that it arose from trickery. He is insistent that his apostolic team was "approved by God" and that the good-news message was "entrusted" to them (2:4a). They were thoroughly inspected by the God who knows and sees all and they were found responsible as trustees of the truth. With that commission, and before the all-knowing God (who tests hearts[5]), their mission is to seek to please God (not merely to please mortals, as con art-

---

4. See Gaventa 1998: 24; Wanamaker, 1990: 92.

5. It is possible, when Paul refers to the God who tests hearts, he has something in mind akin to Sirach 2:1–5: "My child, when you come to serve the Lord, prepare yourself for testing. Set your heart right and be steadfast, and do not be impetuous in time of calamity. Cling to him and do not depart, so that your last days may be prosperous. Accept whatever befalls you, and in times of humiliation be patient. For gold is tested in fire, and those found acceptable, in the furnace of humiliation." Certainly, Paul could have earned a reputation for integrity amidst such persistent persecution (cf. Prov 17:3). He appears to have wanted to assure the Thessalonians that his cohort should be counted among the righteous and upright.

ists do; 2:4b). They never tried to win the Thessalonians with flattery, nor masking greed (2:5).[6] Aristotle clues us into the Hellenistic concern with hucksters when he wrote: "the man who joins in gratifying people...for the sake of getting something for himself in the way of money or money's worth is a flatterer" (*Eth. Nic.* 4.6.9).[7]

Paul was not in the business of making himself the center of attention (2:6). His focus was on bringing glory to the Messiah. But, he notes in 2:7, it was within his rights to demand their respect as "apostles of the Messiah." Literally, he writes that he had "the ability in heaviness," meaning he had the requisite credentials to throw his weight around (so CEB), but he chose not to behave that way with them. His use of the word weight (*baros*) here points forward to his employment of a related word *epibareō* in 1 Thess 2:9b: "night and day we were working to prevent burdening (*epibareō*) any of you." By use of wordplay, he argues that while he had authoritative *weight* (*baros*) as an apostle such that he could make demands on them, he lovingly chose to work extra hard so as not to *weigh* (*epibareō*) them down.

Paul's Tender Care (2:7b–12)

While Paul is firm on the point that he has acted "above-board," as it were, throughout his ministry with and towards them, he also underscores, especially in 2:7b–12, his tender care for the Thessalonians. In 2:7b we find a statement that contains one of most contested textual problems in the whole of the New Testament. Does Paul write that he was *gentle* (*ēpioi*) in their midst, or that he was like an *infant* (*nēpioi*) with them? Translations are divided on this matter, but there is slightly better reason to side with the reading of "infant" (*nēpioi*).[8]

---

6. If Paul worked hard not to burden the Thessalonians with requests for financial support for his livelihood and ministry, how could he be worried about being seen as greedy? In the introduction to this section (2:1–12), I entertained the possibility that, while he did not *ask* for money, he may have accepted gifts (see Phil 4:15). Ambrosiaster, writing in the fourth century AD, made a comment that, in Paul's refusal of "small gifts," some locals may have wondered if he was hoping for larger ones (see Bray 2009: 103).

7. See Bruce 1982: 29.

8. See Weima 2014; Sailors 2000: 81–98.

Excursus: Gentle or Infants? (2:7b)

The reason why we have the question regarding what Paul meant in 1 Thess 2:7 is that some Greek manuscripts show the reading "infants" (*nēpioi*) and others "gentle" (*ēpioi*). The difference between these words is a single Greek letter—*nu* (an "n" consonantal sound) at the beginning of the word. When Greek manuscripts differ on the wording of a text, theories are devised to determine which word (*nēpioi* or *ēpoioi*) was the original one that Paul wrote. Such theories rely on two kinds of evidence: external (based on the quality and dating of extant manuscripts) and internal (based on how one reads the text). From an external standpoint, virtually all scholars agree that the manuscript witnesses for the *nēpioi* ("infants") reading are stronger.[9] However, many scholars find internal evidence persuasive enough to encourage adopting the *ēpioi* ("gentle") variant as original.

Howard Marshall, for example, prefers *ēpioi* ("gentle") on the grounds that it would appear that a rarely-used word (*ēpioi*) was swapped out by a textual scribe for a more common word (*nēpioi*).[10] Most commentators that adopt the *ēpioi* reading do so, though, primarily because it fits well into the flow of Paul's argumentation—Paul could have come on strong in authority with the Thessalonians, but chose to be *gentle*. The *ēpioi* proponents also argue that a *nēpioi* reading would be very confusing as Paul would be mixing metaphors: Paul was *like an infant, like a nursing mother* (2:7). Does it make sense for Paul to link together these two metaphors in this way?[11]

In defense of the *nēpioi* reading, Charles Cousar appeals to a guiding principle of textual criticism called *lectio difficilior*—in general, the reading that makes the text *more* difficult to understand is probably the original reading. Another way to put this principle is that it is far more likely that a scribe

9. Gordon Fee states this quite starkly: "The external evidence is decisively in favor of *nēpioi*, being supported by the earliest evidence in the West (all the Old Latin) and in the East ($\mathfrak{P}^{65}$), as well as by the predominance of what is most often considered the best evidence (in this case, all but Codex A of the Egyptian witnesses). One would seem to need especially strong transcriptional arguments to overrule this combination of evidence. In fact, the evidence for *ēpioi* is so much weaker than for *nēpioi* that under ordinary circumstances no living scholar would accept the former reading as original, which is what makes the note in the NRSV so misleading: 'Other ancient authorities read *infants*.' That note levels the ground on a textual decision that is decidedly not level, not even close" (Fee 2009: 70).

10. Marshall 1984: 70.

11. See Best 1986: 101; Holmes 1998: 64.

would modify a confusing idea in order to make it simpler, rather than make it more inscrutable. In this case, proponents of *nēpioi* find it more likely that a scribe saw "infants" and felt that this may have been a mistake and removed the *nu*, reasoning that "gentle" (*ēpioi*) made more sense.[12] But what about the awkward mixed metaphors where Paul is an infant, one moment, and a nursing mother the next? I concur with Cousar that "The vulnerability of 'infants,' combined with the tender, loving care of the lactating nurse (providing milk and nurture not to someone else's children but to her own) present a double counterpoint to the picture of demanding apostles."[13]

Gordon Fee argues that the awkwardness of the combining of different metaphors is somewhat weakened if they are seen as completely separate ideas. Thus, Fee treats 1 Thess 2:1–7b as its own thought-unit (ending with "But we were like young children among you") and considers 7c-8 ("Just as a nursing mother cares for her children, so we cared for you") as the beginning of another section that reaches until v. 12. He concludes, "seen as separate sentences, they [2:7b and 2:7c in his sentencing] can easily be explained as in keeping with similar sudden shifts of metaphor elsewhere in Paul, where one metaphor triggers another in the apostle's mind, and thus are related primarily by 'catchword' and not by consistency in application."[14] For the reasons given by Cousar, Fee, and others (see footnote 8), I lean in favor of the *nēpioi* reading.

Paul's point in calling himself (and his other apostolic partners) *infants* would be that they neither seek power nor honor, and that they are not flatterers seeking personal fame or fortune.[15]

From the imagery of infants, Paul switches to the metaphor of "nursing mother" (2:7b). What both these images have in common is the kind of innocent love that is given and shared amongst close family members. That sense of intimacy is reinforced by the language of her *own* children—that is, *the children she holds most dear, those closest to her, the ones she nurtures and cherishes and feeds from her own body.*

12. Cousar 2001: 206.
13. Ibid.
14. Fee 2009: 71.
15. See Sailors 2000.

With this in mind, he expresses in 2:8 his affection for the Thessalonians. Paul became so close to them that he went above and beyond the normal call of duty, sharing "not only the good news of God, but also the depths of our souls because you became beloved to us." The word *psychē* is often translated simply as "souls," but does not mean a kind of spiritual self (versus, e.g., a bodily self). He was referring to his most intimate and vulnerable self.[16] Some people guard their lives from their work. Think of a lawyer defending a client, not wanting to get too emotionally involved in every case. Or a surgeon who tries not to become attached to suffering and grieving patients and families. So too with apostles, it can seem professional to maintain a cool distance; but with the Thessalonians Paul simply could not help himself. As Charles Wanamaker surmises, "He committed himself totally to the Thessalonians rather than remaining aloof and uninvolved in their struggles to come to terms with the new faith that had been declared to them."[17] Indeed, they had become "beloved" to him (see Rom 1:7; 1 Cor 10:14; Phil 2:12). Given that Paul already reflected on the Thessalonians as if they were his own children, one could fill out what he means by "beloved": "I am not writing this to make you ashamed, but to admonish you as my *beloved* children" (1 Cor 4:14).

In 2:9 Paul reminds the Thessalonians about his labor and toil and how they worked night and day so to preach the good news without burdening the Thessalonians by asking for money (2:9). He calls them to recall as witnesses his impeccable character (2:10; cf. 2:5). The language of "holy" here means something like "pure and innocent," godly in virtue. So also "just" refers to respectable and upright behavior. "Blameless" means that no fault could be found in them, no blemish on their record, no whiff of suspicion.

Having cycled through various familial metaphors, Paul ends this section with the image of a father (*pater*) who treats his children with care and concern (2:11–12).[18] It is important to note the emphasis Paul places on individual attention (*hos hena hekaston hymōn*). He took special concern for each and every one, in turn. No one was left out or neglected. As a father-like apostle, he was committed to caring for them by encouraging and comforting and insisting so that they might live up to God's standards.

---

16. Bruce interprets *psychē* here as "the seat of affection and will" (1982: 32); Ernest Best is, perhaps, a bit closer to what I think Paul has in mind when he describes *psychē* as "the personality, the real person" (1986: 102).

17. Wanamaker 1990: 102.

18. See Burke 2003: 46–52, 65–67; Best 1986: 106; Morris 1975: 76.

Paul knew that good fathers were invested in seeing to it that their children matured and had opportunities to thrive. He loved them like just that sort of mentor and guardian. The word for comforting (*paramytheomai*) is typically used by Greek writers of Paul's time in view of some occasion of sadness (e.g., John 11:19, 31); hence a common meaning for the verb is "to console" or "to cheer up." Why might Paul have been consoling them? We might learn from the way Jewish historian Josephus used similar language. While recounting the Hebrew war against the Amalekites, Josephus notes that the latter were known to be adroit and advanced in military skills compared to the people of Israel. This terrified the Israelites and they were despondent.

> Moses accordingly proceeded to console (*paramythia*) them. He bade (*parakaleō*)[19] them take courage, trusting in God's decrees, through which they had been promoted to liberty and triumphed over such as set themselves in battle against them to dispute it (*Ant.* 3.44, Thackeray).

It is possible, in light of this sort of usage, that Paul was embodying a kind, Moses-like encouragement to a Thessalonian community troubled by threat and persecution. Just as Moses was compassionate and concerned for his people, so Paul for his own people.

Paul saw his mission as focused, not only on winning converts, but training them up to be worthy of God; that is, to live up to God's high standards (see Phil 1:27). Paul reminds them that God has called them into his own "kingdom and glory" (literally). This is probably a hendiadys that should be translated "glorious kingdom" (cf. 1 Chron 29:25; Matt 4:8). By referring to the calling of God, Paul may have been appealing, again, to their new identity as those who are precious to God and carefully watched over by a God who is near (see 1:4). It could also reflect the sort of idea found in Rom 8:30 that those whom he has graciously called are expected to move along a trajectory of life towards glorification (*doxazō* in Rom 8:30; *doxa* in 1 Thess 2:12). This might have encouraged the Thessalonians that, despite the pressures of conflict and shame from their neighbors and compatriots, the God who adopted them into his family would see them all the way through to an end that would prove them valuable and innocent (see Phil 2:5–11). After all, "The one who calls you is faithful, he will also

---

19. *Paramythia* is closely related to *paramytheomai*; *parakaleō* is the same verb used by Paul in 1 Thess 2:12.

do it" (1 Thess 5:24), that is, he would sanctify them body, soul, and spirit in the end (5:23–24).

Fusing the Horizons: Integrity and Transparency in New Covenant Leadership

Ecclesiastes has proven itself right over and over again when it attests that there is nothing new under the sun (1:9). In Paul's day, there were people of influence, power, education, and charisma who took advantage of the masses and masked greedy motives behind pretenses of benevolence and generosity. The methods may change over time, but the motives stay the same. Over the past few years I have been astonished and dismayed by scandal after scandal making the news regarding pastors who have lied, embezzled, manipulated, and hoarded for themselves. When called to answer for this behavior we hear responses like "God has blessed me" and "I did it for the church." (Cicero once wrote: "So near is falsehood to truth that a wise man would do well not to trust himself on the narrow edge" [*Academici* 4.21].) Paul could not have imagined a day when pastors and Christian leaders became known for a multimillion-dollar net worth, or record-breaking book sales. The temptation to seek the praise of mortals (1 Thess 2:4) is, all too often, overwhelming. One might benefit, though, from remembering the words of St. Augustine inspired by 1 Tim 6:6:

> On all sides its charms decoy us. We like lots of money, we like splendid honors, we like power to overawe others. We like all these things, but let's listen to the apostle, "We brought nothing into this world, neither can we take anything out." [1 Tim 6:6] Honor should be looking for you, not you for it. You, after all, should sit down in the humbler place, so he that invited you may make you go up to a more honored place. But if he doesn't wish to, eat where you are sitting, because you brought nothing into this world. *Sermons* 39.2.[20]

The model that Paul sets for Christian leaders is timeless: integrity, transparency, humility, and hard work. Perhaps one of the major problems that bedevils many modern pastors is the ability to function independent of accountability. However, the tendency to operate in gray areas is only en-

---

20. See Gorday 2000: 212.

couraged by such autonomy. Christian leaders must be challenged to work alongside other leaders and foster mutual accountability for the preservation of the integrity of the church as well as their own conscience.

Praiseworthy Endurance Amidst Persecution (1 Thess 2:13–16)

> 13And on account of this, as for us, we give thanks to God always, because when you received the word of God as you heard it from us, you embraced it not as the word of mortals, but as it truly is—the word of God, which is at work among you who believe. 14As for you, you became imitators, my dear brothers and sisters, of the churches of God in Messiah Jesus in Judea, because you suffered the same things by men in your own country as they did by the Jews there. 15These Jews killed the Lord Jesus and the prophets, and drove us out too. What they are doing does not please God and they make everyone an enemy 16when they prevent us from speaking to the Gentiles so they may be saved. They are filling to full the measure of their sins. God's anger for justice has come upon them and there is no turning back.

Again, in 2:13, Paul praises the Thessalonians for their initial reception of the good news, receiving it as the "word of God," not as a fleeting, unfulfilling message from mere mortals. Throughout 1 Thessalonians, Paul insists that the one God is alive, powerful, and "at work" in an undeniable way amongst the believers in Thessalonica (see 1:5).

Paul compares their faithful endurance to the experience of the believers in Judea—the Thessalonians persecuted by their own fellow citizens, while the Jesus-following Jews by their own neighbors. The main point of this passage is clear: the situation of the Thessalonians (under persecution) is not unprecedented. It is part of a pattern that they share with the believers in Judea. It seems unjust for the holy and faithful people of God who follow the Messiah Jesus to be humiliated and to suffer, and for the persecutors to appear to prevail. *How could God let this happen?* This is clearly a theodicy issue that Paul is addressing. Problems and questions like these can send faith into a tailspin. Paul responds with a prophetic voice, urging that judgment awaits those who lash out against God's innocent people (2:16).

The Thessalonians' unjust suffering is not only analogous to that of the believers in Judea, but also to the situation of Jesus himself and the prophets before him. Paul touches upon a kind of ignorance motif. Ostensibly well-intentioned people are sometimes blind to the horrifically unholy acts they are committing. What Paul communicates here is remarkably reminiscent of John 16:2–3 where Jesus warns his disciples: "They will put you out of the synagogues. Indeed, an hour is coming when those who kill you will think that by doing so they are offering worship to God. And they will do this because they have not known the Father or me." Paul takes his statement a step further to say that, despite the ignorance and opaque judgment of the persecutors, their sinful hostility will meet divine reckoning in the end. In 2:16, Paul writes that God's "wrath" has come upon them "*eis telos*"—literally "to the end." What does this mean? F. F. Bruce is probably on the right track when he explains it this way: "They have reached the point of no return in their opposition to the gospel and final, irremediable retribution is inevitable; indeed, it has come."[1] Thus, we have translated it "God's anger for justice has come upon them and there is no turning back."

While Paul's overall message in this passage (2:13–16) is clear and fits the major concerns of the letter as a whole, scholars have debated intensely whether or not Paul could have written such a negative statement and condemnation about his own Jewish people.

Excursus: Could Paul Have Written 1 Thess 2:14–16?

Paul's words in 1 Thess 2:14–16 are so ostensibly damning in the view of many scholars that some have labeled Paul anti-Semitic, while others conclude that, if Paul could not write such a statement, this section must be a post-Pauline fabrication.[2] Opting for the excision of these verses might bring us some relief, but without support from the extant manuscripts, labeling these verses as a later editorial insertion seems hasty.[3]

So, if Paul *is* responsible for these words, was he prejudicially hateful towards Jews? This seems unlikely coming from a Jew whom we know held his own people so close to his heart (see Rom 9:1–5). It is important to note,

---

1. Bruce 1982: 48 (cf. Ps 52:5/LXX Ps 51:7).

2. See Pearson 1971: 79-94; Koester 1979:33–44; Scholars Version Paul (see Dewey *et al.* 2010). On the matter of which verses in particular are considered an interpolation, theories differ on whether it should be 2:13–16 or 2:14–16.

3. We know of no manuscripts of 1 Thessalonians in existence that do not have these verses. On the folly of cutting out offensive biblical texts, see Johnson 1989: 421.

right off the bat, that Paul was not condemning *all* Jews of *all time* in 1 Thess 2:14–16, but specifically Jews in his present and past who had been implicated in hostile actions towards Jesus and the Jesus-community.[4] Paul is not making a discriminatory statement against an ethnic group as a whole.[5]

In an important article by Luke Timothy Johnson, which treats the subject of hostile rhetorical in early Christianity, Johnson makes a number of critical points that inform our understanding of passages such as the one under discussion here. Firstly, he notes how minority groups (such as the early Christians, what Johnson calls the "messianists") were relatively powerless in the ancient world, and a defensive posture would be reasonably expected.[6] Secondly, though, Johnson points out that the Hellenistic models of slander that we see from Paul's time would have clued readers into the main point of such rhetorical damnation: "The purpose of the polemic is not so much the rebuttal of the opponent as the edification of one's own school. Polemic was primarily for internal consumption."[7] Put another way, Paul's purpose was not to stir up counter-violence against Jews, but rather to give comfort to the afflicted Thessalonian believers, particularly assuring them that *God* is the avenger in all things (cf. 1 Thess 4:6).

What should we do with this language today? It should be clear enough that special sensitivity should be maintained in Jewish-Christian dialogue in view of a history of mistreatment of Jews perpetrated under the flag of Christian witness. When Christians today face pressures from outsiders, it is altogether appropriate to offer pastoral encouragement, especially that violence against the people of God in Messiah Jesus will not be ignored by God. However, Paul always laid the emphasis in human interaction on non-retaliation, benevolence, and generosity towards enemies (Rom 12:19–20).

---

4. Gaventa 1998: 36.

5. Paul refers to fellow Jesus-believers Andronicus, Junia, Herodion, Lucius, Jason, and Sosipater as "my kinsmen," probably recognizing they are fellow Jews (see Rom 16:7, 11, 21). Note also, in Colossians, how Paul makes explicit mention of a few individuals whom he calls "fellow workers for the kingdom of God who are of the circumcision," people who have especially been of comfort to him in his imprisonment (Col 4:10–11). This should be evidence enough that he still maintained a special bond with Jews, even though he dedicated his ministry to Gentiles.

6. Johnson 1989: 424.

7. Ibid., 433.

Fusing the Horizons: A Hospitable Community for All People

While 1 Thess 2:14–16 has become a controversial passage regarding Paul's statement about the "wrath of God" on non-Christian Jewish persecutors, the debate has, unfortunately, masked one of Paul's wider purposes in these verses—namely, to remind the Thessalonians that these local opponents are trying to prevent salvation from reaching the Gentiles. In direct contrast, the new covenant community under Messiah Jesus is meant to be a fellowship that is for the people. *All people.* The local persecutors seek to exclude. But Paul wants to embrace and welcome Jew and Gentile alike.

Most of us in the modern world do not separate people into the categories of Jew and Gentile. Nor do we establish social barriers on the basis of whether or not one is a slave or freeman (Gal 3:28). But it would be a lie to say we do not live by classifications. *Blue collar vs. white collar. White church or black church. Too single. Too old. Do you dress the right way? Know the lingo? Express yourself in worship appropriately?* These filtering questions bar and exclude. So, again I ask, are we a community that is for the people? *All people?*

What is needed desperately in our churches, especially in the West, is a deeper understanding of hospitality. Henri Nouwen says it best when he writes, "Hospitality means primarily the creation of free space where the stranger can enter and become a friend instead of an enemy. Hospitality is not to change people, but to offer them space where change can take place....It is not a method of making our God and our way into the criteria of happiness, but the opening of an opportunity to others to find their God and their way... Hospitality is not a subtle invitation to adopt the life style of the host, but the gift of a chance for the guest to find his own."[8]

One could take some of Nouwen's statements in the wrong sense where "anything goes." That is not what he meant. He is simply emphatic that, though all should have the "mind of Christ," that does not amount to narrow uniformity: "There is a great wisdom hidden in the old bell tower calling people with very different backgrounds away from their homes to form one body in Jesus Christ. It is precisely by transcending the many individual differences that we can become witnesses of God who allow his light to shine upon poor and rich, healthy and sick alike. But it is also in this encounter on

---

8. Nouwen 1996: 49.

the way to God that we become aware of our neighbour's needs and begin to heal each other's wounds."[9]

---

9. Ibid., 121.

Paul's Love, Pride, and Concern (1 Thess 2:17—3:13)

In 2:1–12, Paul's concern is that the Thessalonians have a proper understanding of his motives and behavior when he was with them. The points he made about his own purity of motive, integrity, courage, and affection for them was not only in service of defending his honor, but also to supply a righteous example for them. In 2:17—3:10, Paul continues with this concern, but here the focus is on what happened *after* Paul left Thessalonica. They were not only beloved to him when he was in their presence, but also in absence. This section is concluded with a "prayer-wish," where Paul expresses his concern for their well-being and their maturity before God and especially in view of the impending return of the Lord Jesus (3:11–13).

Paul's Longing for the Thessalonians (2:17-20)

> **17**But, as for us, my dear brothers and sisters, when we were separated from you for a time, in person not in our hearts, we longed more deeply and with great affection to see you in person. **18**For we wanted to visit you—I, Paul, tried again and again—but Satan blocked our way. **19**For who is our hope, our joy, our crown of boasting before our Lord Jesus when he comes, if not you? **20**Yes, you are our glory and joy!

According to Acts, Paul and Silas fled from Thessalonica to Berea to avoid the hostility and persecution of the agitated Thessalonian citizens and city officials (Acts 17:8–10). Paul may be referring to this same situation when he mentions being separated from the Thessalonians for a time (2:17). The word separated (*aporphanizō*) bears the kind of image of being torn away from one's parents and, thus, to be *orphaned* (in fact, we get our word "orphan" from this Greek word).[1] Given how much Paul uses kinship language in this letter, the idea that Paul thought of the Thessalonians as family members fits well into his wider argument that he was just as ill-affected by

---

1. Note the NRSV: "We were made orphans by being separated from you" (2:17a).

his unscheduled departure as they were.² But, though he had to leave, they were always on his mind and he was eager to pay them another visit.

Paul admits that he attempted to see them on several occasions, but Satan blocked the way (2:18).³ What does Paul mean by this? Did Satan literally appear and stand in his way? Or is this an interpretive statement, viewing an obstacle (e.g., the equivalent of a flat tire or cancelled flight) as the work of a hostile power threatening his ministry? Given a text like 2 Cor 12:7–8 where Paul was given a "thorn in the flesh" as a messenger from Satan, and the thorn was probably either a physical ailment or the problem of his own persecutors, one could see how the Apostle could interpret various hindrances to visiting the Thessalonians as schemes of Satan (see 2 Cor 2:11; Eph 6:16; cf. 1 Pet 5:8).⁴ In any case, the wider point is obvious—if there is any suspicion or blame for Paul's distance from the Thessalonians, it should fall squarely on the real enemy, Satan, God's adversary (Rom 16:20; Cf. 1 Tim 5:15).⁵

Paul intends to make his relationship with the Thessalonians as clear as possible. He has shown that he cares for them deeply (see 2:1–12). Here he also acknowledges that they are his "pride and joy," so to speak.⁶ He takes "joy" in them because he recognizes their work, labor, and endurance (see 1:3) and he especially values their trust in God.

What does it mean that they are his "hope"? Paul mentions the coming of the Lord Jesus here. At that future moment, a great light will shine on all people and all history, exposing everything that was hidden (1 Cor 4:5). When it comes to Paul, it seems to be that he will be examined in some way

---

2. See Burke 2003: 157–62. Burke underscores that this language puts the emphasis, not on Paul's power as apostle or father, but as one who is *vulnerable*, "perhaps in order to identify with his own converts' sense of vulnerability, not to mention their social and familial isolation experienced upon turning 'from idols to serve the living and true God'" (1:9; see 2003: 162).

3. Gregory A. Boyd offers a brief, but insightful discussion of Satan according to the New Testament; see Boyd 2001: 38–39.

4. For a succinct and insightful discussion of 2 Cor 12:7–8, see Guthrie 2015: 590–92.

5. See Malherbe 2000: 184.

6. St. John Chrysostom compares this language of pride to that of a parent: "Observe then the words, which are those of women, inflamed with tenderness, talking to their little children." But Chrysostom is quick to add about Paul's remarks in 2:19, "Of what fiery warmth is this! Never could either mother, or father, yea if they even met together, and commingled their love, have shown their own affection to be equivalent to that of Paul" (*Homilies on 1 Thessalonians* III.335); see http://www.newadvent.org/fathers/230403.htm.

based on the fruitfulness of his ministry (see Rom 15:16). He can claim a "hope" and "crown of boasting" based on churches such as the Thessalonians, because his ministry had such an effective impact on them and they responded appropriately to the good news of Messiah Jesus through the power of the Holy Spirit.[7] It may seem strange to us that Paul writes positively about "boasting." Certainly he does occasionally condemn inappropriate self-centered boasting (for example, see 2 Cor 10:17). But that does not preclude a noble kind of "pride" that recognizes the work of God in one's life and ministry.[8] Paul mentions to the Philippians that the maturity of their faith on the "day of the Messiah" will prove that "I [Paul] did not run in vain or labor in vain" (Phil 2:16). Thus, he can boast in his converts as fruit of God's work through him (see 1 Cor 15:31; 2 Cor 7:4).[9] The Thessalonians are Paul's own "glory" because he beams with pride on account of their firm commitment to Messiah Jesus, all of which is a demonstration of the grace and power of God. N. T. Wright offers an apt reflection on how this attitude can nourish and inspire all believers today.

> Each of us has our own work of love to perform, whether it be quiet and secret or well known and public. Each pastor and teacher should look to the future, and see those in their charge as their potential joy, hope, and crown. And each congregation should recognize that this is how they will appear on the last day. Both should be challenged and encouraged, by this forward look, to learn and live the faith, to celebrate the hope, to consolidate and practise the love revealed in the gospel.[10]

---

7. Malherbe 2000: 185; Wanamaker 1990: 123. James W. Thompson offers an excellent discussion of this subject: "In every instances in which Paul declares his pastoral ambition, he indicates that the success or failure of his work will be determined only at the end, when he will either 'boast' of his work or realize that his work has been in vain. The eschatological horizon is a central feature of Paul's pastoral ambition. . . . [T]he ultimate test of his ministry is the outcome of his work with the churches, the ultimate goal defines his ministry in the present." See 2006: 22; generally 31–60.

8. A text like Gal 6:4 gives the impression that a good sense of pride has its place where one can be proud of oneself for a job well done, but a line is crossed when the matter turns into a contest or "us" vs. "them" rally.

9. A helpful place to turn for discussion regarding the relationship between justification by faith and judgment according to deeds is the recently published *Four Views on the Role of Works at the Final Judgment* with Robert N. Wilkin, Thomas Schreiner, James D. G. Dunn, and Michael Barber as contributors (ed. A. Stanley, 2013).

10. Wright 2004: 107.

The Thessalonians' Good News of Perseverance (3:1-10)

1Therefore, when we could no longer bear it, we thought it best to stay behind in Athens, **2**and we sent Timothy, our brother and coworker for God in the good news of the Messiah. We sent him to strengthen you and to encourage your loyalty, **3**so that no one is shaken up by these afflictions. For you know for yourselves that this was inevitable. **4**When we were with you, we kept telling you that we would be persecuted—and so it came to pass as you know. **5**So then, when it became impossible for me to bear, I sent Timothy to learn about your loyalty, fearing that the tempter may have tempted you, and all our toil wasted.

6But now Timothy has come back to us from visiting you and has announced to us the "good news" of your loyalty and love, and that you always carry fond memories of us. He told us how you long to see us just as we long to see you. **7**So we were comforted about you, my dear brothers and sisters, in all of our distress and suffering since we were reassured about your loyalty. **8**For now we feel alive again, knowing you stand firm in the Lord. **9**In what way can we thank God in return for you, for all the joy we feel in the presence of God because of you? **10**Night and day we pray fervently that we may see your faces so that we may meet the needs of your loyalty.

Starting in chapter three, Paul narrates his concern for the Thessalonians while he was in Athens (3:1-12). Timothy, Paul's close companion and co-worker (see 1:1), was sent to check in on the Thessalonians and to strengthen and comfort them during a difficult time (3:2).[11] He carried out an important pastoral task, namely, "helping them both to understand and to live out what it means to be members of God's people."[12] Almost as an aside, Paul reminds them that they were forewarned that true followers of Jesus are bound to face persecution (3:3b). Paul communicates something quite similar to the Philippians: "For he has graciously granted to you the privilege not only of believing in him [Jesus], but of suffering for him as well" (1:29; cf. Rom 8:17). Believers inevitably will suffer for their allegiance to Jesus as Lord, not because God relishes in suffering, but because the

---

11. Todd Still wonders whether the reason Timothy was the right choice for this ministry was because he "was not 'front and center' during the founding visit and as a result would not be on the 'radar screen' of non-Christian opposition." See Still 2011: 30–45, at 33.

12. Holmes 1998: 97–98.

Messiah's kingdom operates in direct opposition to the sinful way of the world—his subjects must maintain a distinctly counter-cultural existence imitating the radically backwards values of holiness as well as self-giving love towards neighbor and God.

Paul offered this reminder about the inevitability of Christian suffering because he feared that, in his absence, their faith and loyalty would be shaken (3:3). According to J. P. Louw and Eugene Nida, the verb that Paul uses here for "shaken," *sainomai*, can be defined as "to be so emotionally disturbed as to give up one's belief."[13] The pressures and pushback the Thessalonians were receiving from their neighbors created cognitive and social pressure that, if not dealt with, could lead to a kind of world-view collapse (see Introduction, 2–3).[14] One way that Paul could manage to avoid this implosion was to warn and prepare believers. However, when push comes to shove (perhaps literally in this case), training can fail. How many soldiers, having theoretically "trained for war," have retreated when things get overwhelming on the real battlefield?

Paul was afraid that the Tempter may have succeeded in undermining their confidence and hope (3:5b). Clearly the "Tempter" is Satan who makes it a habit of preying on the weak (1 Cor 7:5). But the New Testament is quite emphatic that, while the Tempter sees it as his business to tempt, he has no power to control the human will.[15] His role is to distract and confuse, and to promote fear and doubt. One wonders whether the situation of the Thessalonians might have been similar to that of the Smyrnian church (of a later time): "Do not fear what you are about to suffer. Beware, the devil is about to throw some of you in prison so that you may be tested, and for ten days you will have affliction. Be faithful until death, and I will give you the crown of life" (Rev 2:10). As we learn here, the Evil One tests (or tempts) to push people to their breaking point. Revelation encourages the Smyrnians to endure even if it means martyrdom. We do not know what the Thessalonians were facing, but Paul offered critical advice—*keep pressing on*. The subtext of 1 Thess 3:3–4 is that Paul could forewarn and prepare the Thessalonians about suffering and trials precisely because God has all things in hand and such set-backs and challenges cannot thwart his

---

13. L-N 31.66.

14. See also Gaventa 1998: 42.

15. St. Thomas Aquinas reinforces this point: "To tempt is properly speaking to make trial of something. . . . A demon cannot change the will. . . . [This] cannot be forced; it can be inclined." See *Summa Theologiae* 1, qu. 114, art. 2, as cited in Thiselton 2011: 87.

redemptive purposes. God intends not just to work *in spite of* problems, but especially *through* problems as the faith of believers is strengthened by trials[16]—so much so that Paul could write to the Romans that believers can *boast* in their troubles and afflictions because God uses these things to produce godly character (see Rom 5:3-4).

Paul recounts how Timothy returned to him with news that the Thessalonians were, in fact, enduring (3:6). Quite noticeably in the Greek text, Paul uses the word *euangelizomai*, a verb he employs almost exclusively for "preaching the good news." The verb *euangelizomai* appears about twenty times in his letters in the New Testament, but only *here* does he use it in reference to something *other than* the good news of Messiah Jesus (the message of salvation). It has, in a sense, a mundane meaning in 1 Thess 3:6: Timothy shared the *pleasing message* (or *happy news*) of the Thessalonians' perseverance. However, because Paul tends to use language of "good news" for the gospel of Messiah Jesus (i.e., as a sort of technical term), one cannot help but draw that nuance into 1 Thess 3:6 as well. Timothy sharing a *pleasing message* about the Thessalonians is part of the ongoing work of the *sharing of the gospel* because it is the same Spirit that inspires their endurance and the same Messiah Jesus that models and guides their love. It is a beautiful thing for Paul's converts to be responsible for the *"good news"* to be preached *to Paul* on account of their faithfulness and obedience!

Paul is relieved and pleased to hear from Timothy that, not only have the Thessalonians been enduring, but they acknowledge and fondly remember Paul's love for them and they want to see him just as much as he does them (3:6b). The language of longing (*epipotheō*) is the language of intimacy and close friendship. This is the same verb used in the Greek translation (Septuagint) of Ps 42:1: "As the deer *longs* (*epipotheō*) for the streams of water, my soul also for you, O God." Paul and the Thessalonians have a deep, almost unquenchable thirst for being in fellowship together in one place.

Paul, Timothy, and Silas could find some comfort in their anxieties when they came to know of the Thessalonians' *pistis*—a word normally translated "faith," but here seems to refer to their faithfulness, loyalty, and confident hope in God through Jesus (3:7).[17] Paul's next statement could be rather shocking to some modern readers: "For now we feel alive again, knowing you stand firm in the Lord" (3:8; cf. 4:1). What does this mean?

16. See Jervis 2007: 15-36.
17. See Andy Johnson 2016.

There is a sense in which Paul receives vitality and life through the lives of his converts. Imagine parents whose college-age daughter goes off to Europe on spring break and they discover on the news that an airplane crashed after take-off from the airport where she departed. Until they know if it is their child's plane, their hearts stop and deep panic sets in. When they get the phone call from their daughter (who was safely on a different flight), what relief and joy! Given how much Paul and his companions invested in their churches, it is no wonder they became his lifeblood. F. F. Bruce's paraphrase of Paul's sentiment is especially eloquent and appropriate: "the news of your unwavering faith and love is the very breath of life to us."[18] So filled to the brim with joy is Paul at this news that he could not possibly think of a big enough gift to give back to God for God's gift of the Thessalonians to him (3:9).

Once more we come to know of Paul's constant attentiveness to them in prayer ("night and day") in the hopes that he can be with them and "meet the needs of your loyalty" (3:10). It is unclear what Paul means by this, but we may have a clue by looking at similar language in Romans. In the opening chapter of Paul's letter to Rome, he communicates his intent to see the Roman believers in person, and to impart to them a spiritual gift to strengthen them (Rom 1:11). He clarifies: "that is, that we may be mutually comforted by one another's faith, both yours and mine" (Rom 1:12). Similarly, Paul wanted to be with the Thessalonians in their time of distress to give them comfort and encouragement. Perhaps this could happen through additional teaching, but one also imagines that simply catching up together as friends could offer a special consolation and refreshment (as we often see when friends visit loved ones in the hospital and simply provide good company).

Paul's Prayer-Wish (3:11–13)

> [11]Now may God our Father himself and Messiah Jesus our Lord guide us on a path to you. [12]And may the Lord cause your love to abound and overflow both for each other and for all people in the way that we love you. [13]So may he strengthen your hearts so that you may be blameless and holy before our God and Father when our Lord Jesus comes with all his holy ones.

---

18. Bruce 1982: 67.

So moved is Paul by the hope of seeing the Thessalonians that he offers a doxological prayer: "Now may God our Father himself and Messiah Jesus our Lord guide us on a path to you" (3:11). This is the first of three prayer-wishes he expresses in 3:11–13. Firstly, he prays that both God and Jesus open a way to the Thessalonians. This is a rare, but important, glimpse into Paul's Christology in terms of how he views the nature of Jesus himself. Scholars have long debated whether Paul placed Jesus into the category of "divine." This is a complex topic, fraught with historical, theological, and methodological challenges, but the fact that Paul offers his prayer-wish *both* to God the Father *and* Jesus means that Jesus shares with God the Father the power to prepare his way and secure his footsteps.[19]

The second prayer-wish Paul offers (3:12) is focused on a desire for the Lord "to cause your love to abound and overflow both for each other and for all people in the way that we love you." If we look ahead to 1 Thess 4:10, we see that Paul can affirm that there is no serious deficiency in their expression of communal love. He merely prays that they continue to push forward and not lose steam in this area, a temptation common to those under pressure and persecution.

In the third prayer-wish, Paul's focus is on the Thessalonians' character and standing at the return of the Lord Jesus (3:13). In particular, he prays for their holiness (*hagiosynē*) and purity (*amemptos*). This is judgment imagery, where their lives are placed under the divine microscope and Paul desires that they be able to stand proud and unashamed that they lived lives pleasing to God (see 4:1–3).[20]

The mentioning of the "coming" or "appearance" (*parousia*) of Jesus is a special emphasis of 1 Thessalonians (2:19; 3:13; 4:15; 5:23; cf. 2 Thess 2:1, 8). It seems to have been a standard apostolic teaching (James 5:7–8; 2 Pet 1:16; 3:4, 12; 1 John 2:28) and probably reaches back to the Jesus tradition (e.g., Matt 24:3, 27, 37, 39). The early Christians anticipated the return of the Lord Jesus with great excitement, but they knew that they too would face judgment and had to be fully prepared for the careful consideration of

---

19. See Fee 2007: 53–55.

20. See Matera 2012: 181–83. Morna Hooker notes that, while Paul does frequently refer to judgment of believers, he maintains confidence in the grace and justification of the Messiah. The references to the examination of the deeds of believers are not about damnation, but rather accountability; "God's righteous people must be righteous, urged Paul, and that meant that they were required to live out the gospel. They had indeed been righted by God, but might still fall away. The Christian's aim must always be to please the Lord" (Hooker 2008: 161).

their lives and deeds (see Rom 2:6; 2 Pet 3:10). Paul prays, in regards to the Thessalonians, not so that they may be fearful of the coming of Jesus, but rather that they may have confidence and assurance in view of blameless and obedient lives.

Fusing the Horizons: Life Together

"Join us for our fellowship hour after the service!" How many churches conclude their worship by welcoming visitors to have "fellowship" in the next room over coffee and donuts? The motivation behind this is obviously appropriate—many churches recognize how important it is that life in the church is about a community of relationships. However, I fear that by talking about this snack-enriched chatting hour as "fellowship," we define it in a way that would be quite alien to Paul. We in the West generally use the language of fellowship as a way to refer to social gatherings. At its best, these gatherings give encouragement and promote upbuilding. But even with these good things in place, I am concerned that the essence of what *fellowship* is in the sense that the early Christians meant remains obscure for many congregations. The Greek word in the New Testament that is often translated as "fellowship" in English Bibles is *koinōnia*, and it literally means "commonness" or "sharedness." Because this word could be used as a technical term in Paul's world for a business partnership or a marriage contract, one can get a sense for the idea of "shared-ness" associated with *koinōnia*.

In 1 Thessalonians, Paul does not actually use the word *koinōnia* (though he uses it regularly in several of his other letters), but you can easily see the fingerprints of the meaning of *koinōnia* all over this letter and especially in 1 Thess 2:7—3:13. When two people or two groups agree to share life, then being apart is a heavy burden. Hence Paul has the deepest longing to see the Thessalonians, because they became so dear to him (2:17). They became his own hope and joy and glory (2:19–20). When Paul wondered about how adversity might affect the Thessalonian brothers and sisters, he could not stand the thought of their confusion or doubt (3:5). His attachment to the Thessalonian church was so strong that his own life itself was bound to their faith in the Lord—their loss would be his loss, their triumph and loyalty in the face of trials, a kind of resurrection from the dead for Paul himself (3:8).

Again, this vision differs from what I often see in our churches today, because I rarely see the sort of Christian unity that is determined by, what

Paul explains in Philippians, two people who share one soul and heartbeat (see Phil 1:27; 2:2). Christian fellowship and unity are not about agreement and encouragement—though such things are obviously important. Christian fellowship can begin with an hour at church, but must be defined by, to borrow a phrase from the German theologian Dietrich Bonhoeffer, "life together."

Bonhoeffer wrote the book *Life Together* to capture a proper Christian vision of fellowship. In this book, he reminds us that one reason why we have such a hard time understanding how Paul felt about the Thessalonians is because we are often spoiled by too many opportunities to know and have friendship and companionship with other believers. But there have been times and places in history where Christians have not had that luxury – even places around the world today. Here is what Bonhoeffer writes:

> It is by God's grace that a congregation is permitted to gather visibly around God's word and sacrament in this world. Not all Christians partake of this grace. The imprisoned, the sick, the lonely who live in the diaspora, the proclaimers of the gospel in heathen lands stand alone. They know that visible community is grace.[21]

Bonhoeffer ponders why community is so important, and concludes that it is because we are *human*.

> A human being is created as a body; the Son of God appeared on earth in the body for our sake and was raised in the body. In the sacrament the believer receives the Lord Christ in the body, and the resurrection of the dead will bring about the perfected community of God's spiritual-physical creatures. Therefore, the believer praises the Creator, the Reconciler and the Redeemer, God the Father, Son and Holy Spirit, for the bodily presence of the other Christian. The prisoner, the sick person, the Christian living in the diaspora recognizes in the nearness of a fellow Christian a physical sign of the gracious presence of the triune God. In their loneliness, both the visitor and the one visited recognize in each other the Christ who is present in the body. They receive and meet each other as one meets the Lord, in reverence, humility, and joy. They receive each other's blessings as the blessing of the Lord Jesus Christ. But if there is so much happiness and joy even in a single encounter of one Christian with another, what inexhaustible

---

21. Bonhoeffer 2005: 28.

> riches must invariably open up for those who by God's will are privileged to live in daily community life with other Christians![22]

Again, keeping in mind that some believers around the world are less fortunate and do not have the privilege of regular Christian fellowship, Bonhoeffer enjoins us who do have a church community to count our blessings.

> Therefore, let those who until now have had the privilege of living a Christian life together with other Christians praise God's grace from the bottom of their hearts. Let them thank God on their knees and realize: it is grace, nothing but grace, that we are still permitted to live in the community of Christians today.[23]

As Bonhoeffer suggests, we should cherish Christian fellowship when we see how people like Paul hungered and thirsted for the Thessalonians. We also should remind ourselves that Paul had this longing because he opened himself up to sharing *life together* with the Thessalonians. Fellowship, for Paul, was not an event, but a means of life itself. May we dare to entrust ourselves to our fellow believers and share our deepest selves (1 Thess 2:8) with our brothers and sisters such that they become life to us and we to them. And may we thank God that we can.

---

22. Ibid., 29.

23. Ibid., 30. In the same section of the book, Bonhoeffer quotes Martin Luther (one of his favorite theologians) who commented that church fellowship is one of the "roses and lilies" of the Christian life; see Ibid., 31.

Exhortation to Persevere and Grow in Holiness, Love, and Integrity (1 Thess 4:1–12)

¹Furthermore, my dear brothers and sisters, we ask of you and urge you in the Lord Jesus, as you received from us instruction about how you must walk and live to please God—as indeed you do walk this way—we encourage you to pursue this even more passionately. ²For you know what instructions we gave you through the Lord Jesus. ³This is God's will: that you are consecrated to him, namely that you distance yourself from sexual immorality. God wills that each of you knows how to maintain control of his own "vessel" with holiness and honor, ⁵not yielding to lustful passion like the Gentiles who do not know God. ⁶Each of you must not trespass and cheat his brother in this matter, because the Lord repays justice for all these things, just as we forewarned you and testified. ⁷For God called us not to be impure, but to be holy. ⁸Therefore, whoever rejects this teaching is not rejecting a mere mortal but rather rejects the God who gives his Holy Spirit to you.

⁹Now, on the matter of love for siblings, you do not need us to write to you, because you yourselves are taught by God when it comes to mutual love. ¹⁰Indeed, you already do it, you have shown love for all the brothers and sisters in all of Macedonia. And we encourage you, my dear brothers and sisters, to let this love overflow even more. ¹¹And set your ambition on living a quiet life: attend to your own affairs and work with your own hands, just as we commanded you. ¹²Then you will walk in the proper way in view of outsiders and you will need nothing.

In the first three chapters of 1 Thessalonians, Paul's primary concern involved extending compassion and comfort to a suffering and troubled church. There is a gracious, warm, generous tone. He reminds them of how special they are, and how attentive God is to their plight. He reminds them of how God has worked among them in power in the past, he is at work in the present, and he will act again on their behalf through Messiah Jesus at his return. He confesses to them his longing to have close fellowship with them—they are loved and missed.

But Paul's purpose in writing is not purely to offer reassurance and comfort. He also writes to them to remind them of God's expectations for their lifestyle and behavior. It is important for them to know that God has called them into his "glorious kingdom" (2:12), but this "calling" is also a privilege, a lifelong response and responsibility. They are called to live according to kingdom standards. The constitution of their kingdom citizenship requires holiness, not impurity (4:7). Three main topics are treated in this early section of chapter four: holiness (4:1–8), love (4:9–10), and integrity (4:11–12).

God's Call to Holiness (4:1–8)

Paul begins this section by reminding the Thessalonians (through the authority of the Lord Jesus) about the teaching that they had already received from him (4:1). When he originally instructed them, he shared not simply the good-news message, but also counsel regarding "how you must walk and live to please God." We sometimes call this "ethics," but Paul would not have seen a distinction between "theology" and "ethics."[1] For Paul, the free gift of new life in Messiah Jesus automatically entails a new set of personal and social standards under the Lordship of Jesus. The idea behind "walking" (*peripateō*), a Jewish idiom, is that the religious life is lived at all times, not just in temples and religious meetings (Deut 6:4–12).

Paul is quick to note that the Thessalonians are not failing in their obedience to God—he simply wants them to keep their eyes focused on God's will and expectations (4:1–2). He goes on to refer in quite specific terms to the nature of the will of God. God wishes, in particular, that they are "consecrated" to him (*hagiasmos*). To be consecrated is to be dedicated to holiness. Here Paul views holiness as a kind of maintained condition of purity and personal dedication to God.[2] Sometimes this word is explained as if it were simply about *not* doing or being something (i.e., avoiding worldliness), and Paul does point out here what jeopardizes holiness. However, the language of holiness in Jewish thought has an important *positive* value. Holiness involves being close to God and being available and dedicated to serving God wholeheartedly.[3] Given that most of the Thessalonian believers would have been Gentiles (see 4:5), and in the Greco-Roman world at large men had quite a lot of freedom to indulge their sexual passions, it

---

1. See van der Watt 2006.
2. L-N 53.44; see Peterson 2001.
3. See Tidball 2000.

is no wonder that the early Christians had to give new believers directed and repeated teaching about self-control and purity.[4] For example, the early Christian training manual called the *Didache* ("The Teaching of the Twelve Apostles to the Gentiles"), dating perhaps even to the first century AD, impresses upon the readers the need for everyday purity: "Abstain from fleshly and worldly lusts" (1:4); "thou shalt not commit adultery, thou shalt not commit paederasty, thou shalt not practice fornication" (2:2); "My child, be not a lustful one; for lust leadeth the way to fornication" (3:3); "The way of death is this: . . . adulteries, lusts, fornications . . . " (5:1).

Excursus: Sexual Immorality in the Greco-Roman World

The world in which Paul lived offered men a number of sexual opportunities and "privileges," even for those that were married. F. F. Bruce explains it in this way:

> A man might have a mistress [*hetaera*] who could provide him also with intellectual companionship; the institution of slavery made it easy for him to have a concubine [*pallakē*], while casual gratification was readily available from a harlot [*pornē*]. The function of his wife was to manage his household and be the mother of his legitimate children and heirs. There was no body of public opinion to discourage *porneia* [sexual immorality], although someone who indulged in it to excess might be satirized on the same level as a notorious glutton or drunkard. The general attitude is frequently illustrated by a quotation from Demosthenes's oration *Against Neaera:* "We keep mistresses for pleasure, concubines for our day-to-day bodily needs, but we have wives to produce legitimate children and serve as trustworthy guardians of our homes."[5]

Roman poet Horace (65 BC–27 BC) confirms just this sort of sexual license in Roman society:

> If your groin is swelling,
> and a housemaid or a slave boy is at hand,
> arousing constant desire,
> do you prefer to burst with tension?
> Not me: I enjoy love that is available and easy.[6]

---

4. See Hock 1999: 159–70.
5. Bruce 1982: 87; see also Morris 1975: 118; Hubbard 2014.
6. Horace, *Sermons* 1.2.116–19; as cited in Elliott and Reasoner 2011: 252.

From Pompeii a piece of graffiti was discovered that reads: "If anyone's looking for tender embraces in this town, he should know that all the girls are available."[7] Even when observing these few examples, it is easy to see why instruction regarding sexual purity was so standard in Paul's ethical teaching.[8]

Paul offers much the same kind of clarity regarding what dedication to God entails: "that you distance yourself from sexual immorality" (4:3). This advice goes beyond a simple "don't do it." Rather, Paul essentially counsels them, "Get as far away from it as possible!" (One thinks of Joseph running with haste away from the temptress in Potiphar's household [Gen 39:12]; see also below.) Too many Christians (of every generation) have desired a kind of minimum-standard moral system to follow which often results in believers lining up as closely as possible to the boundary of sin, but just barely on the "holy" side. This is not Paul's mindset whatsoever. The only way for believers to have real integrity is to put any hint of sin or dubious behavior at a far distance.

The concern was not just with public witness, though that was also something of which Paul was mindful (4:11–12). The immediate issue is with mastery over carnal passions and lusts (4:4–5). Each one needs to know how to "control his own 'vessel' with holiness and honor" (4:4). There is hardly another verse in Paul's letters that has generated more debate and discussion than this one.[9] Obviously Paul is concerned with self-control, but what does he mean by "vessel" (*skeuos*)? This word *skeuos* is the normal Greek word for container (see, e.g., John 19:29), but in this context it is obvious that Paul is being metaphorical.

Three interpretive options are possible. First, it could be that the *vessel* is the man's *wife* and the text is encouraging marriage (see RSV: "to take a wife for himself").[10] Scholars and translators who prefer this reading argue, firstly, that Paul employs a verb here (*ktaomai*) that is also used in a semi-technical phrase "acquire a wife" (so Sirach 36.29; Ruth 4:10; Xenophon,

---

7. *CIL* IC 1796, trans. Berg; as cited in Elliott and Reasoner 2011: 251.

8. Another route into this topic is the study of sexual themes in Greek and Latin Graffiti; see Williams 2014: 493–508.

9. See Still 2007: 207–19.

10. This interpretation is favored by Patristic interpreters such as Theodore of Mopsuestia and Augustine; also Frame 1912, Best 1986, Holtz 1986, Malherbe 2000, and Witherington 2006; for detailed argumentation, see Yarbrough 1985.

Conviv. 2.10). Thus, on this reading, Paul would be adapting conventional language. He would be urging believing men in the Thessalonian church to "restrict their sexual activity to their own wives and to enter on this with them in sanctification and honour."[11]

A second option is to see *skeuos* in reference to the person's own body (see NRSV; NET).[12] So, Paul writes in 2 Cor 4:7, "We have this treasure in earthen vessels (*skeuos*), that the surpassing power belongs to God and not to us" (NASB). This view comports well with the idea that the body is sacred and not meant for sexual immorality, so what we do with our bodies matters greatly to God (1 Cor 6:13, 18; 9:27; 2 Cor 12:21; Rom 6:19). The greatest challenge with this view involves the verb *ktaomai*. If the primary meaning of this verb is "to acquire," what would it mean for Paul to urge the Thessalonians to "acquire" their own bodies? It is possible that one heard excuses for promiscuity like "I couldn't help myself." Paul would, then, be responding, "Get ahold of yourself!" Thus, G. K. Beale, for example, looks at the use of *ktaomai* in this way: "those not presently living holy lives must begin to do so, that is, take possession of their bodies and begin to control them and then continue to do so."[13]

A third option (perhaps viewed as a more specific subset under option two) would be to see *skeuos* as a euphemism for the male genitalia. Gordon Fee has made a reasonable case that the desire to use a euphemism may be the reason behind Paul talking about "vessel" versus simply using the literal words for "wife" (option one) or "body" (option two).[14]

Of these options, I lean in favor of the second, that Paul refers to control over the body.[15] Paul saw the problem of sin as a battle for control: "do not let sin reign in your mortal bodies, to make you obey their passions"

---

11. Best 1986: 162–63. Some interpreters in the past who have defended this view made appeal to 1 Peter 3:7 where *skeuos* is used in reference to the wife, but this so-called parallel has been largely debunked because the text implies that both the husband and the wife are *vessels*; see Smith 2001: 65–105.

12. While it is not commonplace for the word "vessel" (*skeuos*) to be used metaphorically to mean "wife," it is more frequently used in reference to the body in Jewish literature; see, e.g., *Apocalypse of Sedrach* 11.2, 6; *Testament of Naphtali* 2.2.

13. Beale 2003: 117.

14. See Fee 2009: 149; also further possible evidence from Elgvin 1997: 604–19.

15. How should translations approach this matter? Beverly Gaventa wonders whether it is best to render it literally as "vessel." She explains: "It is important to see . . . that one reason this debate has emerged is precisely that *Paul himself gives us few clues* as to what he means by the use of the word *skeuos*. He writes in terse aphorisms that call out for explanation. Presumably this is because he has already instructed the Thessalonians, and they know what he means, even if we do not" (1998: 53).

(Rom 6:12; cf. 1 Pet 2:11). Because of the bondage-breaking power of God, one can "put on the Lord Messiah Jesus," as it were, and his power can enable believers to "make no provision for the flesh, to gratify its desires" (Rom 13:14). This is not automatic. It is a choice—a daily, hourly choice to let Jesus rule and to live according to the Spirit (Gal 5:16). It is not a matter of pure will-power, but the believer must fully assimilate the idea that "those who belong to Christ Jesus have crucified the flesh with its passions and desires" (Gal 5:24).

The choice to indulge in sexual vices, to degrade the body with lust and promiscuity, is not a symbol of freedom—just the opposite; it is a mark of imprisonment (see Rom 1:18–32). Inversely, holiness is not a barrier or restriction, but true freedom in God. Controlling one's body is not a prohibitive rule, but a natural corollary of one's honor (4:4) or value in God. What many Christians lack today is a deep sense of self-worth or dignity. Believers will have a mature sense of dignity when they truly understand their incalculable worth to God. It actually degrades the sacrifice of Jesus when we do not ascribe worth and value to ourselves. If we put value in his giving of his life, such "worth" is ascribed to us for whom he gave that blood. Paul wants each believer to weigh his or her own body on the scale of worth in God's perspective and to treat that commodity in a way commensurate with what God has invested in it through Messiah Jesus.

In 4:5, Paul draws a sharp qualitative distinction between the Thessalonian believers' lifestyle and that of "the Gentiles who do not know God." Almost certainly the Thessalonian believers themselves were not ethnically Jews (and, thus, they were Gentiles, "non-Jews"), so how can he tell Gentiles not to act like Gentiles? It could be that Paul is comparing "Gentiles who do not know God" with "Gentiles who *do* know God." But I think Paul's thought runs deeper than this point. The idea is that they have been written into a new story through Jesus, the story of Israel; they do not literally become "Jews," but they are adopted into the family of Yahweh through Jesus and they live out a different set of values (see Rom 11:17).[16]

Furthermore, Paul seems to draw from a common Jewish criticism of Gentiles who are "godless" despite having many idols, and their state of

---

16. Notice in 1 Corinthians, Paul also corresponds with a church composed mostly of Gentiles and he writes to them in regards to lessons learned from the Israelite wilderness period that "*our ancestors* were all under the cloud, and all passed through the sea" (1 Cor 10:1; NRSV). As Richard Hays explains, "the story of Israel is for the Gentile Corinthians not somebody else's story; it is the story of their own authentic spiritual ancestors" (Hays 1997: 160); see also Garroway 2012.

being disconnected from the one true God (hence the life-transforming conversion of the Thessalonians in 1:9–10). The Jewish philosopher Philo (roughly a contemporary to Paul) made this statement about the difference between Jews and Gentiles:

> And there are some of the Gentiles, who, not attending to the honor due to the one God alone, deserve to be punished with extreme severity of punishment, as having forsaken the most important classification of piety and holiness, and as having chosen darkness in preference to the most brilliant light, and having rendered their own intellect blind when it might have seen clearly (*Special Laws* 1.54).

This is, more or less, what Paul expresses in Rom 1:18–32: when people reject the one God, it is as if they choose to live in darkness—ignorance of (the one, true) God is ignorance of life itself (Rom 1:21). But Paul's point is precisely that the Thessalonians are *not* in darkness (1 Thess 5:4) like their neighbors (or even their pre-Christian selves). They are people of the day who are, or certainly can be, at their full wits to live holy and upright lives (1 Thess 5:8; cf. Rom 13:12).

While there are obviously some interpretive conundrums in 1 Thess 4:3–5, Paul's overall concern for sexual purity and holiness is clear. However, when we transition to 4:6, we are at a loss to make sense of what he means that "each of you must not trespass and cheat his brother in this matter." What is "this matter"? Probably the meaning is that, when a man commits adultery with a married woman, he is violating the boundaries of that marriage and sinning against his Christian brother (see NLT). We may gain some insight on these concerns by, again, turning to the situation of Joseph and Potiphar's wife according to Josephus' retelling (*Ant.* 2; cf. Gen 49). Josephus explains Joseph's righteous refusal of Potiphar's wife in this way:

> She made known her naughty inclinations, and spoke to him about lying with her. However, he rejected her entreaties, not thinking it agreeable to religion to yield so far to her, as to do what would tend to the affront and injury of him that purchased him, and had vouchsafed him so great honours (*Ant.* 2.42).

While Joseph shows concern for proper holiness ("religion"; *hosios*), he demonstrates particular respect for Potiphar himself. He would never do anything, no matter how tempting, to damage and mistreat Potiphar. This is an apt analogy for what Paul is concerned with. It is improper for a man to gratify his urges with a married woman, lest he *trespass* and sin against the marriage covenant of his brother. God will refuse to turn a blind eye to such unholy behavior (4:6b). The calling of God is gracious, but also formative—God's people must direct their lives towards holiness, not impurity (4:7). In 4:8, Paul threatens anyone who would stubbornly reject this teaching.

Even More Love (4:9–10)

Paul transitions from teaching on holiness to the subject of love (*philadelphia*; "sibling love"). Much as he did at the outset of this chapter, he makes clear that they are not failing in this area, but perhaps need a bit of a push to press on in expressing this kind of deep love for each other. So excellent have they been in loving the family of faith, their love has extended out to the wider region of Macedonia.

Excursus: "Sibling Love" (*philadelphia*)

I lived for a year near Philadelphia, Pennsylvania, so the word "philadelphia" sounds very commonplace to me. We must recognize, though, how truly unusual it would have been for Paul to be so comfortable using this term for a group of people that were not related biologically.[17] So distinctive (and strange) was the early Christian use of siblingship language that second-century Roman Marcus Cornelius Fronto criticized them with these words: "They recognize each other by secret marks and signs; hardly have they met when they love each other, throughout the world uniting in the practice of a veritable religion of lusts. Indiscriminately they call each other brother and sister, thus turning even ordinary fornication into incest by the intervention of these hallowed names."[18] Christian believer Minucius Felix responded to Fronto thusly: ". . . it is true that we do love one another—a fact that you deplore—since we do not know how to hate. Hence it is true that we do call one another brother—a

---

17. Reidar Aasgaard notes that the term was used less than a dozen times in all the Greek literature of which we know before Paul's time (Aasgaard 2004: 151).

18. See *Octavius* 8-9, in *The Octavius of Marcus Minucius Felix* 1974: 123; ANF 4.177. It should be noted that it was unlikely that Fronto was aware of actual sexual deviance amongst the Christians. Rather, Christians meeting privately in houses (and not publicly in temples) probably led to the kinds of suspicions noted here.

fact which rouses your spleen—because we are men of the one and same God the Father, copartners in faith, coheirs in hope."[19]

Writing a few decades after Paul's first letter to the Thessalonians, Greek historian and moralist Plutarch produced an essay called *Peri philadelphia/ De fraterno amore*—"On brotherly love." Plutarch underscores how a sibling relationship is superior to one of friendship because brothers and sisters are bound together within the same family and have a special obligation to love and protect one another. As Reidar Aasgaard explains, Plutarch notes that a sibling form of love is necessarily characterized by "tolerance, loyalty, and forgiveness."[20] This is noticeably relevant to what Paul has to say to the Thessalonians, especially when there may have been situations where some were inappropriately taking advantage of others in the church. Thus, reinforcing their siblingship relationship in the Messiah, Paul would be reinforcing what can be called "other-regarding morality."[21]

In 4:9, Paul mentions that they hardly need explicit instruction because they have been "God-taught."[22] What does this mean? Some have proposed that Paul is referring to particular "love" teachings from the Old Testament or to Jesus' earthly words about love recorded and passed down in the Jesus tradition, but this seems unlikely because Paul appears to be comparing normal human instruction with a unique kind of divine instruction. If Paul were referring to Jesus' teachings or Old Testament instruction, the Thessalonians would have learned it from *Paul's* own apostolic instruction, and then it would be unclear why he would calls this "God-taught."[23] Rather, it seems most probable that Paul is talking about the inward, transformative work of the Spirit. John Calvin captures this idea with particular eloquence:

> Their hearts were framed for love; so that it appears that the Holy Spirit inwardly dictates efficaciously what is to be done, so that there is no need to give injunctions in writing.[24]

19. Minucius Felix, *Oct.* 31.18.

20. Aasgaard 2004: 106.

21. See this language used by David Horrell (2005: 115).

22. As far as we can tell, Paul made up a new word—*theodidaktoi* ("God-taught" or "taught by God"). See Witmer 2008: 153–64.

23. See Best 1986: 173.

24. Calvin, *Commentary on 1 Thessalonians* 4:9, see http://www.ccel.org/ccel/calvin/

Paul's point in saying this would be to comfort and encourage the Thessalonians who have suffered physically and emotionally in light of recent events (especially the death of community members). No doubt they were wondering—*what is happening? What should we do? How do we move forward?* Paul, the excellent pastor that he is, reminds them of who they are as part of the family of God in Messiah Jesus, and he gently exhorts them to excel in the love that God has already taught them how to share.[25]

Fusing the Horizons 5.1: A New Covenant Community of Love

When I was in seminary, I experienced a kind of crisis of faith. Some of the students in my classes expressed their serious interest in "theology," and read their textbooks with utter devotion. They wrote impressive term papers and even met with professors outside of class for further instruction. However, as I lived with many of these students in the dorms, I became uneasy with a startling realization: they excelled in academic knowledge but many did not dedicate themselves to holiness, discipleship, and Christian love. Some went to the pub and got drunk on a regular basis. Others destroyed school property for fun. And the term "humility" could hardly characterize many of these students.

They had been taught *about God*, but it could hardly be said that they were *theodidaktos*—"God-taught." In Paul's reckoning, the Christian cannot be merely engaged in intellectual exercises and call it Christian "teaching." To be taught by God, to be taught by God *the Spirit*, is to be transformed. St. Augustine reflects on this idea of true Christian teaching in this way.

> It is through grace that we not only discover what ought to be done but also that we do what we have discovered. That is, not only that we believe what ought to be loved but also that we love what we have believed. If this grace is to be called "teaching," let it at any rate be called "teaching" in such a manner that God may be believed to infuse it, along with an ineffable sweetness, more deeply and more internally. This teaching, therefore, would be not only by

---

calcom42.vi.vi.iii.html; see also Bruce 1982: 90; Richard 1995: 216.

25. Given the emphasis in chapter five on prophecy, it might be the case that the unexpected death of community members led the Thessalonians on a hunt for more divine revelation. If so, Paul's point here might be that their focus should not be on learning something *new* from God (in terms of information), as much as growing in what they already know (i.e., love).

> their agency who plant and water from without but likewise by God also who ministers in secret his own increase. All this is in such a way that God not only exhibits truth but likewise imparts love. . . . Thus the apostle speaks to the Thessalonians, "As touching love of the brothers, you have no need that I write to you, for you yourselves have been taught by God to love one another." *On the Grace of Christ* 12.13—13.14.[26]

Augustine makes the point that, for the new covenant people, their "way" must be unique at its core. These people do not simply receive written or verbal teaching for intellectual consumption, but, rather, the instruction they receive (even when through humans) is imbued with the presence and power of the Holy Spirit itself. And the people are not simply informed by God, but they are moved. This is why Paul can talk about the God who *gives* his Spirit to the people (4:8). "Thus you will know them by their fruits" (Matt 7:20). As we recognize the powerful work of God in us, his transformed people, may we sing together a song of exhortation to love like this one.

> Gracious Spirit, Holy Ghost
> taught by you, we covet most,
> of our gifts at Pentecost,
> holy, heavenly love.[27]

Living with Integrity (4:11–12)

In 4:11–12, Paul exhorts the Thessalonians to live quietly, manage their own affairs, and work with their own two hands. Throughout the whole letter, Paul underscores the importance of work and labor (1:3; 2:9; 3:5; 5:12–13; cf. 1 Cor 4:12). Despite the fact that he can refer to the importance of being ready for the return of Jesus (1 Thess 5:6, 8), there is also the need for faithfulness and integrity in everyday work, not least as a testimony to the outside, unbelieving world that followers of Jesus are respectful, trustworthy citizens and neighbors. Wherever need exists in the community, Paul assumes that believing brothers and sisters will step in and offer support (1 Thess 5:14). However, where "grace" is the watchword, there is always the temptation for some to exploit the kindness of others for their own gain and to gratify their own laziness. Paul rejects this spirit of exploitative dependence. This comes across clearly in Galatians as well. Each person is

---

26. See Gorday 2000: 82.
27. Written by Christopher Wordsworth, 1862.

expected to carry her own load (Gal 6:6), though there are obvious occasions when we must carry one another's burdens (Gal 6:2).

Sometimes scholars have argued that Paul operated, especially in such an early letter (like 1 Thessalonians), under an "interim ethic" where certain moral expectations were hastily put into place in view of the imminent return of Jesus. Certainly Paul had no reason *not* to think Jesus would come soon and suddenly, but the fact that in 1 Thess 4:12 he moves the churches towards having no one directly dependent on another (and that everyone paid their own way, as it were) means that he desired, as a matter of first principle, that believers live in a self-sustaining community.[28]

Excursus: Work and Quietness

Paul's instructions in 4:11 are peculiar for a number of reasons. First, why does he tell these Thessalonians to work with their *hands?* Should the emphasis fall on *hands* (i.e., manual labor) or simply on *work* (versus inactivity)? Second, why does he tell them to be quiet and to mind their own business? Is the "quietness" about silence or about tranquility/peace?

There was a time when some scholars connected problems of idleness and unproductive fervor with the Thessalonians' misunderstandings about the end times. In 1912, James Frame made this comment: "It may be assumed that the belief in the coming of the Lord had created in the midst of some of the converts a feeling of restlessness and excitement which manifested itself outwardly in idleness and meddlesomeness in the affairs of the brotherhood. The idlers, we may imagine, being in want, had asked support from the church, and being refused on the ground that they were able to support themselves, had attempted to interfere in the affairs of the group."[29]

However, some scholars have wondered, if the "problem" was presumptions about the impending end of the world, why does Paul wait until 5:1–11 to talk about the true timing of the return of Jesus (instead of right after 4:9–12)?[30] Others relate this issue of idleness with more typical social problems in society. Richard Ascough has argued in favor of viewing the Thessalonian church as a converted "voluntary association," a kind of social club.[31] In

---

28. For a recent treatment of Paul's ethics, see Gupta 2009.
29. Frame 1912: 160; see also Best 1986 175–76; Morris 1975 131.
30. See discussion in Furnish 2007: 97–98
31. See Introduction for more on the history and composition of the Thessalonian

such clubs, it was common for members to compete for status and privilege (in terms of social value and honor). In reference to "aspire to live quietly" (4:11), Ascough notes a Greek inscription related to a voluntary association which reads: "let the association increase by aspirations." The word used here for "aspirations" (*philoteimia*) is related to the word Paul employs in 1 Thess 4:11 for "aspire" (*philotimeō*). In the voluntary associations, it was expected that members competed for honor and status—it was obviously encouraged. If Ascough is right, Paul would have been discouraging Christians from engaging in races for honor and status.

My concern with Ascough's theory is that the terminology of aspiration (*philoteimia*) is quite common and does not restrict Paul's language to that of the association. Rather, I think Bruce Winter's theory has more to commend it. Winter argues that believers should not forsake regular work in view of tying themselves to wealthy benefactors. Ben Witherington supports Winter's view and expresses Paul's reasoning in this way.

> They were to be quietly busy, not busybodies, which is to say not living on the dole of some patron and then spending their time spreading the patron's name around and seeking to win friends and influence people for the patron. Christians, by contrast to the patron-client system, were all to work as they were able, avoid being a burden to others, and earn money to do good to others without thought of return. Love and doing good to all, especially the household of faith, rather than reciprocity, was to be their guiding principle.[32]

The reality in Thessalonica may have been that some tragedy struck the Christian community (leading to unexpected deaths), for some reason some community members were stirred up by eschatological concerns, and in a troubled state they came to over-rely on patrons as they tried to discern what was going on. Paul's counsel to these is, to borrow a British morale-boosting motto, "keep calm and carry on." Despite unanswered questions, even amidst the confusion and chaos, the life of the community requires consistency and self-discipline. As Richard Hays writes, "The eschatological hope should leave them, according to Paul, neither in a state of passivity nor in a state of fevered striving; instead, they should gladly acknowledge that God is at work among

---

church (6–16).

32. Witherington 2006: 122; see Winter 1994: 42–60; Winter 1989: 105–19; also cf. Green 2002: 209.

them preparing them for the day of the Lord precisely through the works of love that characterise their common life."[33]

Fusing the Horizons: Living Quiet Lives in a Noisy World

There is an ironic twinge in Paul's phrasing in 4:11 that is not readily apparent in English. When Paul tells the Thessalonians to *aspire to live quiet lives*, "aspire" and "quiet" are not usually put together in a Greek sentence. Aspiration, in the way it was commonly used in the Greco-Roman world of Paul's time, was about struggling, persevering, and, most importantly, *competing*—essentially, trying to get ahead in a dog-eat-dog world. Given that the Greco-Roman world was fiercely competitive, "to aspire" was to fight and claw your way to be king of the hill.

Paul cleverly turns this somewhat natural inclination on its head—*aspire to . . . live quietly*. What he is saying here is that believers do things differently, they march to the beat of a different drummer. When *they* struggle and persevere, the goal is not to conquer the world by trampling over others. Paul is basically saying *don't copycat the way of the world, the world's values and models for success*.

The redeemed, grace-rich people of God do not need to add extra noise to a noisy world. To live "quietly" does not mean to sequester yourself, to step out of the world (see 1 Cor 5:9–10). Rather, it is to respond to your God-given vocation and feel comfortable in your own skin and place in the world, such that your focus is not on being so loud about yourself that you get the right attention and boost your reputation up in the right ways in public. Heart-quietness, life-quietness, is the by-product of contentment. Contentment can only come from peace with God.

---

33. Hays 1996: 22–23.

The Hopeful Fate of the Christian Dead
(1 Thess 4:13–18)

> **13**We do not want you to be uninformed, my dear brothers and sisters, on the matter of those who are "asleep." We do not want you to grieve as the rest who have no hope. **14**For if we believe that Jesus died and rose, so also God will bring those who have "fallen asleep" thorough Jesus with him. **15**For we say this to you in a word from the Lord: we who are left alive at the coming of the Lord will absolutely *not* go ahead of those who have "fallen asleep." **16**The Lord himself will descend from heaven with a command, with the voice of an archangel, and the dead in the Messiah will rise first. **17**Then we who are left alive, along with them, will be swept up in the clouds to meet the Lord in the air. And henceforth we will be with the Lord forever. **18**Therefore comfort one another with these words.

Paul addresses in 4:13–18 a topic that seems to be of particular interest to the Thessalonians—that is, the fate of the Christian dead. The fact that he gives such emphasis to the notion that "we . . . will absolutely *not* go ahead of those who have 'fallen asleep'" (4:15) is probably a clue that there were some who thought that those who died (recently) were somehow doomed or separated from the Lord Jesus. Paul is insistent that those dead will be appropriately reunited with them (the Thessalonians) and the Lord Jesus.

Why refer to the dead as "asleep"? It could be pointed out that this language is somewhat conventional in the Greco-Roman world. Roman poet Catullus wrote, "The sun can set and rise again / But once our brief light sets / There is one unending night to be slept through."[1] Indeed, historians and archaeologists have discovered a repeated pattern on ancient Greek vase-paintings that depict twin-brother gods *Thanatos* (Death) and *Hypnos* (Sleep) lifting or carrying a dead body together.[2] But even with some of

---

1. See Bruce 1982: 96.
2. See Heinemann 1913.

these death-sleep associations "in the air," as it were, there seems to be a more theological purpose behind Paul's word-choice.

It is almost certain that Paul's depiction of death as sleep is influenced by teachings from the Jesus tradition.[3] There is the well-known story in the Synoptics where Jesus visits the house of a synagogue leader and heals his daughter. According to Matthew, he proclaims, "the girl is not dead but sleeping" (Matt 9:24; cf. Mark 5:39; Luke 8:52). The point is not that the mourners were wrong to think the young girl dead (for she *was* dead). Rather, the point of this saying is that death is such an unequal match for the life-giving power of Jesus that it does not even deserve to be called "death." Jesus is so bursting with vitality that restoring her from the dead, something no human could do with this kind of authority and ease, is as simple for Jesus as rousing a sleeping child. No doubt Paul's point in referring to death as merely "sleep" is to remind the Thessalonians that death is not the end. There is something more—resurrection life/wakefulness is waiting just as morning waits for the sleepers until they meet sunrise.[4] Cyril of Alexandria once wrote, "To him, as being life by nature, there is nothing dead. Having a firm hope of the resurrection of the dead, we call the dead 'those that sleep' for this reason. They will arise in Christ, and as the blessed Paul says, 'They live to him,' because they are about to live."[5]

This is what it means to grieve *with hope*. Paul here implies that most pagans grieve *without* hope. While there is evidence that some Greeks and Romans did believe in a kind of afterlife (see Plato, *Georgias* 52D),[6] there is the impression that many expected little beyond the grave.[7] So, Greek poet Theocritus famously wrote "hopes are for the living; the dead are without hope" (*Idyll* 4.42) and some ancient grave markers have been discovered that bear the abbreviation NFFNSNC (*non fui, fui, non sum, non curo*): "I was not, I was, I am not, I care not." One Roman tombstone bore this inscription, "Into nothing from nothing how quickly we go."[8] And with a

---

3. On the wider subject of Paul's use of the Jesus tradition in 1 Thessalonians 4–5, see Wenham 1995: 305–16.

4. Consequently, I think it is unfortunate that several translations render the verb *koimaomai* as a form of "died" instead of "asleep" (see NRSV, NLT, CEB).

5. Cyril of Alexandria, Commentary on Luke, Homily 46; see Just 2003: 146.

6. See Smith 2000: 724.

7. As Martin Goodman writes, "It would be quite wrong to imagine many people in the Roman world preoccupied with the world to come or weighed down by guilt for sin"; see 2013: 313.

8. See Abbott 1911. Abbott makes the case that many Romans probably did believe

more lighthearted tone, we might note this inscription also: "Friends who read this, listen to my advice: mix wine, tie the garlands around your head, drink deep. And do not deny pretty girls the sweets of love. When death comes, earth and fire consume everything."[9]

Let us now spend time examining closely the statement of comfort Paul offers in 4:15–17. First, we should note what Paul does *not* do here. His concern is that he wishes to encourage the Thessalonians who are left alive in light of the recent death of fellow believers of their community. I would imagine that if a similar situation happened today, I might hear a pastor or priest say (for example, at a funeral), "Charlie is gone from this world, but take comfort, because he is in heaven with Jesus and the angels enjoying eternal peace and rest." No doubt Paul had a sense for the "silver lining" of death sending one somehow into the immediate realm of the Messiah (see Phil 1:23); but for the early Christians, they placed the weight of their hope on the "Day of the Messiah" (so Phil 1:10; 2:16; cf. 1 Cor 15:23; 2 Thess 2:8; 2 Peter 3:12–13). So even in 1 Thess 4:15–17, Paul does *not* tell the Thessalonians—*the dead in the Messiah are at peace with God in heaven*. However he understood their present existence, it was *more* important that he tell them about what lies ahead. And he does so with such fantastic images, like something out of a science fiction novel. But as unusual as his language is for our daily, chastened religious vocabulary, it was rather common for Jews like Paul who had an "apocalyptic imagination."[10] This kind of thinking carried the expectation that the God of Israel was a God who would not let human sin and the power of evil consume the world He created. An apocalyptic mindset expected God to break into time and space in a radically powerful way to reset the balance of power and restore all that had (re)turned to chaos. So, Isaiah 63 reflects on the problem of Israel (in exile) suffering under foreign oppression—where is God? The whole chapter recounts a sad tale of Israel sinning, being punished by God, Israel crying out in pain (because of the mess they caused for themselves), and God coming to their aid. Life in exile seemed to be the end of the road, a place of utter hopelessness (see Isa 63:17). The lament comes to a climax with Israel pleading with her God, enjoining Him to "burst forth from the heavens and come down, so that the mountains would quake at your presence" (64:1).

---

in some kind of post-mortem existence, but it seems to be that there was no clear idea of what that existence would look like, or whether it was consciously happy or not.

9. *CIL* VI 17985a; Rome n.d., as cited in Ascough 2004: 522.

10. Cook: 2003: 177–78.

The mood of the apocalyptic imagination was born in this kind of context where Israel began to hope for a dynamic, cataclysmic act of God on their behalf, protecting and restoring them (not least from their sin), and punishing and destroying their enemies. While there are some disagreements among scholars about how the term "apocalyptic" should be used and what its essential components are, many scholars find an "apocalyptic" perspective/worldview to have the following six elements.[11]

> *Cosmology.* The "world" is not just material molecules in motion, not just a world of human work and wars and food and drink. Rather, there is a much larger stage where "players" at work include demons and angels and all kinds of forces of good and evil that are not detectable to the naked eye. Apocalypticists are attentive to such goings on (Rom 16:20; 2 Cor 2:11; cf. Eph 6:11). We see this in 1 Thessalonians when Paul refers to the voice of the "archangel" (4:16).[12]

> *Revelation.* The word "apocalyptic" comes directly from the Greek word *apokalypsis* which means "revelation" or "disclosure." An "apocalypse" is a writing (at home within early Judaism) where a "seer" typically has his eyes opened in visions or dreams to the operations of an unseen world and to important events yet to come. I am convinced that this "revelatory" aspect accounts for Paul's appeal to the "word of the Lord" (1 Thess 4:15; see 96–99).

> *Eschatology.* As noted above, one key purpose of divine revelation for a seer is knowledge of significant future events, in the case of Paul the information about the return of the Messiah found in 4:15–17 underscoring the priority of the resurrection of "the dead in the Messiah" and the sure hope that all believers will be together with the Lord Messiah Jesus henceforth.

> *Dualism and Conflict.* Most apocalyptic texts (like Daniel [esp. chs. 2, 7–12] and Revelation) narrate a kind of good-versus-evil battle (or battles). This is absent from 1 Thess 4:15–17, but probably because Paul's focus is specifically on the fate of the recently deceased.[13]

---

11. The following categories are of my own making, but are influenced largely by Aune 1993: 25–35; Murphy 2002: 127–66; see also Collins 1998: 264–68.

12. The only other appearance in the New Testament of the word "archangel" (*archangelos*) is Jude 9 which specifically mentions the angel Michael.

13. Note, however, 2 Thess 1:8–9; 2:8.

Divine Sovereignty. Unfortunately, the language of "divine sovereignty" has sometimes been used to imply that God controls everything with puppet strings. However, the more general use of this phrase simply means that believers are expected to have full confidence that God has ultimate power over evil, and when he promises to make things right, to rescue and redeem and renew, we can rest assured that it will happen by his will. Thus, Paul can write to the Thessalonians with a sense of boldness and sureness—"we who are left alive at the coming of the Lord will absolutely *not* go ahead of those who have 'fallen asleep'" (4:15).[14] It is because of the faithfulness of the all-powerful Father God and Messiah Jesus that Paul can have such confidence (1 Thess 5:24).

Radical Transformation. Apocalypticists tend to have a keen sense that what God intends to do in the future will change everything. Paul already believed a major "change" happened with the first coming of Jesus (1 Cor 10:11; 2 Cor 5:17). However, Paul believed that God was not yet finished with his redemptive work, and the Parousia, the reappearance of Messiah Jesus, would complete his plan to make all things like new. That sense of "radical transformation" is notable in 1 Thess 4:17 where Paul claims, "And henceforth we will be with the Lord forever." That word "forever" (*pantote*) is essential, because it means there is no going back, there is no threat of disruption, corruption, or separation at the threat of any hostile force. While *pantote* is technically a temporal word ("for all time"), the force of what Paul is saying has to do more with "unalterable togetherness."[15]

Going back to Paul's rhetorical purposes in chapter four, we can contextualize his apocalyptic discourse in view of comforting the Thessalonian believers who remain alive. Again Paul, in contrast to pagan grief, sets his converts' eyes on a hope beyond the grave. Paul does not discourage or dismiss grief. He simply wants believers to know the power and plan of God. God intends to restore the Christian dead, and he will do it. Through a "word of the Lord," Paul goes on to reveal a glimpse of eschatological events that are yet to unfold (4:15–17).[16] Paul seems to underscore that "the

---

14. The NET is one of the only translations I could find that tries to capture the rare Greek negative construction *ou mē* (with the subjunctive verb following), which expresses absolute certainty that something will *not* happen (NET employs "surely"; compare, similarly, CEB "definitely").

15. Cook 2003: 179.

16. Scholars have vigorously debated the meaning of Paul's phrase, "word of the Lord"

dead in the Messiah will rise first." For Paul to go into such detail in 4:16–17 about the fate of the Christian dead almost certainly means that the living Thessalonian believers had concerns and questions. However, contrary to the arguments of many scholars, it seems to me that more is going on than simply that they are confused about whether or not the dead will be able to rise again. The keyword that stands out for me is *protos*—"first" (4:16). Paul underscores the *priority* of these dead believers in the Messiah. The living Christians will only go up to meet the Lord in the air *after* (*epeita*; 4:17) the dead have risen. Why is this so?

My own suggestion is that it has something to do with how these particular believers died. A handful of scholars have wondered whether it is possible that a group of believers died due to persecution.[17] While there is no definitive evidence to support this, theoretically it could explain Paul's focus on the priority of the resurrection of those Thessalonians who died (see Introduction, 14–15). No doubt, from their community's perspective, the sudden and traumatic death of such members of their church would have brought great shame. Highlighting that these martyrs would come *first* in the resurrection might be Paul's way of expressing God's ability to reconcile their dignity and honor. Chapter four verse seventeen has been the subject of much attention because of two words: "caught up" (*harpazō*) and "meeting" (*apantēsis*). As for the former, this is where we get the language and idea of "the rapture" which has been popularized as an eschatological idea by the *Left Behind* books and movies. The word "rapture" is taken from a Latin translation (*raptio*) of the word Paul uses here for "caught up" (*harpazō*). The idea behind "rapture" theology is that Jesus' return (the first of two future appearances) involves a secret snatching away of believers from the earth. However, nothing in Paul's words here in 1 Thess 4:17 lead us to believe that the appearance of Jesus is anything but public, visible, and

---

(*logos kyriou*). Is Paul referring to something Jesus said during his earthly ministry, but which is not recorded in the canonical gospels (see John 21:25)? Or perhaps could this be the tradition behind Matt 24:30–31, but in Paul's own words? I find neither of these options very persuasive. Rather, if we look at the patterned use of the language "word of the Lord" in Scripture, it is associated with special prophetic insight. Following Victor Furnish, I lean in favor of viewing this as a revelatory message from the Lord given to Paul himself. This view would account for the specificity and the uniqueness of what Paul writes in 4:15–17; see Furnish 2007: 104–5.

17. See Marxsen 1969: 24; Donfried 1985: 349–51; Pobee 1985 113–14; Witherington 2006: 140–41; cf. Gorman 2004: 150; Johnson 1999: 285; see also Bruce 1988: 327–28; Donfried 1997: 215–23.

loud![18] Thus, many scholars believe that there will not be two appearances of Christ, but only one, *the Day of the Lord*.[19]

The second controversial word is *apantēsis*. The basic meaning of the word is not in dispute, it simply translates as "meeting." However, much scholarly discussion has swirled around whether this is a technical word in the Greco-Roman world that refers to the official visit of a dignitary whereby the townspeople go to "meet" this person-of-importance and escort him to the city with an honorary parade. Raymond Collins explains this imagery

> The lord's arrival in a town, with military escort, was announced by a herald. A blast from a trumpet would announce the impending arrival. Perforce the inhabitants of the city would go out to meet the lord. More often than not the lord would arrive as a "Savior" bestowing various benefactions on the citizens.[20]

Some scholars have shown skepticism because, while *apantēsis* (and words related to it) were sometimes used in reference to such occasions in Greek literature, the word does not *necessarily* assume this whole scenario by virtue of its usage. However, given that Jesus is referred to in 1 Thess 4:16–17 as *kyrios*, lord, a term with strong political resonances, the case becomes much stronger.[21] But what is Paul's purpose in his borrowing of this procession motif if Paul did indeed intend it here? Collins continues:

> Paul evokes the scene to create an impressive image of the coming of the Lord. The Lord himself will give the command to start the parade. The beginning of the parade will be announced with the archangel's cry and a blast of the herald's trumpet. The Lord will be accompanied by 'all the saints,' the heavenly host. The arrival of the Lord descending from heaven and accompanied by hosts of angels will be an impressive sight.[22]

---

18. See Keener 2009: introduction, under "Misinterpretations of Revelation 1–3."

19. For two excellent studies, critical of "rapture theology," see Rossing 2004; Gorman 2011.

20. Collins 2008: 29.

21. Scholars who are in favor of reading *apantēsis* with this imagery in mind include Bruce 1982: 102–3; Holmes 1998: 151; Witherington 2006: 141; Shogren 2012: 190n.40 (see also Smith 2004: 48). Less convinced are Wanamaker 1990: 175–76; Malherbe 2000: 277. Best 1986: 199 and Byron 2014 are neutral and open to the possibility, but reluctant to force such a reading without stronger evidence.

22. Collins 2008: 29.

No doubt the Thessalonians could set their hope on this certain future course of events as a kind of "reversal of fortune" for their Christian community. From a very narrow perspective, it might have felt to them like life was bleak as they struggled with bereavement and ongoing persecution—feeling perhaps like Paul did as he expressed his trials to the Corinthians later on: "afflicted in every way . . . perplexed . . . persecuted . . . struck down" (2 Cor 4:8–9). But Paul encourages the Thessalonians in a way similar to how he later comforts the Corinthians. *Things seem too far gone to change, too hopeless to redeem. But in the snap of the fingers—a moment so fast you may blink and miss it—God will change everything forever* (1 Cor 15:52). *And thanks be to God that he will stand the great conqueror Messiah Jesus* (1 Cor 15:57)!

And Paul can finish out his discourse with this: "comfort one another with these words" (4:18). Again, the emphasis falls on restoration, particularly bringing together what feels torn apart. Believers left alive were separated from those who died. They will be reunited. Furthermore, there is great encouragement in knowing that we will be *with the Lord* always because he is our rock and our refuge. As Beverly Gaventa remarks, "To be with the Lord is to be beyond the reach of evil."[23]

To put into historical perspective the important choice of words here for Paul, we might appeal to an ancient letter found from Oxyrhynchus (Egypt) that dates to the second century AD. It is a letter of sympathy to a couple who lost their son.

> Irene to Taonnophris and Philo, good cheer. I was as much grieved and wept over the blessed one, as I wept for Didymas, and everything that was fitting I did and all who were with me, Epaphroditus and Thermouthion and Philion and Apollonius and Plantas. But truly there is nothing anyone can do in the face of such things. Do you therefore comfort one another. Farewell. Hathyr I.[24]

As for some today, Irene faced the morose reality that loved ones die. She tries to maintain a positive spirit by encouraging her friends to take comfort. And yet there is no clear referent of that hope. But for Paul it was not this way. Yes, of course people must grieve. But believers face the loss knowing the impending work of God to wipe away every tear and quiet mourning and shouts of agony (Rev 7:17; 21:4).

---

23. Gaventa 1998: 67.
24. P. Oxy. 115 (see Milligan 1912: 95–96).

Fusing the Horizons: The New Covenant People of Hope

In the few weeks that I was writing this chapter, there was a shooting at Seattle Pacific University (SPU) where I had been a faculty member only two years prior. A couple of students were very seriously injured and one young man lost his life. Even though I was living 2700 miles away when the incident happened, the reality of this event hit home for me because one SPU student tackled the shooter and immobilized him, and that brave student was in the introductory Bible class at SPU I taught when he was a sophomore.

The United States has endured a long string of these school shootings in its recent history, but rarely does this happen on the campus of a Christian college. Newspapers were quick to notice the SPU community response to this tragedy. On the one hand, students did not shortcut the need to express grief and lament. On the other hand they dared to cling to Christian hope. One SPU staff worker who was interviewed by the Seattle Times said this: "Each of us felt the weight of this horror and grief, but we were not lost. The essence of the Christian faith that we teach and try to embody on this campus gave us the words and the vision we were looking for. The central proclamation of our faith is that our crucified Lord was raised back to life. God has the power and the will to restore and redeem all that has been terrorized and lost."

Another noticeable response from the SPU community was authentic fellowship. A graduate student at SPU shared with reporters her appreciation for this community of support: "What I'm seeing most is the desire to really be together, to find each other, to look after each other. To both give and receive the love of Christ." To these statements no doubt Paul would say *amen and amen*. The new covenant community grieves with hope in the radically transformative work of Jesus that has come and will come again in a consummating way. For now we are called to be a *with-each-other* and *for-each-other* fellowship. This is not only good medicine for the soul, but it is a part of Christian testimony, the bearing of the likeness of Jesus in the world. Observe these words that SPU professor Richard Steele shared with the community after the SPU tragedy.

> We can experience anger, even rage, but we do not give vent to vengefulness. We can experience intense grief but we do not lose hope. We recognize the brokenness in ourselves and therefore try to extend compassion and mercy to other people whose broken-

ness has been unleashed. This is our darkest day and our finest hour.[25]

This tenacious clinging to hope, expressed above in 2014, is mirrored in these lines from William Cowper's eighteenth-century poem called "Hope."

> These shall last when night has quench'd the pole,
> And heav'n is all departed as a scroll:
> And when, as justice has long since decreed,
> This earth shall blaze, and a new world succeed,
> Then these thy glorious works, and they who share
> That hope which can alone exclude despair,
> Shall live exempt from weakness and decay,
> The brightest wonders of an endless day.

---

25. The shooting happened Thursday, June 5, 2014. All of the quotes come from the Seattle Times article "At Faith-Based Seattle Pacific University, Grief Without Despair," published June 7, 2014. Online: http://seattletimes.com/html/localnews/2023794834_spufaithxml.html.

The Day of the Lord: Preparedness and Perseverance, not Prediction (1 Thess 5:1–11)

> **1**Now on the matter of "times and seasons," my dear brothers and sisters, there is no need for us to write to you. **2**For you know accurately for yourselves that the Day of the Lord is coming like a thief comes at night. **3**Whenever they might say, "peace and security," then suddenly destruction falls upon them just as labor pains for a pregnant woman. And there will be no escape. **4**As for you, my dear brothers and sisters, you are not in the dark for the day to overtake you in surprise like a thief. **5**For all of you are children of light and children of day. We are not night-people or darkness-people. **6**Therefore let us not fall asleep as the rest, but rather let us be awake and fully alert. **7**For those who sleep sleep at night and those who drink get drunk at night. **8**But as for us, day-people, let us stand at the ready, having dressed in the breastplate of loyalty and love, and having donned the helmet of the hope of salvation. **9**For God did not destine us to suffer God's anger for justice, but instead he destined us to obtain salvation through our Lord Messiah Jesus. **10**He died for us so that, whether we are "awake" or "asleep," we will live with him. **11**Therefore, comfort one another and each of you build up the other, as you are already doing.

From 4:13–18 to 5:1–11 we can sense a clear change of subject from the fate of the dead ("sleeping") in the Messiah to the fate of those Thessalonian believers still alive.[1] The introductory phrase, "Now on the matter of" (*peri de*), clues us into the nature of the subject (see 1 Cor 7:1; 8:1; 12:1; 16:1), "times and seasons." Some interpreters argue that this *peri de* construction shows that the Thessalonians raised the matter of "times and seasons." Others believe that Paul simply wanted to offer a relevant teaching. However, it very well could be that there is a both-and going on—perhaps the Thessalonians wondered about the nature and timing of future events (*what is going to happen next?*) and Paul chose to word the matter in his own way (*"times and seasons"*). In any case, the subject of "when" is quickly

---

1. See Holmes 1998: 165.

addressed and Paul focuses on the more important question regarding the "how" of Christian living. He switches from a purely temporal view of "days" and "nights" to an ethical discussion of "day/light"-people and "night/darkness"-people. The key theme that pervades this passage is *vigilance*—Christian mental sobriety and alertness in a time of spiritual torpor and ethical perversion. While this section is brief, there are three parts: Ready for the Night Thief (5:1–3), You are Day and Light People (5:4–7), and Battle as Day People (5:8–11).

Ready for the Night Thief (5:1–3)

Again, as noted above, Paul commences this section with a clear interest in the topic of "times and seasons."[2] This phrase appears to refer to phases in a timeline, as we read in Eccl 4:1: "for all things, there is a *time* and *season* for every matter under heaven." A couple of Jewish texts focus on the mysterious nature of how God plans periods and events (Dan 2:21; Wisdom 8:1–8).[3] One can only guess why the Thessalonians should be taught (or reminded) about the eschatological timing. Perhaps it was that some wanted details regarding the Parousia because they were uncertain that it was going to happen. In that case, Ernest Best is right that Paul's point is its "unpredictability, and yet its inevitability."[4] I think the situation, though, is closer to what Malherbe proposes, namely that the Thessalonians were confused by the predictions of local prophets. Now, Malherbe and Furnish suggest that it was *Christian* prophets who made such prognostications. However, we should entertain the possibility that it was Jewish (non-Christian) prophets who may have predicted impending doom for the Thessalonians because of their apostasy and failure to continue to respect and revere

---

2. In the past scholars have tried to make a distinction between the meaning of times (*chronos*) and the meaning of seasons (*kairos*), but there appears to be no such distinction made by Paul. In terms of this being a kind of stock phrase, I could find no evidence that it was such in the Greek world. Out of hundreds of ancient (pagan) Greek texts, only one appears to use this collocation, though not exactly in the order we find in 1 Thess 5:1 (Dem. 23.141; "seasons and times").

3. The closest parallel to Paul's own wording is Acts 1:6–7 where the disciples ask about the time of the restoration of the "kingdom of Israel" and Jesus replies: "It is not for you to know the times or periods that the Father has set by his own authority." Jesus tells his disciples that the Spirit-empowered mission takes priority over eschatological knowledge—no doubt Paul echoes this sentiment.

4. Best 1986: 203.

The Day of the Lord: Preparedness and Perseverance, not Prediction 103

the true God.⁵ Imagine how easily their attention could turn away from day-to-day faithfulness to Jesus towards signs and omens that might divine this ill-fated destiny.⁶

Paul tries to refocus the Thessalonian believers' attention on the singular future event that really matters: the Day of the Lord that is coming like a thief in the night. One can easily sense the irony in this: they know *accurately* (*akribos*) that the Lord Jesus will come *unexpectedly*! How can they know precisely about an event that is meant to take them by surprise? This may be a slight against accepting "accurate" timeline prophecies. As far as Paul is concerned, the *only* thing about the future that matters is that believers should be ever at the ready in anticipation of Jesus' arrival.

The language of the night-thief as a metaphor for the sudden nature of the Lord's return appears to be a common Christian convention that likely traces back to a Jesus saying such as we have recorded in Matt 24:36–44 (cf. Luke 12:38–40): "if the owner of the house had known in what part of the night the thief was coming, he would have stayed awake and would not have let his house be broken into. Therefore you also must be ready, for the Son of Man will come when least expected" (Matt 24:43–44).⁷ Similarly, we read in 2 Peter 3:10: "But the day of the Lord will come like a thief, and then the heavens will pass away with a loud noise, and the elements will be dissolved with fire, and the earth and everything that is done on it will be disclosed." In view of this total devastation, the readers are exhorted to live lives of holiness and godliness, signposts of the righteousness that will characterize life in the "new heavens and new earth" (2 Peter 3:11–13).

First Thessalonians 5:3 continues on the theme of the unexpected (especially wrath-bearing) nature of the Day of the Lord. Paul warns them about people who might say "[there is/will be] peace and security." Such people cannot make absolute guarantees—the only one who can ensure true safety must be the one who holds all power. Whatever the Thessalonians might have feared, in Paul's mind, only the Lord Messiah Jesus has such executive powers, both for deliverance and for retribution.⁸

---

5. Malherbe 2000: 287; Furnish 2007: 106–8. See a developed hypothetical scenario with explanation in the Introduction 5–6.

6. Again, while this is only an imaginative situation, the hints and clues on which I build are explained in the Introduction 5–6.

7. See also Rev 16:15; see Bruce 1982: 109.

8. So Witherington: "rather than offering theological comfort food promising an escape from extreme suffering or death, Paul ramps up the eschatological pressure on the audience to remain faithful and be prepared to suffer and if need be die, before the

Excursus: Whose Peace and Security?

First Thessalonians 5:3 offers many questions to the interpreter. Who are the "they" that offer peace and security? What exactly is the danger or threat? Why should the judgment of God come upon them? In the nineteenth century and into most of the twentieth century, the common assumption was that Paul was borrowing this language ("peace and security") from a prophetic tradition such as we find in Jer 6:14 and Ezek 13:10.[9] In the latter text, the thirteen chapter involves Ezekiel's responsibility to condemn the false prophets of Israel. Ezekiel decried "they have misled my people, saying, 'Peace', when there is no peace" (13:10a); and "the prophets of Israel who prophesied concerning Jerusalem and saw visions of peace for it, when there is no peace, says the Lord God" (13:16).

In the last few decades there has been a shift towards a reading that sees "peace and security" as a slogan in support of Roman power and protection, a source of security towards which Paul himself is apparently quite skeptical.[10] The literary and archaeological evidence for a similar (though not exact) Roman motto is intriguing, though it seems many scholars appeal to this interpretation without fleshing out *why* Paul raises this matter at this point in the letter. For my part, I do not find this theory compelling for three reasons: (1) if the "Roman slogan" reading is correct, it would have to pertain somehow to 5:1–11 as a whole which is related to the aftermath of the traumatic death of the Thessalonians whom Paul mentions—if they died due to a tragedy or disease, how could Roman "peace" have stopped it? If they died due to local persecution, *why* would Rome have stopped it, or why would they be promising security *now*, and did not safeguard it *before*? (2) Secondly, the fact that the main verb is specific ("they say") makes it seem that there are *particular* people in mind who are saying this, rather than an appeal to a generic imperial saying.[11] Who would these people be? A scenario must be suggested to account for a local and direct appeal to this so-called Roman slogan. (3) Finally,

---

Lord returns, implying in effect 'blessed are those who die in the Lord henceforth'" (see 2008: 167).

9. See Eadie 1877: 178; Bruce 1982: 109, Plummer 1918: 83.

10. See Bammel 1960: 837–40; Wengst 1987: 17–20, 76–79; Harrison 2011: 61–62; Carter 2006: 89; cf. Weima 2012: 331–59.

11. For a more generic reference, you might have expected a phrasing like "when you hear . . ." as in Deut 13:12; cf. Mark 13:7; Luke 21:9

Joel White has written an insightful article acknowledging that, indeed the language of peace and safety does crop up in imperial texts and on inscriptions and coins, but there is little evidence for a distinct "slogan" and the terms *eirēnē* (peace) and *asphaleia* (security/safety) are extremely common and can be found in relation to a number of contexts political, religious, and otherwise.[12]

It is my contention that the Thessalonian believers may have been falsely comforted by the "predictions" of local Jewish prophets who promised protection from future tragedies and deaths on the condition that they appease the God from whom they have turned away, assuming they were Gentile godfearers who had taken an interest in the Jewish synagogue.[13] This hypothesis, then, would lean in favor of the older reading of 5:3 which detected an allusion to texts like Ezek 13:10, issuing warning of the deceptive safety offered by counterfeit prophets.

You are Day—and Light—People (5:4–7)

From a more temporal discussion of what is to come (the surreptitious appearance of the Lord like a night-thief), Paul transitions to an ethical statement about two kinds of people: those associated with night/dark(ness) and those associated with day/light. What we find here is classic dualistic imagery.[14] Going all the way back to the early chapters of Genesis we find reference to light and darkness, night and day. And throughout the Old Testament night and darkness are symbolically related to hiddenness (Job 12:22; 29:3), ignorance, evil (Ps 139:11–12), sin (Isa 5:20), and judgment (Amos 5:18). And, of course, conversely, light is related to revelation (Dan 2:22), wisdom (Ecc 2:13), and salvation (Ps 18:28). As we move into the second temple period of Judaism, we see a more consistently agonistic and apocalyptic use of light imagery. People and groups are regularly

---

12. White 2013: 382–95.

13. Again, see the Introduction, 6–16.

14. The edited volume *Light Against Darkness: Dualism in Ancient Mediterranean Religion and the Contemporary World* (ed. Lange, 2011) offers a number of fascinating essays including one on the Hebrew Bible (Meyers 2011: 92–16), Second Temple Judaism (Stuckenbruck 2011: 145–68), and the New Testament (Horton 2011: 186–208).

categorized as either on the side of "light" or the side of "darkness."[15] Paul himself establishes a clear line dividing day-people from night-people. This is similar to his portrayal in 2 Cor 6:14–16 ("what fellowship is there between light and darkness?"). Paul also underscores that, at the Parousia, the Lord himself will "bring to light the things now hidden in darkness and will disclose the purposes of the heart" (1 Cor 4:5). Perhaps the one passage that parallels most closely 1 Thess 5:4–11 with its night/darkness/sleep language is Rom 13:11–14:

> Besides this, you know what time it is, how it is now the moment for you to wake from sleep. For salvation is nearer to us now than when we became believers; the night is far gone, the day is near. Let us then lay aside the works of darkness and put on the armor of light; let us live honorably as in the day, not in reveling and drunkenness, not in debauchery and licentiousness, not in quarreling and jealousy. Instead, put on the Lord Jesus Christ, and make no provision for the flesh, to gratify its desires.

Again, it should be obvious that in these kinds of hortatory passages, Paul's concern is with godly behavior. For the Thessalonians, Paul desires for them to be prepared, to know what really matters, and to focus less on being "in the know" and more on being "in the right" in their behavior.

Battle as Day-People (5:8–11)

In keeping with the dualistic language introduced earlier, Paul encourages the Thessalonians to take up the spiritual armor necessary to challenge their enemies. It is probably not necessary or useful to try to read too much into each component; the total picture portrays the kind of people (soldiers) who were recognized in society to be disciplined and prepared. Perhaps, due to bickering about "times and seasons" and questions about recent events, there was in-fighting in the church at Thessalonica. This may have created a kind of spiritual and moral fog that made it difficult for them to fully have their wits about them. With their guard down, it would be easy for members of their community to slip into sinful habits that prevailed in their former lives before they turned to the living and true God.[16]

---

15. See, for example, the language of "sons of light" and "sons of darkness" in the Dead Sea scrolls texts 1QS and 1QM.

16. Best points to the important study by Lovestam (1963) where it is argued that here sleep and drunkenness are "metaphors for absorption in the affairs of the world" (in the words of Best 1986: 212; see Lovestam 1963: 34–56). See also Beale 2003: 147: "To be

The "armor" that the Thessalonian believers wear consists of loyalty, love, and hope—the Pauline triad of virtues that first appeared in 1 Thess 1:3.[17] So, here at the close of the letter, Paul returns to the attitudinal and behavioral distinctives that already characterize the Thessalonians. Paul simply emphasizes that the key to vanquishing their fears lies in the power of these virtues rather than any kind of preparation based on knowing dates and times. By reminding the Thessalonians that God has destined them for *salvation* and not divine *anger*, he is affirming again (see 1 Thess 1:4) their identity in the Messiah. Almost certainly the tragic recent events (that involved the death of some in their community) made some wonder if God was on their side or against them. Paul directs their attention to the fact of their security in and through Jesus who died for them (5:9–10). Not only did he give his life for their salvation, but he will be with them forever.

The final word he offers in this section is the exhortation to encourage and build one another up (5:11). Mutuality and other-centeredness lies at the heart of Paul's concern. He is quick to acknowledge that they have already demonstrated faithfulness in these areas, but perhaps the "fog" of their current concerns clouded their vision of these standards and goals. In the next section of the letter (5:12–22), Paul gets into more detail regarding what this community-orientation requires—respect towards leaders, setting the rebellious straight, comfort for the discouraged, dedication to the weak, patience and peace overall.

Fusing the Horizons: War and Peace: The New Covenant Community in Action

Oftentimes, when I read Bible stories to my children at night, I am struck anew by how violent and even gruesome the Bible can be. Cain murdering Abel. A devastating flood. Death in Jericho by wall and weapon. The decapitation of Goliath. If the Old Testament were a movie, it would certainly be R-rated for violence! It is no wonder many Christians prefer to read the New Testament, trusting in the "meek and mild" Jesus. Yes, certainly we do not get bloody battle scenes in the gospels and, yes, Jesus is depicted as patient and non-violent when he goes to the cross as a sheep to slaughter. In keeping

---

drunk spiritually is to imbibe too much of the world's way of looking at things and not enough of the way God views reality."

17. See Gaventa 1998: 72.

with the model of Jesus, the New Covenant Community should be known for being peacekeepers, lovers of reconciliation, patient forgivers, and servants to the wounded, abused, broken, and downtrodden. The image of the slaughtered lamb ought to be a key symbol for the church—absorbing violence, not perpetuating the cycle.

And yet we must also set that image of the lamb next to the kind of picture we have here in 1 Thess 5:8–11 of the people of God as warriors. Try as we may, we cannot take warfare out of the Bible, even the New Testament. Even though the Gospels do not portray Jesus as a literal warrior, combative language permeates the New Testament:

- "Do not think that I have come to bring peace to the earth; I have not come to bring peace, but a sword" (Matt 10:34).

- "And then the lawless one will be revealed, whom the Lord Jesus will destroy with the breath of his mouth, annihilating him by the manifestation of his coming" (2 Thess 2:8)

- "From his mouth comes a sharp sword with which to strike down the nations and he will rule them with a rod of iron" (Rev 19:15)

Now the point that should be obvious here is that none of this is literal, physical violence with fists and swords. Jesus did not really bring a metal sword. These are word-pictures. However, just because the weapons are not those of flesh and blood (2 Cor 10:3–6), we should not neglect the reality that the New Testament writers (and Jesus himself) used combat imagery. If the ultimate goal is peace, if gentleness and meekness are ideals, then how could this be? What fellowship can peace have with war?

The point of the warfare language in Paul and the rest of the Bible seems to relate to an emphasis on the wider battle versus good and evil. Believers cannot drift through life just spending hours and days waiting to die and go to heaven. Believers are engaged in a conflict against "the rulers, against the authorities, against the cosmic powers of this present darkness, against the spiritual forces of evil in the heavenly places" (Eph 6:12). Just because the battle is not waged with tanks and bombs doesn't make it any less serious or necessary. According to Paul, the cosmic battle is the important one and it is a contest in which all believers must partake. Believers are not called to be physically violent, but they are taught to engage in spiritual battle, knowing the enemies and knowing the proper equipment to win the war (e.g., loyalty, hope, and love).

If we, today, ignore or shun the violent imagery of warfare and soldiering used in Scripture, we will miss the wider point. Model soldiers know the enemy, trust their training, cooperate with their regiment, obey the army commander, serve the king loyally, and live in a state of readiness-for-action. For Paul, these are relevant to believers who live in a world hostile to the living God and his kingdom. Until the new heavens and new earth, the kingdom will still need soldiers committed to King Jesus and his reign. We would do well, then, to ask, are we, as the New Covenant Community, ready for battle? Do we know our enemies (sin, injustice, evil)? Do we recognize that it is the will of the emperor, the Lord Jesus, that we fight against the injustice around us?

Is "peace" the Christian watchword? Absolutely, but to that we must add bravery and vigilance, because the days are evil, the enemy is cunning, and the war is not yet over.

Final Instruction (1 Thess 5:12–28)

¹²Now we ask you, my dear brothers and sister, to acknowledge those who are laboring among you, who guide you in the Lord, and who admonish you. ¹³Show them deep respect for their work by your love. Live peacefully with each other. ¹⁴And we urge you, my dear brothers and sisters, admonish the idle, comfort the discouraged, devote yourself to the weak; be patient with everyone. ¹⁵See to it that no one pays back evil with evil; instead, always pursue goodness both with each other and with everyone. ¹⁶Rejoice always. ¹⁷Pray all the time. ¹⁸Give thanks no matter the circumstance. This is God's will in Messiah Jesus for you. ¹⁹Do not put out the Spirit's fire. ²⁰Do not disregard prophecies. ²¹Instead, put everything to the test: cling to what is good, ²²distance yourself from whatever has even a hint of evil.

²³Now may the God of peace himself make you completely holy, and may your whole spirit, soul, and body be kept blameless at the coming of our Lord Messiah Jesus. ²⁴The One who calls you is faithful, and he will see it is done.

²⁵My dear brothers and sisters, pray for us. ²⁶Greet all your brothers and sisters with a holy kiss. ²⁷I solemnly command you in the Lord to have this letter read to all the brothers and sisters. ²⁸The grace of our Lord Messiah Jesus be with you.

Paul has a tendency to conclude his letters with a series of final instructions and statements. When approaching these last words, we must be careful to avoid two problematic approaches. First, it is not uncommon in popular Christian devotionals to extract a snippet as a motto, such as "pray without ceasing" (1 Thess 5:17). No doubt, this is good advice from Paul overall, but you will appreciate what he is writing on a far deeper level if you try to make sense of these statements in their context. That leads to the second tendency, a scholarly one. There is a tradition of scholarship that treats the cluster of Paul's final instructions as "generic." That is, many interpreters in the past assumed that what Paul says about "Do's" and "Don'ts" have no connection to specific concerns that Paul has for the Thessalonians.

Now, when we see Paul refer, in a rapid-fire sort of way, to a series of broad comments—*rejoice, pray, discern carefully*—it does give a kind of one-size-fits-all impression. However, clearly other things he talks about in this section seem more contextually-focused, regarding, for example, the "rebellious idle."[1] Below we will also discuss other themes and key terms from earlier in the letter that reappear in the final section of the letter. So, is Paul writing generically or specifically? The most likely scenario is that there is some of both going on here. Most of the Gentile churches to which Paul ministered would have benefited from all kinds of general advice about holiness, purity, peace, and love. Think of the American missionary on furlough who travels around the United States and speaks at numerous supporting-churches. She is bound to tell the same stories and give the same kind of encouragement and wisdom. However, there are enough unique, peculiar, or specific elements in this section that convince me that this is *more than generic* counsel *per se*, as Paul appears to be addressing local issues. One more caveat is warranted. To say that Paul was writing with a specific focus on the Thessalonian community does *not* presume that problems were severe or that Paul had all the information he wanted or needed about their lifestyle and behavior. We should entertain the possibility that Paul combined general apostolic wisdom with concrete things he heard from Timothy's report, as well as even some guesses as to what the Thessalonians may have been struggling with.[2]

Leadership and Life Together (5:12–15)

This initial section of the final instructions offers an important, albeit small, glimpse into the inner workings of life in the church in the first century. Paul gives instruction regarding how the church in Thessalonica should show proper respect for the leadership. Beginning, as he so often does in this letter, with his exhortation to his beloved "brothers and sisters" (*adelphoi*), he encourages them to acknowledge their leaders, the ones who carry the responsibility of looking after them. It is vital to note that Paul presents them as people who *toil* or *labor* (*kopiaō*) in their midst. Hard work is a virtue that Paul has repeatedly noted throughout the letter (1:3; 2:9; 3:5), and

---

1. See Malherbe 2000: 309.

2. Many modern interpreters of Paul opt for this both-and approach to Paul's final instructions here; see Wanamaker 1990: 191; Furnish 2007: 114; Fee 2009: 201–2. For a methodology discussion regarding how to reconstruct the historical situation based on the text (as possible), see Gupta 2012: 361–81.

here he aims to underscore the diligence, endurance, and reliability of these leaders. It is possible that some people in the church resented the corrective teaching of the leaders (hence Paul's mention that they "admonish" them), but since his focus is on *acknowledgment* and not *obedience*, the focus for Paul seems to be on the leaders serving as role models.

Let's say that the community was thrown into a bit of tumult and uncertainty due to the recent and sudden death of some of their own, as well as other issues related to the circumstances of their death. Throughout the whole letter, Paul has emphasized endurance and faithfulness, staying on course, and ongoing commitment to holiness and obedience to the will of God. Paul may be setting up hard-working leaders as models of these virtues for others who had decreased their steady walk of faith down to a snail's pace or nearly a halt.

When tragedy strikes a community, when it feels pressure and is forced through change, there is a natural, even instinctual focus on self-preservation. All too often a church can be divided and smaller constituencies or individuals lash out against one another, trying to salvage their piece of stability.

Paul preaches here *peace* (*eirēnē*). Regardless of the status of the community, Paul holds tenaciously to an ethic of other-regard (non-retaliation, patience, seeking good for all; 5:15). In 5:14 Paul specifically mentions the "faint-hearted" (*oligopsychos*) and the "weak" (*asthenēs*). It is difficult to know who these people are. If the community faced a local tragedy (which led to deaths in their church), it is possible the "fainthearted" were scared and fearful of their safety.[3] They needed consolation. As for the "weak," the Greek word (*asthenēs*) is quite broad in meaning and could refer to a weakness of conscience or spirit, or perhaps to those who are physically weak. It is almost impossible to know without more information about the situation, but it could be that some believers were physically injured in the event that led to the deaths in their community. No doubt such ones would need attention and care.[4] And what about the "rebellious idle?" Some translations have opted to read this as people who were "lazy," but at least since John Chrysostom many interpreters understand them as "unruly" or "insubordinate." Malherbe surmises that Paul is calling out these insubordinates for

---

3. For more information regarding how this situational hypothesis might look, see 14–15.

4. For a discussion of the term *asthenēs* ("weak") in its context here, see Black 1984: 22–53.

causing trouble.⁵ One can imagine, in a crisis, troublemakers who complain, gossip, and stir up problems, rather than bring peace to the community and help everyone to move forward in hope.⁶

I would be remiss not to point out Paul's emphasis on love (*agapē*), the driving force that sustains the welfare of the church. Love is the antidote to a malicious spirit and it is the highest and purest form of goodness.

Attitude, Obedience, and Discernment (5:16–22)

The next section of Paul's final instructions appears to stem from the question, no doubt "live" in the minds and hearts of the Thessalonians, *what is God up to? What does he want? What is his will?* We, even now, make it a regular habit of trying to tie events in our life to ways that God might be leading us. Some of this is good and natural (see John 9:1–3), but there is a way we can overthink our circumstances and work too hard trying to hear a message that no one said! Perhaps in view of the recent deaths of multiple members of the believing community, they wondered how this related to the will of God (cf. Luke 13:4–5). What if their neighbors told them, "This all happened because you have turned away from our gods, and now they are cursing you. Seek their will and appease them!" The Thessalonian believers themselves may have wondered whether their own one living and true God was punishing them for some reason (cf. Jonah 1:6). We must remember the kind of religious assumptions and sensibilities these Gentiles would have brought to their new faith. What did you do when you wanted to know how the world of the gods related to the mortal realm, what their will was, and how to ensure blessings and avoid curses? You consulted an oracle or a prophet.⁷ An oracle offered divine revelation and wisdom regarding matters unknown to mortals, and Greeks and Romans placed a great deal of trust in divination.⁸ Thus, it would have even been instinctual for the Thessalonians to consult oracles about the meaning of recent events, or the path that lies ahead regarding the divine will.

Notice in 5:16–18 how the focus is on the *will of God*: "This is God's will in Messiah Jesus for you." (5:18; cf. 4:3). Paul takes what I believe is a

---

5. See Malherbe 2000: 325.

6. See Paul's protracted discussion of these idlers in 2 Thess, cf. pp. 148–54 below.

7. See the outstanding study of Greco-Roman prophecy, and especially the use of oracles, in Aune 1983: 23–80.

8. See Bonnechere 2010: 145–60.

very specific, time-related, event-oriented concern on the Thessalonians' behalf with regard to the will of God (the recent deaths), and he changes the focus to the overall devotional and covenantal "will" (*thelēma*) of God "in Messiah Jesus." Instead of trying to "divine" the future, they should focus on divine virtues and habits: joy, prayer, thanksgiving. These three are closely linked for Paul. A prayerful disposition places God at the center of life and knowing his sovereignty (i.e., that he reigns over all things) and his presence (through the Spirit of Jesus) can and should produce joy and inspire thanksgiving.

This is related to Paul's concern that, first, the Thessalonians not suppress the Spirit, and, second, that prophecy is not flat-out rejected, but cautiously considered after testing. Malherbe considers whether Christian "prophetic pretenders" appeared and Paul was warning them not to be enchanted by their prophecies without discernment.[9] Some believing Thessalonians may have written off prophecy altogether, but in this case Paul discourages unilateral rejection. Paul is quick to address too the equally problematic uncritical acceptance of prophetic knowledge. Prophecies must be carefully judged. But how *did* one judge a prophecy such that it could be determined to be good and true? Unfortunately Paul does not tell us! I think, though, Ben Witherington makes a strong case for seeing acceptable prophecy as the kind that builds up, encourages, and comforts.[10] One should keep in mind that Paul had just placed the focus on joy and thanksgiving in this section, and then transitions to a wish-prayer to the God of *peace* in the next section. Good and true prophetic words should not have the ultimate effect of stirring up fear and anxiety, but should lead the recipients (even sometimes through a healthy dose of exhortation and rebuke) towards obedience to and peace with God.

Wish-Prayer for Holiness (5:23–24)

Transitioning from the subject of discerning good and evil, Paul commences a second wish-prayer in this letter (cf. 1 Thess 3:13–14). In keeping with themes found throughout the letter, Paul's focus is on the Thessalonians

---

9. Given the ubiquity of interest across cultures in prophecy and oracles in the ancient world, I find it equally possible that local pagan or Jewish prophets attempted to dissuade the Thessalonian believers from their faith, arguing that their new religion kindled the anger of the local deities (or in the case of Jews, the One God, if they had been Gentile god-fearers attached to the synagogue).

10. Witherington 2006: 169–70.

being formed by God. The divine will is set upon guiding believers towards completeness and maturity in holiness. Perhaps for some Thessalonians, their concern was set on *information—what happened in our community? What will happen next? How can I be spared? How can I appease an angry god?* But according to Paul, their concern should be set on *formation—how can I grow in holiness and obedience to God? How can I bring wholeness to my entire self? How can I ensure that I have nothing to hide when Jesus returns?* But even in the area of formation, Paul assures the Thessalonians that this is not an area where believers should be driven by fear. God will see this through, he is both powerful enough and faithful to his promises.

One item of scholarly interest should be noted here. In this text, Paul refers to the Thessalonian in view of "spirit, soul, and body" (5:23), namely that these should be preserved at the Parousia. Theologians have been fascinated with this description of the nature of the person, and debate has ensued over exactly what is meant by this triple designation. Ambrose is a good example of a "trichotomist" who viewed the person as a "mixture" of three separate components:

> We are a composite of diverse elements mixed together, cold with hot, and moist with dry. This mixture is the source of many pleasures and manifold delights of the flesh. But these are not the first fruits of this body of ours. Since we are composed of soul and body and spirit, the first place is held by that mixture in which the apostle desires that we find sanctification.[11]

There are several problems with a tripartite view of the person, not least of which is that the mention of all three items (body, soul, spirit) is found only in this one verse in all of Paul, and, indeed, in all of the Bible.[12] N. T. Wright has recently summarized a helpful re-thinking of how to approach Paul's anthropological language. He writes,

> These words sometimes appear to designate different "parts" of a human being, but, as many have pointed out, it is better to see them as each encoding a particular way of looking at the human being *as a whole* but *from one particular angle*. . . . Each of these aspects means what it means because of all the others; but one would use different language to draw attention to these different

---

11. Gorday 2000: 100.
12. For a helpful study of biblical anthropology, see Gundry 1976.

facets or aspects of it, without implying that this facet or aspect could be split off from all the others.[13]

So, then, what do these terms mean? "Body," Wright argues, relates to the person's "public, visible and tangible physical presence in, and in relation to, the world."[14] "Soul" refers to the "human seen in terms of the ordinary human life with its consciousness, self-awareness, memory and imagination."[15] And, as for "spirit," this is "the human seen in terms of an interiority which is open to the presence and power of the creator (not least by his [Holy Spirit])."[16] Paul can use a wide range of anthropological terms to highlight these various angles and perspectives precisely because the work of divine redemption and sanctification is multi-faceted and each one (body, soul, and spirit) can be "rescued, redeemed, and redirected."[17]

Last Words (5:25–28)

At the close of the letter, Paul requests three things from the Thessalonians. First, he asks for prayer for himself and his co-workers. For what in particular were they supposed to pray? Obviously Paul is not specific, but perhaps he assumes that they will pray for his work of sharing the good news and forming communities of Jesus-believers amongst the Gentiles.[18] It should not go unnoticed that, at the end of his letter—a place where what he has written will be most easily remembered—he shows the humility and vulnerability to ask for prayer. Not only does it speak to his trust in God as ruler over all, but it also shows how much he relied on the prayer ministry of churches to sustain his apostolic work.[19]

Next, Paul tells the Thessalonians to greet and exchange a holy kiss. Obviously in the modern Western church this Pauline request comes across

---

13. Wright 2013: 490–91.
14. Ibid., 491.
15. Ibid., 492.
16. Ibid.
17. Ibid.
18. Note the much longer explanation in 2 Thessalonians: "Finally, brothers and sisters, pray for us, so that the word of the Lord may spread rapidly and be glorified everywhere, just as it is among you" (2 Thess 3:1); cf. Col 4:3: "At the same time pray for us as well that God will open to us a door for the word, that we may declare the mystery of Christ, for which I am in prison, so that I may reveal it clearly, as I should" (Col 4:3–4).
19. On the subject of the importance of the final subject matter and how Paul closes his letters, see the important study Weima 1994.

as a strange practice, uncomfortably intimate, even erotic. However, Ernest Best does well to explain the socio-cultural dimensions of kissing in Paul's world: "The kiss was given on the lips (normally only in sex), on the cheeks, brow and shoulders (among kinsfolk), on the hands and feet (in honouring a superior)."[20] Two things are safe assumptions based on what we know from the New Testament about this practice in the early churches. First, it was not a kiss on the lips. And, secondly, the pervasiveness of this tradition and the fact that Paul mentions it to the Thessalonians without further explanation means that it became a common church practice very early on. Ben Witherington is wise to suggest that this tradition "caught on" because it was a very clear symbol and gesture of the unique bond and relationship between "brothers and sisters" in the Messiah—they were part of a special family through Messiah Jesus under God the Father.[21] Again, it was common for family members to kiss one another and a perfect example is found in Jesus' Parable of the Prodigal Son: "But while he was still far off, his father saw him and was filled with compassion; he ran and put his arms around him and kissed him" (Luke 15:20). With this example in mind, it is no wonder 1 Peter 5:14 refers to the ecclesial holy kiss as a "kiss of love!"

Those who become part of the people of God in Messiah Jesus are now family. How radically counter-cultural it was for these early Christians to embrace and kiss one another *as family members do* even though some were Jews and others Gentiles! It makes sense in my modern Western culture *not* to practice the holy kiss tradition, but do we have ways in which we share love, fellowship, and friendship with one another on a regular basis as brothers and sisters in Messiah Jesus? If Paul made it a point to give this command on so many occasions, how can we honor the spirit of what he asks, even if we cannot fulfill the specific request?[22]

Next, Paul requests, in no uncertain terms, that his letter should be read publicly in the church (5:27). It could be that he wanted to ensure that the exhortations were heard by any who have caused problems (such as the *ataktoi*). However, a plainer assumption would simply be that Paul did not want the "leadership" of the church to be the sole parties responsible for the health and growth of the church. There is something refreshingly transparent and egalitarian about his solemn request. Each one, whatever status or role, is responsible for the health of the body. Each one is called to

---

20. Best 1986: 245.
21. See Witherington 2006: 175–76.
22. See 1 Cor 16:20; 2 Cor 13:12; Rom 16:16.

upbuilding, unity, and peace. Each one must hear the call to holiness and maturity.

Finally, as in all his subsequent extant letters, Paul extends his word of grace from Messiah Jesus.[23] This offers a nice book-end close to his opening wish for grace (1:2)[24] and serves as a reminder that, in spite of difficult and troubling circumstances, the Lord is with them and desires to pour out his favor and goodness upon them.

Fusing the Horizons: The New Covenant Community, A People of Prayer

Most Christians set aside time for prayer, and rightly so, but Paul refers here to praying with no beginning or end (1 Thess 5:17). How is this possible? Paul is not talking about never leaving one's prayer closet physically, but he is referring to a prayerful disposition where the believer always lives within the presence of God. We cannot separate our lives physically into sacred spheres (church) and secular spheres (office). God is everywhere and this is his world. We cannot simply segment our lives into spiritual times (prayer, devotional reading, ministry) and other times (work, leisure, chores). The eternal God is king from dawn to dusk and beyond.

In the context of this letter, Paul tells the Thessalonians to be always-pray-ers so that they recognize the presence and goodness of God at all times and especially in difficult circumstances. "Prayer," then, becomes a term associated with a believing will that trusts God's benevolence and promises. To be an always-pray-er is to be constantly attentive to the work of God around us.

To "pray without ceasing" does not mean a life of prayer-words and no action. Part of this prayer-filled disposition is the fostering of a kind of spiritual instinct that acts on behalf of God's will. May the people of God, a people of prayer, be known for both their patient intercession and thanksgiving towards God, and also their gracious will and actions as agents of Messiah Jesus' redemption in the world.

---

23. See 2 Thess 3:18; Gal 6:18; 1 Cor 16:23; 2 Cor 13:13; Rom 16:20; Phil 4:23; Phm 25; cf. 1 Tim 6:21; 2 Tim 4:22; Titus 3:15.

24. See Bruce 1982: 136.

Thanksgiving and Hope (2 Thess 1:1–12)

2 Thessalonians 1:1–12

Prescript (1:1–2)

> ¹Paul, Silvanus, and Timothy to the church of the Thessalonians in God our Father and the Lord Messiah Jesus, ²grace and peace to you from God our Father and the Lord Messiah Jesus.

Theologian Thomas Oden recounts a vivid dream where he was walking through New Haven cemetery and happened across his own tombstone. The epitaph read: "He made no new contribution to theology." For many theologians, this moment would signal that the dream was actually a nightmare, but Oden woke up relieved. He came to the realization that being a successful theologian did not require constant novelty.[1]

This story might help the reader of 2 Thessalonians to put an obvious feature of this text into perspective: it's not terribly original. In many ways, 2 Thessalonians is a re-expression of 1 Thessalonians, repeating many of the earlier text's themes, arguments, and sometimes even its wording. In fact the opening greeting of 2 Thessalonians is almost identical to 1 Thess 1:1–2.[2] But for Paul, some things do not need to be said differently. He, Silvanus, and Timothy wrote again to this church and desired to underscore that who they are, as a community, is defined by their relationship with God the Father and the Lord Messiah Jesus.

---

1. See Oden 2014: 144.

2. 2 Thessalonians adds "our" before "Father" in v. 1, and in v. 2 includes after "grace and peace" the following: "from God the Father and the Lord Messiah Jesus."

Thanksgiving for Faithful Endurance (1:3-4)

> 3 We ought to thank God for you all the time, my dear brothers and sister, as it is a worthy thing to do, because your loyalty is growing beyond measure and your love is increasing—each and every one for the other and vice versa. 4 Therefore we ourselves boast about you to all the churches of God thanks to your loyal endurance in the face of all the harassment against you and the troubles you are enduring.

As is typical in most of his letters, Paul offers thanksgiving to God for the lives of those to whom he is writing, particularly for their fidelity and devotion. In 2 Thessalonians, Paul commends their loyalty (*pistis*) and love (*agapē*) that marks communal life, and all this in spite of persecution and trials.

While 1 Thessalonians also includes a thanksgiving, in the second letter there is more of an official-sounding tone—*we ought to...as it is a worthy thing.* . . . It is possible, as F. F. Bruce suggests, that Paul felt the need to explain *why* he had such optimism and joy in regards to their perseverance, even if some of the Thessalonians had felt his earlier commendation was exaggerated. In such a case, Paul responded in this second letter that he is not only led to thanksgiving towards God on their account, but indeed he sees it as his "bounden duty" to honor God for how he works mighty things among and for his people.[3]

The language of doing what is "proper" and "of worth" in thanksgiving to God also implies that Paul had taken up a more formal liturgical tone here, one reminiscent of several Jewish texts of his time. For example, Roger Aus observes how Philo (an Alexandrian Jewish writer) encourages the sacrifice of praise, noting that the Jew who has lived a blessed life "has as his bounden duty to requite God, who has been the pilot of his voyage . . . with hymns, and songs, and prayers, and also sacrifices, and all other imaginable tokens of gratitude in a holy manner; all which things taken together have received the one comprehensive name of praise" (*Spec. Leg.* 1.224).[4]

Aus notes that this liturgical rhetoric of propriety and fittingness passes on into the early Christian tradition. As an example, one notably similar to 2 Thessalonians, Aus refers to the *Hermas Similitudes* 9 which includes a discussion of persecution against Christians. An angel shares

---

3. See Bruce 1982: 144.
4. Aus 1973: 433-44.

with Hermas about the blessings and honor bestowed on martyrs: "all who once suffered for the name of the Lord are honorable before God; and all these the sins were remitted, because they suffered for the name of the Son of God" (9.28.3). The angel goes on to explain that when these faithful believers were brought to trial, they did not renounce their faith, but "suffered cheerfully."

Thus, "these are held in greater honor with God" in comparison to those who succumbed to doubt (9.28.4). The angel warns Hermas that suffering brings out either the weakness of doubt and lack of commitment to Jesus, or it demonstrates the depth and genuineness of faith: "And ye who suffer for His name ought to glorify God, because He deemed you worthy to bear His name" (9.28.5).

What all this implies is that Paul is deeply sensitive to the suffering and shame that the Thessalonians are experiencing and he is concerned with how they respond to this problem. No doubt some Thessalonian believers were having their honor diminished by criticism and rejection from friends, neighbors, coworkers, and fellow citizens. Looking at Paul's rhetorical strategy from the perspective of honor discourse, he was interested in re-constituting the Thessalonians churches' "court of reputation." According to David deSilva, this language is used by social-scientists to refer to "that body of significant others whose 'opinion' about what is honorable and shameful, and whose evaluation of the individual, really matters."[5] By focusing in 2 Thess 1:3 on the apostles' own compulsion to give thanks to God, Paul was transferring the "court of reputation" from hostile Thessalonian neighbors to God "whose central place is assured because of God's power to enforce his estimation of who deserves honor and who merits censure."[6]

What is Paul specifically thankful *for*? He commends their growing *pistis* and their increasing *agapē*. These are virtues that peppered the text of 1 Thessalonians (1 Thess 1:3, 8; 3:2, 5, 6, 7, 10, 12; 4:9, 10; 5:8, 13).[7] *Pistis* is usually translated "faith," but one should not take that to mean that Paul was grateful merely for their inner faith, personal spirituality, or

5. deSilva 2000: 40.

6. Ibid., 55.

7. Some scholars are quick to note that Paul does not add "hope" (*elpis*) in 2 Thess 1:3 (as is found in 1 Thess 1:3), and the argument has been made that this lacuna is meaningful, i.e., the Thessalonians were struggling in the historical context of this letter with lacking Christian hope in a way not yet true when Paul wrote the first letter. This is possible, but the mere absence of *elpis* ought not to carry too much weight by itself.

doctrinal orthodoxy. In 1:4, Paul mentions their *pistis* again along with their *hypomonē* (perseverance). *Pistis* and *hypomonē* seem to function as a hendiadys and can be translated as something like *loyal endurance (loyalty [pistis] + endurance [hypomonē])*—there is an active, observable nature to this *pistis*.[8]

As for their *agapē*, Paul notes that they are excelling in love, and his emphasis is on reciprocity and mutuality. In reference to both of these, "loyalty" and "love," Paul is probably making the case that the suffering they are experiencing has not plunged their community into chaos; rather, by the grace of God, they are marching forward in honor of the Lord Jesus.

According to 1:4, Paul informs the Thessalonians of his boast before the other churches regarding their "loyal endurance" in the face of resistance. The language of persecution is found here, but it is unclear what kind of afflictions are involved. Todd Still, in his extensive research on the subject, makes this conclusion about the persecution: "it is best understood as vigorous, non-Christian opposition which likely took the form of verbal harassment, social ostracism, political sanctions and perhaps (some kind of) physical abuse."[9] In light of these afflictions, Paul turns the Thessalonians' attention away from shame and disgrace by expressing his pride in their tenacity, spiritual resilience, and faithfulness to God.

Justice at the Day of the Messiah (1:5-10)

> **5**This is a sign of the right judgment of God, so that you may be worthy of the kingdom of God, the kingdom on behalf of which you are suffering. **6**For it is right for God to repay troublemakers with trouble, **7**and for you who are troubled it is right for God to give you relief along with us, when the Lord Jesus is revealed from heaven with his mighty angels; **8**his revealing will be with a fiery flame, dispensing retribution to those who do not know God and those who do not obey the good news of our Lord Jesus. **9**They will pay the penalty of permanent destruction, separated from the presence of the Lord and from his glorious power **10**when he comes on that day to be glorified among his holy people and to be an object of glorious wonder by all those who have believed. And this includes you, because our testimony to you was believed.

---

8. See Richard 1995: 303-4; Gaventa 1998: 100.

9. Still 1999: 226; see also Barclay 1993: 512-30; Dunn 2009: 704. For a sociological analysis of persecution and control of deviance, see deSilva 1999: 93-94.

In this next section of the first chapter of 2 Thessalonians, Paul transitions from a word of thanksgiving for the Thessalonians' perseverance in persecution to a theological reflection on the meaning of this suffering. It is easy for someone who is suffering to wonder if the affliction is a form of punishment or retribution from God. Perhaps unbelieving neighbors and family members of the Thessalonians even *told them* that their communal sufferings were due to wrath from above.

Paul's goal in this section is to reassure the Thessalonians in regards to (a) the path they have chosen in Messiah Jesus (and for which they are suffering) and (b) the just work of God not only in spite of persecution but even within and through it. The problem that interpreters face is that 1:5 addresses "evidence" (*endeigma*) of the right judgment of God, but modern readers are simply unsure about what Paul is counting as this "evidence." Is the evidence or proof that the Thessalonians are *persevering*? Or is the evidence that the Thessalonians are *suffering*? Which option (suffering or perseverance) is the basis for Paul's appeal to God's fairness (=right judgment)?

Scholars are divided on this interpretive crux. There is strong support for the view that Paul considers the "evidence" to be the suffering itself.[10] The rationale behind this tends to appeal to Jewish tradition. There are some Jewish texts that carry an idea that God might see it fit to punish his people in the present time, so that they do not have to face damnation at a day of reckoning. *Psalms of Solomon* 13:10–12 is typically used by scholars as a representative of this viewpoint:

> For the Lord spares his pious ones, and blots out their errors by his chastening. For the life of the righteous will be forever; but sinners will be taken away into destruction, and their memorial will be found no more. But upon the pious is the mercy of the Lord, and upon them that fear Him His mercy. (Pss 13:10–1)

Similarly, even more explicitly, we have the statement from R. Akiba in Genesis Rabbah 33.1:

> [God] deals strictly with the righteous, calling them to account for the few wrongs which they commit in this world, in order to lavish bliss upon and give them a goodly reward in the world to come; he grants ease to the wicked and rewards them for the few good deeds which they have performed in this world in order to punish them in the future world.[11]

---

10. See Menken 1994: 85–86.
11. See Talbert 1991: 15.

Clearly there is Jewish conceptual precedent if Paul were to be making this kind of point in 2 Thessalonians. However, there has been strong pushback against this interpretation. For example, Beverly Gaventa wonders whether Paul would endorse such a perspective in view of a suffering community that would lead them to wonder: "Shall I measure my standing with God by my misfortunes (since God is punishing me now and will reward me later)?"[12]

The other interpretation of 1:5 suggests that the proof of God's right judgment is seen, not in the Thessalonians' suffering *per se*, but rather in their *response* to the afflictions—their faithfulness, loyal endurance, and growth.[13] The problem with this view is that it is hard to see their *growth* as evidence of God's *judgment*.[14]

Perhaps the best solution is to consider the possibility that Paul is playing with the Greek word "judgment" (*krisis*). Just as in English, so also in Greek, this word can have a negative meaning, as in *damnation* (i.e., "He cast judgment on me"). However, it can also have a neutral or positive meaning, as in "I trust the teacher's judgment." The second meaning has to do with someone's wise decision-making. Here is how this might be relevant to 2 Thess 1:5—perhaps neighbors of the Thessalonians told them that their trials served as evidence of divine wrath (i.e., negative judgment). Paul's response here is that the trials they face are not unrelated to God, and involve his *judgment*, but it is his *krisis* in the positive sense—he has *deemed it right and appropriate* to allow his Thessalonian people to face persecution, just as he showed Paul how much Paul must suffer for God's name (Acts 9:16). This coheres with the narrative of Acts 5:41 where the apostles left the council celebrating that "they were considered worthy to suffer dishonor for the sake of the name."[15]

Here is how I understand what Paul is saying in 1:5: *You Thessalonians are suffering and you wonder, "Who is pulling the strings up there in heaven? Is God in control? Is he punishing us? Is he trustworthy? I say to you, God is in control and he is acting according to his good pleasure and looking after you at the same time. The afflictions you are suffering are not a negative reflection of your worth and value to God, but you should consider it a privilege that he*

---

12. Gaventa 1998: 102–3; for further critique, see Shogren 2012: 249.
13. See Richard 1995: 305; Malherbe 2000: 395.
14. Fee prefers this reading, but acknowledges this hurdle; 2009: 253–54.
15. See Jervis 2007: 31.

would let you represent his kingdom and that he trusts you to rise above the persecution in faithfulness and hope.

Paul goes on to explain that God is in fact just (*dikaios*), and it may be difficult to recognize this in the midst of suffering, but believers also expect that God's justice will be even clearer when he shines the light of his judgment on all works and people in the end. Those who have taken up the role of afflicter will be "repaid" (1:6). To the unfairly troubled and harassed, God will finally give rest and relief as well. It is critical to note, even if subtly, that Paul includes *himself* (and his fellow apostles) as those who endure persecution (1:7). The future, final appearance of the Lord will publicly declare what can only be known by faith in the present—only those who know, love, and obey the Lord Messiah Jesus *as* the unique embodiment and image of the one eternal God are the true servants of the kingdom of God (1:8).

Those who persecute the Thessalonian believers will not "get away with" their harassment, but will face the punishment of eternal destruction and will be withheld from the presence of the Lord (1:9).

Excursus: Eternal Destruction (2 Thess 1:9)?

The language of damnation that Paul uses here has been of interest to theologians with a view towards the Apostle's understanding of "hell." Did Paul believe in a hell of unending torment, or did he believe that the damned would be annihilated?[16] The language of "eternal destruction" is not a clear indicator either way—how can something be destroyed eternally? The better approach in this passage is to try and make sense of why Paul raises this matter at all. His focus is on the punishment of the oppressors; hence "destruction" represents damnation, God plunging them into ruin. What about "eternal"? I am persuaded by the direction that C. S. Lewis goes, where the language of eternality is less about *duration* than it is about *finality* - their verdict is complete, it cannot be undone or overturned. So, Lewis writes, "That the lost soul is eternally fixed in its diabolical attitude we cannot doubt: but whether this eternal fixity implies endless duration—or duration at all—we cannot say."[17] I believe Lewis' eschatological agnosticism is wise. The little bits and pieces

---

16. The literature on this subject is voluminous; see Fudge and Peterson 2000; Morgan and Peterson 2004; Date, Stump, and Anderson 2014.

17. Lewis 1996: 129; see also Bruce 1982: 152.

of references to hell do not build a complete picture: "We know much more about heaven than hell, for heaven is the home of humanity and therefore contains all that is implied in a glorified human life: but hell was not made for men. It is in no sense *parallel* to heaven: it is 'the darkness outside,' the outer rim where being fades away into nonentity."[18] Gordon Fee interprets Paul likewise: "Paul had little or no interest in 'hell' as such. For him eternal glory has to do with being in the presence of the Father and the risen Lord. The eternal judgment of the wicked is the absolute loss of such glory."[19]

Paul's concern as he rounds out this section (2 Thess 1:5–10) is that the Thessalonians who are suffering shame will experience vindication along with the risen Messiah Jesus when he comes to be honored at last and even to inspire wonder when he is glorified for all to see (1:10). Paul points to the co-glorification of *believers*—those who have been willing, in this time now of trial, to trust in the Lord who is invisible, but will finally be revealed. What Paul says here is echoed elsewhere in the New Testament in 1 Peter 1:8, "Although you have not seen him, you love him; and even though you do not see him now, you believe in him and rejoice with an indescribable and glorious joy, for you are receiving the outcome of your faith, the salvation of your souls."

Prayer for Vocation, Obedience, and Honor (1:11–12)

> [11]With this is mind we always pray for you, that our God would make you worthy of his calling, and that he would bring to fruition by his power every desire to be generous and every act of loyalty. [12]Then the name of our Lord Jesus will be glorified because of you, and you will be glorified because of him, according to the grace of our God and the Lord Messiah Jesus.

Paul concludes the first chapter of his letter with a wish-prayer, giving attention to their calling and faith, and also the sure hope that Jesus will be glorified in their midst. We should be reminded here of the relationship

---

18. Lewis 1996: 129; there are striking similarities between Lewis here and the words of Theodore of Mopsuestia: "the punishment of those wicked who have died is completed in a reality that transcends time itself and is forever" (See Gorday 2000: 105).

19. Fee 2009: 206; cf. Best 1986: 262; cf. de Villiers 2011: 1–9, at 4.

between human and divine co-participation that Paul expresses. The fact of his praying and the expectation of the mighty work of God remind us that Paul relies on the Almighty to transform and change human lives. In addition, though, Paul clearly reminds the Thessalonians here that they too are responsible to cooperate with the work of God in their midst, to honor and glorify the Lord Jesus and live according to the standard of his kingdom. How do we hold the divine work and human responsibility together? Some have balked at the idea that humans *do* anything; including human agency comes across to these as *synergism* or semi-pelagianism.[20] But it would seem that Paul imagines some kind of co-participatory dynamic.

John M. G. Barclay has attempted to develop an understanding of Paul's logic in this regard. In the first place, Paul begins with the grace of God, the gift of his power and presence in and through the Messiah and the Spirit. Becoming one with Messiah Jesus through divine grace empowers the believer to become an agent.

When human and divine work are properly situated in a context of co-participation, this deconstructs any attempt to talk about agency as a ratio, as if more work from one equals less from the other. Rather, Barclay refers to an "entanglement of the two agencies." When it comes to the ethical and active dimensions of what it means to participate in Messiah Jesus, he writes this:

> Some account must be given of the prepositions "in" and "through" as well as "toward" and "with," and there remains the puzzling pattern of "I, yet not I." At the very least we must speak here of a transformation of the self, a refashioning of the human agent that becomes capable of agency (with a freed will competent to obey or to "fall from grace") and is embedded within the agency of divine grace.[21]

Paul's prayer is, if we follow along Barclay's thinking, a means of grace as well as a summons to growth.

Fusing the Horizons: Can Suffering for the Kingdom be a Blessing?

As I was spending time recently pondering how and why suffering makes one worthy of the kingdom, as Paul writes in this chapter, I was struck by the

---

20. See the rich study on the subject of "synergism" by Yinger 2009: 89–106.
21. Barclay 2008: 372–89, at 384.

news this month that an American televangelist hit national headlines with his request for his megachurch to help him buy a new private jet for his family to do international ministry—a "Gulfstream G650," the fastest, most luxurious, longest range and most technologically advanced jet known to humankind, with a price tag of $65 million. Is this the destiny of believers and the model of a pastor—luxury and wealth, a life of comfort and ease?

In 2 Thess 1:3–5, Paul seems to link *suffering* with being worthy of the kingdom of God. At the very least, Paul appears to be reflecting on a positive feature of persecution from the world in the life of believers. For many Christians, back then but also today, this can be counter-intuitive. Isn't Jesus supposed to make my life *better and easier*?

Paul seems to reflect a general attitude amongst the earliest Christians that it is a mark of Jesus and his people that they will be rejected by the world. According to Luke, Jesus taught that you ought to consider yourself blessed "when people hate you, and they exclude you, revile you, and defame you on account of the Son of Man. Rejoice in that day and leap for joy, for surely your reward is great in heaven; for that is what their ancestors did to the prophets" (Luke 6:22–23). In John Jesus says "In this world you will have trouble" (16:33). According to Romans, Paul explains that being true children of God is confirmed by sharing in the sufferings of Jesus "in order that we may also share in his glory" (Rom 8:17). In the book of Acts, we learn that a band of persecuted apostles, after being beaten and threatened, left the Sanhedrin with joy because "they were considered worthy to suffer dishonor for the name" of Jesus (Acts 5:41)—Paul and Barnabas warned the disciples in Lystra, Iconium, and Antioch about this truth: "It is through many persecutions that we must enter the kingdom of God" (Acts 14:22).

The idea is neither that sufferings *earn* salvation, nor that God's desires to see his people suffer. Rather, we often misunderstand what it means to be a Christian if we think accepting Jesus gets us "off the hook" of any suffering or pain. Instead, recognizing Jesus as redeemer and rescuer, we enter into fellowship with him, and part of what it means to be a united with Jesus is to enter *both* into his *death* as well as his *life*. Regarding Paul and Barnabas' message in Acts 14, Richard Longenecker writes—"They encouraged them to remain in the faith, telling them that many persecutions must necessarily (*dei*) be the lot of Christians in order to enter into the kingdom of God—that is, that the same pattern of suffering and glory exemplified in Jesus' life must be theirs as well if they are to know the full measure of the reign of God in their lives."[22] F. F. Bruce sums this up aptly: *no cross, no crown.*[23]

Persecution, resistance, afflictions—the earliest disciples could find joy in this because they felt they had been considered worthy of re-tracing the steps of Jesus, fighting for hope and justice in a way that threatened the world order.

The rationale with which Paul and the other NT writers operate is that everyone will face suffering. Either one experiences worldly fame, luxury, and glory now—and will suffer judgment later. Or one chooses to follow Jesus, and with him to suffer as a believer, but with the hope of being glorified at his return. In 1 Peter, the choice is made clear: stand firm with Jesus now and suffer for (in eternity's perspective what will be) "a little while," and afterwards "the God of all grace, who has called you to his eternal glory in Christ, will himself restore, support, strengthen, and establish you" (1 Peter 5:10).

When this is put into perspective, Paul's words in Philippians make more sense: God "has graciously granted you the privilege not only of believing in Christ, but of suffering for him as well" (1:29). How can suffering be a form of grace, a blessing? The early Christians believed and taught that joining the kingdom of Messiah Jesus meant signing on to live with him and become like him. To defy the world in the way Jesus defied the world leads to afflictions. It is an honor and privilege to suffer for his Name.

---

22. Longenecker 1995: 234.
23. Bruce 1990: 326.

Perseverance and Hope (2 Thess 2:1–17)

2 THESSALONIANS 2:1–17

In the first chapter of this letter, Paul offered a broader perspective on the challenges that were facing the Thessalonians. He encouraged them to see that their tenacious and intrepid fidelity to God and love for one another was an inspiration to Silvanus, Timothy, and himself (1:1–3). Indeed, it brought encouragement to other churches (1:4). Paul also explained that they could live in the sure hope that God would ultimately afflict the afflictors and relieve the afflicted when the Lord Jesus returns in glory (1:5–10). Paul rounded out chapter one with a wish-prayer that the Thessalonians hold fast to their calling to endure for the glory of Jesus and by the grace of God (1:11–12).

In the second chapter, Paul engages more specifically with the matter of "the coming of our Lord Messiah Jesus" and his concern that the Thessalonians not have their walk with Jesus thrown off balance in light of what seems like recent events, circumstances, or information. In 2:1–12, Paul engages in what appears to be his primary concern in this letter.[1]

There are many details in this chapter that have caught the attention of readers throughout the centuries—*what is the "apostasy"? Who is the "Man of Sin"? What is the "mystery of lawlessness"? Who or what is "the restrainer"?* Unfortunately, we are not in a good position to ascertain the referents to these figures and terms; presumably the original readers were privy to this information. Still, we must be careful not to get too lost amongst the "trees" that we miss the "forest" of Paul's wider concerns. It would seem that Paul adumbrates eschatological events, not as a kind of apocalyptic calendar to follow, but rather to underscore that despite a series of dark happenings to come ultimately Messiah Jesus will prevail and his loyal people will be vindicated. The central imperative of his eschatological discourse, then, is

---

1. Bruce 1982: 162.

explicitly stated in 2:15: "stand firm and hold firmly to the traditions you were taught." *Stay the course.*

Encouraging Perseverance (2:1-2)

> ¹Now, we ask you, my dear brothers and sisters, with regard to the coming of our Lord Messiah Jesus and our gathering together with him, ²that your mind not be easily unsettled or alarmed, whether it be through a spirit, an audible message, or through a letter (as if written by us), leading you to believe that the Day of the Lord has come.

In this introduction to the main topic at hand, Paul refers to the coming of the Lord Jesus and also "our gathering together with him" (2:1). As Howard Marshall explains, "this motif goes back to the Jewish hope of the gathering together of the scattered exiles in their own land and was taken over by Jesus and the early church to refer to the gathering together of his people with the Messiah."[2] Paul had already reminded the Thessalonians of this end-time ingathering in his earlier letter (1 Thess 4:17), but for some reason their hope in this had become unsettled. The language Paul uses of being "stirred up," as Ernest Best notes, "suggests the sudden onslaught of a storm that is quickly past but leaves its effects on insecure buildings."[3]

But what was the issue, why were they thrown into panic and alarm? Verse 2:2 implies that something or someone led them to believe that the "Day of the Lord" had already come. The Day of the Lord was mentioned in 1 Thess 5:2 and goes back to the Old Testament's reference to a "day of Yahweh" (e.g., Amos 5:18, 20) that would involve, as Dale Allison notes, "a dramatic intervention of God in history, a judgment that will condemn God's enemies and save God's people."[4] Paul clearly associated this Day of Reckoning with Jesus, even sometimes referring to it as the "Day of the Messiah" (Phil 1:10; 2:16).[5] But what would it have meant for the Thessalonians to have believed this day *had already come*?

---

2. Marshall 1984: 185; see *Psalms of Solomon* 17.26, 28.

3. Best 1986: 275; cf. Marshall: "being so perturbed as to lose one's normal composure and good sense" (1984: 186).

4. Allison 2007: 2.46.

5. Interestingly, some Greek manuscripts have the wording "Day of the Messiah" instead of "Day of the Lord" in 2 Thess 2:2; see Shogren 2012: 274.

It is unlikely that any of the Thessalonians believed that the Day of the Lord had "come and gone"—wouldn't they have expected to see Jesus himself? Maarten Menken has indeed tried to argue that somehow the Thessalonians thought that "Christ had already returned to earth and was already performing his task, or was on the point of doing so."[6] I do not see the evidence for this in 2 Thessalonians. Instead, Jeffrey Weima offers a stronger interpretation arguing that certain troublemakers in Thessalonica had sowed the seed of fear that this Thessalonian church was facing judgment associated with the Day of the Lord, and it did not take much to whip them into a frenzy. Weima compares this to the story of Chicken Little:

> As revealed in the classic fable "Chicken Little" in which Henny Penny has an acorn fall on her head and immediately runs around yelling "The sky is falling! The sky is falling!," fear is often as irrational as it is contagious. Thus, even though the claim "the day of the Lord has come" may have seemed obviously false, it nevertheless caused the young church of Thessalonica to be scared out of their wits, fearful of whether they would avoid the wrath connected with the day of judgment and instead experience salvation.[7]

In such a case, Paul's concern was to put their concerns to rest and offer a proper vision of what was in store and how they would fit into the events yet to come.

Events Yet to Come: Apostasy with Lawless One, Final Victory of Messiah (2:3–12)

> 3 Let no one trick you in any way. For that day will not come unless the rebellion happens first and the Lawless Man, the Son of Destruction, is revealed. 4 He treats everyone as an enemy and thinks himself superior to anything called "god" or any object of worship, and so he takes his seat in the temple of God to demonstrate his divinity.

---

6. See Menken 1994: 101, more generally 99–101.
7. Weima 2006: 77–78; see also Weima 2014: 503; Eadie makes a similar case: "The day of the Lord, the epoch of the Second Advent had now dawned upon them, and the persecutions now falling on them were tokens of its presence. They regarded the day of grace as apparently at an end, so that in fact they were in the period of judgment, which was to witness the dissolution of society and the introduction of a new state of things"; see Eadie 1877: 263–64.

> ⁵Don't you remember that when I was still with you I used to tell you these things? ⁶And now you know what holds him back from being revealed until his time comes. ⁷For already the lawlessness is operating in secret, but only until the one who holds it back no longer blocks the way. ⁸And then the Lawless One will be revealed, the one whom the Lord [Jesus] will slay with the breath of his mouth; he will obliterate him by the spectacle of his coming.
>
> ⁹The coming of the Lawless One will be by the work of Satan, and will happen with all kinds of demonstrations of power, and deceiving signs and wonders, ¹⁰and with all kinds of wicked deception for those who are perishing. They will perish because they refused to love the truth and thus be saved. ¹¹So, on account of this, God sends them a deluding influence to make them believe what is false ¹²so that all may be judged who did not believe the truth, but instead took please in wickedness.

Paul's approach to soothing the Thessalonians' eschatological distress is to give them a run-down of "events yet to come." He begins with the coming of a great rebellion (2:3). But who is rebelling and against whom? Because this rebellion appears to be associated with the Lawless One, it would seem to imply an attack on the one God and his sovereign rule.[8] The human participants in the rebellion are left unstated, but it does not make sense for Paul to be talking about worshippers of the one God. In the context of this letter, it could be that Paul is referring to the kind of Jews who attack Jesus' followers supposing they these Jews are defending the honor of God.[9] In that sense, they are rebelling against their own God, but unaware that it is such.

Associated with this rebellion is a figure Paul calls "the Lawless Man" or "the Lawless One." He appears to be more than one who disregards the law/way of God; he could be better understood as the Anti-Law One. He is "Anti-Law" insofar as he stands against God, his commandments, and ways.[10] He is also called the "the Son of Destruction." Most scholars and translators take this to mean he is destined for destruction, but it makes

---

8. Morris 1975: 218.

9. This would reflect the same kind of thought expressed in John 16:2: "They will put you out of the synagogues. Indeed, an hour is coming when those who kill you will think that by doing so they are offering worship to God." Again, though, it is worthwhile to be reminded that Paul would not be condemning all Jews, since he himself was Jewish and he loved his people. Rather, he could speak harshly against certain Jews who persecuted believers-in-Jesus. See comments on 1 Thess 2:14–16, pp. 61–65.

10. Holmes 1998: 231; Fee 2009: 282.

good sense to see this language as comprehensive—for someone who is anti-Law and anti-God, destruction follows wherever he goes, and his own demise is inevitable.[11]

Paul does not specifically identify the Lawless One, but the language he uses for him is reminiscent of notorious enemies in Israel's past. In the second century BC, the tyrant Antiochus Epiphanes persecuted the Jews and desecrated their temple. In the first century BC, Roman general Pompey also profaned the Jerusalem temple. According to *Psalms of Solomon* 17:11–15, Pompey is called "the lawless one," enemy, and one who corrupted God's holy house.[12] Paul's description of the Lawless One seems indeed to be based on the archetype of these kinds of anti-God figures. But for Paul the Lawless One is a person yet to come in the future. Christians have speculated (sometimes wildly) regarding the identity of this person.[13] All we can gather from Paul's brief remarks is that he will be a grandiose rebel in league with Satan (see 2 Thess 2:9). Whether he is superhuman[14] or mortal[15] is unclear from the little that Paul writes, but it could be that even Paul did not know the answer to this.[16]

As far as the Lawless One's activity in "the temple of God," did Paul imagine this as the Jerusalem temple (still standing when he wrote 2 Thessalonians, but destroyed in AD 70) or someplace otherwise (like the "new

---

11. The New Testament language of "destruction" (*apōleia*) is sometimes positioned within binaries; the opposite of destruction is life (Matt 7:13–14) and salvation (Phil 1:28); Paul, in 2 Thess 2:3–11, is contrasting the work of the Lawless One (destruction) with the work of Messiah Jesus (peace and justice).

12. See Menken 1994: 105.

13. Some of the Reformers pointed to the Pope as the "man of sin" and "son of perdition" because, as Luther writes, he is the one "who with his doctrines and his laws increases the sins and perdition of souls in the church, while sitting in the church as if he were God"; see Whitford 2011: 103. Obviously this interpretation is ridiculous (see discussions by Morris 220–21; Malherbe 431). There is also a tradition throughout church history and Christian scholarship of associating the Lawless One with the emperor Nero, or at least a kind of "new Nero." Nero died in AD 68, but many believed he was still alive, but in hiding. Christians so much had a deep sense that Nero would return in power that, as Craig Keener notes, "in the Armenian language 'Nero' actually became the equivalent for Antichrist" (see Keener 2009: 338). The challenge with associating Nero with Paul's description in 2 Thessalonians is that Nero did not persecute Christians until after Paul wrote this letter; the Nero *redivivus* theory is only plausible if 2 Thessalonians was written late in the first century and probably not by Paul; see van Kooten 2005: 177–215.

14. Best 1986: 288.

15. Marshall 1984: 189

16. Morris 1975: 284.

temple" of the Church)? Given the metaphor-laden nature of this entire section (2:3-12), we should be wary of pressing for too many details. Paul is not trying to work out the specifics for the Thessalonians, but to inform them of a great dividing line between the wicked and the righteous, and that there will be a great rebellion where the Lawless One will try to dethrone God himself.[17]

In 2:5, Paul, with some frustration it would seem, reminds the Thessalonians that he had taught them these things in person previously.[18] Apparently, he informed them regarding what was "now restraining" the Lawless One. Again, Paul writes in cryptic language; in 2:5 the restrainer is a "what" (neuter), but in 2:6 the restrainer is a "who" (masculine). And, again, there is almost no end to the speculation regarding the identity of this figure or force. The most common interpretations are these:

> *Restrainer as Roman Empire.*[19] This interpretation argues that Paul would have had a positive view of Rome such that he could see the Roman empire as establishing order in such a way as to prevent the Lawless One from taking power.[20] A related view is that Paul appeals not to Rome alone, but the orderliness of governance in general, with Rome as the present one; so one commentator explains that the restrainer could be "the principle of law and order, of which Roman rule was but one instance and of which there have been many others."[21]
>
> *Restrainer as Paul.*[22] A few scholars have tried to make the case that the Restrainer is Paul himself and the restraining power is his

---

17. See Marshall 1984: 191-92; Holmes 1998: 231-32

18. Weima: "eschatological matters were of such importance to the apostle that they were at the core of his gospel presentation [see 1 Thess 1:9-10] and also, in light of the weightiness of the subject, were frequently the subject matter of Paul's preaching" (Weima 2014: 524); also Dunn 1998: 302-3.

19. See Bruce 1982: 188; Richard 1995: 338-39; so John Wesley's Explanatory note: "The power of the Roman emperors"; according to Wesley, what keeps the "son of perdition" at bay is the successive "potentate" coming after Rome, i.e., "the emperors, heathen or Christian; the kings, Goths or Lombards; the Carolingian or German emperors" (see note 2:7).

20. Earl Richard observes that Jewish texts like *Wisdom of Solomon* 6.1-4 could attest that some Jews believed that God entrusted pagan rulers with their authority and could bless their governance as long as they ruled justly; see Richard 1995: 339.

21. Williams 1999: 127.

22. See Cullmann 1936: 210-45; Munck 1959: 36-42.

apostolic ministry. Paul must complete his mission of proclaiming the gospel to the Gentiles before the rebellion.

Restrainer as Spiritual Power.[23] Some interpreters have advocated for understanding the Restrainer in terms of a variety of good spiritual powers, whether God, Jesus, the Spirit, or an angel. It does not make much sense that the Restrainer would be Father, Son, or Spirit since it is difficult to see how any of these could be "removed" to make way for the Lawless One (2:7). But there is much support for the view that he is an angel, and more specifically the archangel Michael (see Dan 12:1; Jude 9; Rev 12:7).[24]

None of these views can be proven from the meager information Paul offers to us, but the third view has garnered the most support in recent years and has much in its favor. If an angel (like Michael) is currently restraining the Lawless One, he is doing so according to a divine timetable: "it is ultimately God who will allow the rebel to be manifested only when the present opportunity for preaching and hearing the gospel is brought to an end by the removal of the angelic figure who is now in charge. Then the power of evil, which has been at work secretly in the world, but nonetheless effectively, will be openly manifested so as to produce the final showdown."[25]

In 2:7, Paul emphasizes that, in spite of the present operation of a restrainer, the *mystery of lawlessness* is already at work. The modern use of the word "mystery" tends to involve something enigmatic, a riddle or puzzle. That is not how Paul uses the word here. Rather, the work of lawlessness is a *mysterion* (Paul's Greek word) insofar as it is kept hidden.[26] This mystery of lawlessness is apparently active, but "bears only a provisional character."[27]

---

23. See Marshall 1984: 198–99; Menken 1994: 113. For example, in the book of Tobit, the demon Asmodeus flees to "the remotest parts of Egypt," but the angel Raphael follows him there and binds him hand and foot (Tob 8:3).

24. See especially Nicholl 2004: 225–49; Shogren 2012: 287–88; Weima 2014: 567–77.

25. Marshall, 200. In all these matters, though, Raymond Brown's caution is appropriate: "Much of the discussion assumes that the author was clear in his own mind as to the identity of both the lawless man and the restrainer. It is not impossible, however, that the author received the imagery from tradition and that, without being able to identify them, in the current situation he believed only that the lawless one had not come and therefore the restrainer must be at work" (Brown 1997: 597); also, regarding an agnostic view towards the identity of the restrainer, Gordon Fee: "From our present distance the best position would seem to be, 'Wait and see'" (2009: 288).

26. See Beale and Gladd 2014: 215–36.

27. Ridderbos 1975: 522.

The restrainer holds back the full presence of the Lawless One.[28] Paul makes it a point to identify the present operation of lawlessness not to scare the Thessalonians, but rather because he did not want the delineation of an eschatological timeline to give them the wrong impression. Just because the Lawless One is not fully "at-large" does not mean that the Thessalonian believers can rest on their laurels. On the contrary, Satan and his minions are presently active. Vigilance is required.

This whole passage (2:3-12) comes to an important climax in 2:8, where Paul first notes the unveiling of the Lawless One, the great villain of the story, the beast that is expected to rampage and ruin. But no sooner has Paul made mention of the Lawless One than he immediately turns the attention of the Thessalonians to "the Lord Jesus." Paul refers to the "appearance of his presence" (*tē epiphaneia tēs parousias autou*); this may seem like a redundancy because Paul could have simply referred to Jesus' presence (*Parousia*) as he does in 1 Thessalonians (1:10; 4:16). However, the addition of the word *epiphaneia* (appearance) seems to be significant. There appears to be an emphasis on the brilliance and splendor of the presence of Jesus. The term *epiphaneia* was sometimes used in reference to "any conspicuous intervention on the part of higher powers."[29] In Jewish tradition, one could implore God to reveal himself to save them.[30]

The very appearance (*epiphaneia*) of Jesus is enough to abolish the Lawless One, but Paul adds that Jesus will slay him by the breath of his mouth. According to the Old Testament, the "word of the Lord" is uniquely powerful: "By the word of the Lord the heavens were made, and all their host by the *breath of his mouth*" (Ps 33:6). The book of Isaiah contains the most striking imagery regarding the judging-breath of God. Regarding the judgment of Assyria, we read that the "breath of the Lord" sets ablaze the funeral pyre of the Assyrian king (Isa 30:33; cf. 40:7). The most important passage in Isaiah for our understanding of 2 Thess 2:8, though, comes in

---

28. So Shogren's paraphrase: "lawlessness is already at work, but forced to operate in part as a mystery or as it were 'underground' until God takes the restraint out of its way" (2012: 286).

29. See M-M 2015; also Trebilco 2013: 25-48, at 44-46.

30. See 3 Maccabees where a helpless band of Jews cry out to God "imploring the Ruler over every power to *manifest* (*epiphaneia*) himself and be merciful to them, as they stood now at the gates of death" (5:51). At the very nadir of their despair, "the most glorious, almighty, and true God revealed his holy face and opened the heavenly gates, from which two glorious angels of fearful aspect descended, visible to all but the Jews. They opposed the forces of the enemy and filled them with confusion and terror, binding them with immovable shackles" (6:18-19).

chapter eleven. In Isaiah's vision of the peaceful kingdom, he refers to a shoot from the stump of Jesse (the Davidic messiah) who will have the spirit of the Lord (11:1–2). He will be a just judge and will take up the cause of the needy.

> With righteousness he shall judge the poor, and decide with equity for the meek of the earth; he shall strike the earth with the rod of his mouth, and with the breath of his lips he shall kill the wicked (Isa 11:4)

In the Jewish apocalyptic text 4 Ezra, we read about the messiah who defeats a great multitude of enemies: "When he saw the onrush of the approaching multitude, he neither lifted his hand or held a spear or any weapon of war; but I saw only how he sent forth from his mouth something like a stream of fire, and from his lips a flaming breath, and from his tongue he shot forth a storm of sparks" (4 Ezra 13:9–10).

When it comes to 2 Thess 2:8, the important thing to note here is that, as with the imagery of 4 Ezra, *there is no battle*. There is no moment when it looks like Jesus might lose. He appears in glory and power and vanquishes the Lawless One effortlessly.

In some ways, 2:9–11 is a digression—Paul stops the clock and goes back to zoom in on the events surrounding the coming of the Lawless One (though he clearly wanted to insure that he established the certain downfall of the Lawless One as a matter of first importance in his discussion). The Lawless One is associated with the work of Satan. Paul elsewhere depicts Satan as the arch-tempter and deceiver (1 Cor 7:5; 2 Cor 2:11; 11:14; 12:7), the ultimate opponent of God (1 Thess 2:18; Rom 16:20; cf. 1 Tim 5:15). Apparently Satan will empower the Lawless One to perform all manner of false "signs and wonders" (*sēmeiois kai terasin*). Signs and wonders were meant to be proof of someone's legitimacy (see Deut 13:1–3). Note that when Peter preaches to the men of Israel, he comments that Jesus was endorsed or accredited by God *via* his miracles, wonders, and signs (Acts 2:22, see NIV "accredited"; CEB "credentials"; cf. Acts 15:12). Paul himself performed signs and wonders, no doubt to authenticate his own ministry (Rom 15:19; 2 Cor 12:12).[31]

By referring to these so-called "signs and wonders" of the Lawless One as "false" (*pseudos*), Paul was not implying that they were mere parlor tricks. It is not as if the Lawless One will be *pretending* to do miracles;

---

31. For a helpful discussion of this, see Twelftree 2013.

presumably the miracles will be supernatural, insofar as Satan can conjure incredible things.[32] Rather, the descriptor "false" means that the Lawless One will do miracles *as if* God were authenticating his work, but rather he will be in league with Satan. So, note Matt 24:24: "For false messiahs and false prophets will rise up and perform great signs and omens, to lead astray, if possible, even the elect" (cf. Mark 13:22); and Revelation 19:20a: "And the beast was captured, and with it the false prophet who had performed in its presence the signs by which he deceived those who had received the mark of the beast and who worshiped its image."

The cooperative work of Satan and the Lawless One will deceive "those who are perishing, because they refused to love the truth and so be saved" (2 Thess 2:10). Throughout the New Testament, there are warnings about false prophets who seek to lead others astray into wickedness (Matt 7:15; 24:11; Mark 13:22; 1 John 4:1; Rev 19:20); so 2 Peter 2:1, where false teachers have infiltrated churches and secretly sowed "destructive opinions," even denying the Lord.

Paul adds the enigmatic statement that "For this reason God sends them a powerful delusion, leading them to believe what is false" (NRSV). It would seem that Paul is saying that God *made them sin*—but how can God force people to sin? No doubt this is an alarming idea, but a similar statement is made in Rom 1:18–32 regarding those who stubbornly refused to acknowledge God; in their intractability, their resistance to God (of their own will) became, as it were, *supercharged* by God, such that "God gave them up in the lusts of their hearts to impurity" (1:24); "God gave them up to degrading passions" (1:26); and "God gave them up to a debased mind and to things that should not be done" (1:28). I hope it is not too trite of an example to compare this to when a teenager who is smoking is caught by dad, and dad makes him finish the whole pack—*by forcing one to dig himself/herself deeper into their own slough of sin, the judgment stings, but with a burn that still feels self-inflicted* (cf. Ps 81:12).[33]

Paul's words here may rest uneasy with us—the idea of God impressing a delusion upon people that leads to their own downfall—but it may help to keep Paul's wider concern in sight. His aim in this letter is to comfort the Thessalonians, by assuring them that the injustices of the persecutions they are presently enduring will be overturned. In this context, it would make

---

32. See Fee 2009: 294; though note Ezek 13:9 where the Lord stands against prophets "who see false visions and utter lying divinations" (cf. 22:28).

33. On the issue of ethics and divine sovereignty, see Best 1986: 310.

Appointed for Consecration and Glory (2:13-15)

> **13**Now, as for us, we ought to give thanks to God always when it comes to you, dear brothers and sisters beloved by the Lord, because God chose you as first fruits for salvation in consecration by the Spirit and by trust in the truth, **14**to which also he called you through our gospel for the possession of the glory of our Lord Messiah Jesus. **15**So then, my dear brothers and sisters, stand firm and hold firmly to the traditions that you were taught whether by word or a letter from us!

Paul transitions here to the proper response to his teaching on these eschatological events. First, Paul expresses thanksgiving to God (again, see 2 Thess 1:3), because they have chosen the better path of following in the way of truth, i.e., the gospel. Despite the tribulations and trials they are facing, their hope should be in the Lord Messiah Jesus and the inevitable fellowship with his glory. It is easy, when times get tough, to feel as if God were not with us or not for us—*is God punishing me? Did he abandon me?* No doubt the Thessalonians felt as if perhaps they had landed on the wrong side somehow and were doomed.

Here Paul offers a number of words of comfort that reinforce the Thessalonians identity in God through Jesus, over and against what their accusers were saying. First, he calls them "beloved by the Lord"—similar to 1 Thess 1:4, "loved by God." Of course it is a comfort to know one is loved and cherished by the Lord, but the intertextual resonances are important here—the language of the Lord *loving* and *choosing* is classic Deuteronomic language of the adoption of God's people, Israel, in the Old Testament:

> **7**It was not because you were more numerous than any other people that the LORD set his heart on you and chose you—for you were the fewest of all peoples. **8**It was because the LORD loved you and kept the oath that he swore to your ancestors, that the LORD

---

34. Not a few scholars believe that Paul is framing the very persecutors of the Thessalonians as the deceived followers of the Lawless One; see Weima 2014: 540; cf. Gaventa 1998: 115–16.

> has brought you out with a mighty hand, and redeemed you from the house of slavery, from the hand of Pharaoh king of Egypt.
>
> 9Know therefore that the LORD your God is God, the faithful God who maintains covenant loyalty with those who love him and keep his commandments, to a thousand generations, 10and who repays in their own person those who reject him. He does not delay but repays in their own person those who reject him. (Deut 7:7–10)

No matter what the Thessalonians were going through, they could count on the Lord's covenantal love, a love that does not waver, is not fickle, is not evanescent. These Gentile Thessalonians were *written into the story of Israel*, so to speak, by virtue of their faith in and loyalty to Messiah Jesus. And, to borrow a line from Romans, *if God is for us, who can be against us* (Rom 8:31)?[35]

Secondly, Paul points out that God chose *these Thessalonians* to be the "first fruits" for salvation.[36] What does he mean by this? Again, the imagery derives from worship language in the Old Testament. Israel was often called upon by God to bring forth the first fruits of their field labors as a sign of trust and commitment to the Lord (e.g., see Deut 26:1–16; Neh 10:37). In the context here of 2 Thessalonians, for Paul to call *them* "first fruits," he is most likely referring to the fact that they are the first believers in Jesus in Thessalonica.[37] This, in and of itself, would be a privilege and would help them to see the amazing work God has been doing all along to make a people for himself in that place. Furthermore, given that the Thessalonians were being persecuted, no doubt they felt alone; one thinks here of the plight of Elijah who complains to the Lord that he is all alone, rejected by those around him (1 Kings 19:10, 14). But, just as God desired to comfort Elijah, so Paul undoubtedly was eager to encourage the Thessalonians—*there will be more!* To call the Thessalonians "first fruits" is to say that, not only have they blazed a trail for more to come, but surely there *will be more*

---

35. Matera 2007: 108–9.

36. Some Greek manuscripts have a slightly different reading here: "he chose you *from the beginning*" (so see NET, RSV). Textual critics are in disagreement on which reading ("from the beginning" or "first-fruits") is original; it would seem that there is a little more support for the "first-fruits" reading, hence the translation choice in this commentary. However, it is interesting to note that Ambrosiaster, writing probably in the late fourth century AD, knew this verse to read "from the beginning" and comments: "He has known from the beginning who would become believers and which of them will increase in faith and not decrease"; see Bray 2009: 116; cf. also Chrysostom, *Homily 4*.

37. See Gaventa 1998: 121.

to come; after all, as Raymond Collins notes, "First fruits are the harbinger of the harvest to follow."³⁸

The path God has laid out for them involves consecration by the Spirit and by trust in the truth. This is Paul's way of helping the Thessalonians to see what is right and good from *God's* perspective, not from the viewpoint of mere mortals. As much as neighbors, "friends," and enemies are telling them—*this new religion is bizarre, suspicious, a distraction, harmful*—Paul, on the other hand, tells the Thessalonians—*see with new eyes, listen to the Spirit, search for the truth (about Jesus and about what Jesus means for understanding who God is and how to understand His world)*. To walk by the Spirit is to live intentionally in a way contrary to the so-called "truth" of the world; it is to walk by faith and to walk blindly, but by blindly Paul means living according to the invisible reality of God (2 Cor 5:7).

An important final word of comfort Paul offers the Thessalonians is that they are called to share in the glory of Messiah Jesus. As noted in 2 Thess 1:5–10, the plight of believers-in-Jesus is, indeed, to suffer in this world, but suffering and shame are not the last words; earlier Paul pointed to *relief* (2 Thess 1:7), and continues on to explain the judgment of Messiah Jesus against the Thessalonians persecutors (1:8–9) and the worst forces of evil (2:8). Here he explicitly acknowledges that the Thessalonians' *final state* will be glory.

After explicating their secure identity, consecration, and vocation in Jesus (2:13–14), Paul gives his charge: "So then, my dear brothers and sisters, stand firm and hold firmly to the traditions which you were taught whether by word or a letter from us!" The problem is obviously that the Thessalonians were growing faint of heart and losing their confidence and zeal for the Jesus way, mostly due to outside pressure, resistance, and shame. Paul, like an army commander to a weary troop, on the brink of "breaking rank," inspires perseverance. It is significant that he enjoins the Thessalonians not simply to trust *him*, but the traditions of the apostles.³⁹

---

38. Collins 2008: 240.

39. For more on the language of tradition in the New Testament, see Humphrey 2013; Best argues that Paul's reference here to "traditions" includes central doctrines, though need not be limited to eschatology *per se*. Best observes that Paul's reference to "our gospel" implies that the traditions in question relate to "the central teaching of the meaning of Jesus Christ (1986: 317; see 1 Thess 2:13; Col 2:6; Gal 1:9).

Wish-Prayer for Strength and Comfort (2:16-17)

> ¹⁶Now, then, as for our Lord Messiah Jesus himself and God our Father who has loved us and given to us eternal comfort and good hope by grace, ¹⁷may they comfort your hearts and strengthen you in every work and word.

Paul's concluding statement in this section is a wish prayer that gives attention to their situation (comfort and strength), but also to the gracious pair—the Lord Messiah Jesus and God the Father—who continue to care for the Thessalonians. At the same time Paul prays for the comfort of God, but also desires divine empowerment to lead the Thessalonians onward in goodness.

Fusing Horizons: Living beyond Fear

So much of this chapter of 2 Thessalonians involves Paul's very specific responses to concerns and confusion in Thessalonica. At first glance, then, it may seem like there is little here to teach the Church today. However, the central problem amongst the Thessalonians was that they were paralyzed with fear about *what is yet to come*. The specifics change in every generation, but many Christians today are also worried about the future. Global warming. Potential nuclear war. Depleting energy sources. Increasingly scarce clean water. Paul does not preach the hope of an easy future—in some ways things will get worse before they get better; *but* he still encourages believers to put their hope in God and trust that God will lead his people towards a good end. And—just as with Paul's expectations for the Thessalonians—*hoping* does not mean sitting on one's hands and waiting for the predetermined future events to unfold. Rather, Christian hope walks *into* that future and remains faithful in what God gives us today as long as it is called today.

Mission and Community (2 Thess 3:1–18)

In the second chapter of this letter, Paul took his discourse into the stratosphere to provide a glimpse into the cosmic realm of an apocalyptic engagement between the Lord Jesus and Satan's Lawless One. Here, in the third and final chapter, Paul touches back down onto *terra firma* to provide some final exhortation and instructions—and encouragement—for this distraught church in Thessalonica.

He treats three main topics. First, he asks for prayer for the apostolic mission and the worldwide glorification of the gospel (3:1–2). Secondly, he appeals to the Thessalonians to put their trust in their trustworthy Father God and the Messiah Jesus (3:3–5). Finally, Paul warns the Thessalonians not to associate with or go the way of those in the church he refers to as "idle" (*atakteō*). The problem was not just that these believers were not working (3:10), but that they were *refusing* to work and, instead of working, they meddled and became mere busybodies (3:11). While such were not meant to be pushed out of the community (3:15), they ought to be corrected and recognized as disobedient to apostolic teaching (3:6–7).

Paul's final teaching "word" comes in 3:16 and strikes the right note regarding why he takes such a stern approach to the troublemakers and disobedient in the church. His desire is to see a healthy church that models holiness and integrity. The church cannot *be* the church unless it lives in peace. Thus, he concludes with a *shalom*-benediction: "Now may the Lord of peace himself give you peace at all times in all ways. The Lord be with all of you" (3:16).

Hoping in the Faithful Lord (3:1–5)

> Finally, my dear brothers and sisters, pray for us, so that the word of the Lord may sprint forward and be glorified everywhere, just as it did among you, ²and pray that we be rescued from wicked and evil people; for loyalty does not belong to everyone. ³But the Lord is faithful; he will strengthen you and guard you from the evil one. ⁴And we have confidence in the Lord concerning you, that you are

doing and will go on doing the things which we command. 5May the Lord guide your hearts to the love of God and to the steadfastness of the Messiah.

At the beginning of this chapter, Paul (with Silas and Timothy) requests prayer for their apostolic work, specifically that the "word of the Lord" (*ho logos tou kuriou*) would *sprint forward* with the final goal that the gospel of Messiah Jesus might be honored and glorified throughout the world (3:1; cf. Matt 24:14; Mark 16:15). The first thing to note here is that Paul humbly asks for prayer; as Leon Morris aptly notes, "He did not feel himself as high above them, but as one with them. He valued their intercessions and sought their prayers."[1]

Also, in the midst of all the persecution and suffering the Thessalonians were facing, Paul was undoubtedly reminding them that they are not *powerless*. Despite the plots and schemes of wicked and evil people (whether subverting Paul or troubling the Thessalonians), the people who follow Jesus can rely on the strength of God through prayer in the name of Jesus.[2]

Who are the "wicked and evil people" that apparently seek to impede Paul's ministry and from whom he needs to be delivered (3:2b)? If Paul was writing this letter from Corinth, than this would probably be the context from which his concerns arise. According to Acts 18:5–17, Paul was facing Jewish opposition in Corinth (see also 1 Thess 2:14–16).[3] Perhaps the Thessalonians were experiencing similar kinds of persecution from certain upset Jews in Thessalonica and, in that case, Paul was showing a sense of solidarity with their own struggle.[4] Paul qualifies the wickedness of these opponents by explaining that "loyalty" does not belong to everyone (3:2c). Here Paul uses *pistis* (often translated "faith") in an absolute sense, implying *trust in Jesus* or *trust in the gospel*. This is similar to "faith" language in Galatians where Paul could simply refer to "the *pistis*" he once tried to destroy (Gal 1:23), living by *pistis* (2:20), the coming of *pistis* (3:23, 25), and the family of *pistis* (6:10). When it came to the nature of Torah, the Law of Moses, Paul told the Galatians that the Law is not "from *pistis*" (3:12). It

---

1. Morris 1975: 224.

2. See Marshall 2004: 248.

3. Furthermore, in terms of Jewish opposition, note the similar language in Romans 15:30–31: "I appeal to you, brothers and sisters, by our Lord Jesus Christ and by the love of the Spirit, to join me in earnest *prayer* to God on my behalf, that I may be *rescued* from the unbelievers in Judea . . ." See Malherbe 2000: 444.

4. See Marshall 1984: 214.

is difficult to pinpoint exactly what Paul means when he uses *pistis* in this independent, unqualified way in 2 Thess 3:2, but it appears to mean something like *thought and life transformed around and committed in loyalty to the gospel of Messiah Jesus*. *Pistis* is a load-bearing word for Paul, central to his understanding of the gospel, multi-faceted, and, thus his use of the word tends to imply more than one simple thing like "faith" or "belief."

When Paul reminds the Thessalonians, then, that "loyalty" is not a characteristic of everyone, he does not mean "loyalty" generically, but that idea of *thought and life transformed around and committed in loyalty to the gospel of Messiah Jesus*. It is my working theory that those who were troubling the Thessalonian believers were *claiming* to understand God and what God wants, and were attempting to move the Thessalonian church away from the true gospel. Paul was making a link between his own opponents in Corinth (wicked and evil people) and those in Thessalonica, reminding his converts to beware of those who seem to know what is right, but actually do not have *pistis* (loyalty) in Jesus.[5]

In 3:3–5, Paul shows his pastoral concern for the Thessalonians clearly by reminding them, despite the bleakness of shame and resistance coming from people around them, the Lord is faithful, and they are in his care. Paul is effusive with the encouragement that they are obedient to the truth of gospel taught by him, and they will continue in that obedience (3:4).

Paul follows this encouragement with a "wish-prayer" that the Lord might direct their hearts towards the love of God and perseverance of the Messiah (3:5). Does Paul mean *love for God and perseverance in view of the Messiah's return?* Or, does Paul mean *God's love for them and the perseverance shown by the Messiah?*[6] Perhaps this is one of those cases where Paul intended some ambiguity with a meaning like this: May the Lord direct your hearts towards the love God has shown and the perseverance Messiah Jesus has demonstrated *so that you can imitate them.*[7]

---

5. While Weima does not get into the kind of details I have described, and perhaps would not agree with my reading in its entirety, he does understand this verse along similar lines: "since there are many who do not have faith, such 'evil and wicked people' (and 'the evil one' who is working through these individuals) pose a threat not just to Paul but also to his converts in Thessalonica . . ."; see Weima 2014: 590.

6. In view of the grammatical construction of these phrases in Greek, scholars refer to the former as the "objective genitive" reading and the latter as the "subjective genitive" reading; either interpretation is possible from the standpoint of Greek syntax, so the decision involves which option makes the most sense when it comes to the point(s) Paul is making; see Weima 2014: 598–99.

7. See Wanamaker 1990: 279; see also Gupta 2008: 179–94.

Warning Against the Idle Troublemakers and Disobedient (3:6–12, 13–15)

> ⁶Now we command you, my dear brothers and sisters, in the name of our Lord Messiah Jesus, to stay away from any brother who is behaving as an idle troublemaker and not living according to the tradition received from us. ⁷For you yourselves know how you should imitate us—we were not idle when we were with you, ⁸and we did not eat anyone's bread without paying for it; but with toil and labor we worked night and day, so not to burden any of you. ⁹This was not because we do not have that right, but we did this to offer ourselves as an example to imitate. ¹⁰For even when we were with you, we gave you this command: Anyone unwilling to work should not eat. ¹¹For we hear that some of you are living in idleness, mere busybodies, not doing any work. ¹²Now such persons we command and exhort in the Lord Messiah Jesus to do their own work quietly and to earn their own living.
>
> ¹³My dear brothers and sisters, do not let it wear you out to do what is right. ¹⁴Take note of those who do not obey what we say in this letter; have nothing to do with them, so that they may be ashamed. ¹⁵Do not regard them as enemies, but warn them as brothers and sisters.

Paul's warm word of encouragement turns to a stern warning regarding a meddlesome group within the church. The whole section of 3:6–12 describes these troublemakers and establishes them as deviants who have strayed from proper apostolic teaching regarding work, integrity, and proper communal life. The keywords Paul uses here to describe these deviants are *atakōs* (adverb, "in an idle/unruly way"; 3:6, 11) and *atakteō* (verb, "to be idle/unruly," 3:7). In 1 Thess 5:14, Paul made passing reference to the "idle" (noun, *ataktos*), but in that letter he instructed the Thessalonians only to admonish them. The fact of such a lengthy warning about these people implies that they have become a more serious problem.[8]

A fundamental interpretive issue involves the meaning itself of this word-group in this particular socio-historical context. The root *takt** means "order"; when you add the *a*-prefix, it means "disorder."[9] In the history of the use of this word in Greek literature before and around the time

---

8. Skeen 1999: 288–90.

9. For example, in the Septuagint (Greek) translation of Prov 30:27, we read: "The locusts have no kind, and yet march *in good order* at one command." "In good order" translates the Greek adverb *eutaktōs* (the prefix "eu" means "good").

of Paul, it could be used for those who are *lazy/idle*, or it could be used for those who are *rebellious*. Only context, in the case of 1–2 Thessalonians, can offer further specificity. Until relatively recently, there has been a trend for translations to default to the meaning "idle" (so RSV, ESV), however the case for this kind of interpretation is somewhat misguided. The inspiration for referring to these people as "idlers" probably comes from the idea that they were not working for a living (2 Thess 3:8, 11). However, as Michael Holmes demonstrates, "the people in question are in fact *active*, not 'idle' or 'lazy.'... The problem, in other words, was not *inactivity*, but the wrong kind of activity (as busybodies)."[10] Marshall adds the point that Paul is not addressing people who simply *don't* work, but rather people who do not *want* to work (*theleō*, 3:10).[11] Perhaps the best solution is to try and represent in translation *both* the non-working *and* the unruliness.[12] Gordon Fee uses "disruptive-idle," we have offered the translation "idle troublemakers."

But *why* were they causing trouble? This is one of the most debated issues in the study of the Thessalonian correspondence. The traditional interpretive view is that their idleness is linked to an expectation of the imminent return of the Lord Jesus; so Leon Morris writes: "The thought of the nearness of the Parousia had thrown them into a flutter, and this had led to unwelcome consequences of which their idleness was the outstanding feature."[13] In the last few decades, though, this view has been questioned, especially because Paul does not explicitly link the eschatological problems with the unruly behavior of this group. Some have proposed that this was a socio-economic problem whereby some were leeching off of wealthier members of the church.[14]

10. Holmes 1998: 272.

11. Marshall 1984: 220.

12. See NIV for 2 Thess 3:6: "idle and disruptive"; see Gaventa 1998: 128; Skeen 1999: 290; deSilva 2004: 548. Ceslas Spicq sums up what might be going on in Thessalonica in light of his lexical study of *atakos* and its cognates: "the *ataktos* is the one who is defective in action, irregular, against the rule...The *ataktoi* Thessalonians free themselves from the rule of community life. One thinks of sins against brotherly love, a propensity to favor discord, a refusal to accept the customs or discipline of the church. Certain 'troubled' ones seem particularly stormy, befuddled types who disturb the peace (1 Thess 4:11–12). At any rate, 'their walk is not in line' (Gal 2:14). They are 'culpable' and probably stubborn"; see Spicq 1994: 226.

13. Morris 1975: 256; more recently, Gaventa: "The writer does not provide an explanation, but the most obvious possibility is that apocalyptic frenzy has triumphed over responsible behavior" (Gaventa 1998: 129).

14. In the Roman empire, it was not uncommon for ambitious persons ("clients") to

Another theory, recently championed by Gary Shogren, is that some Thessalonians set themselves up as local leaders in the church and tried to claim a unique right of exemption from labor for the sake of leadership. As such, they desired support from the Thessalonians. Shogren explains, "they are not lazy and perhaps are very busy; but they do not have gainful employment, and they are proving to be disruptive."[15] While any of these views struggle with lack of clear evidence, the third view is most convincing. Firstly, it would account for Paul commanding the church to set these meddlers at a distance (3:6). Secondly, it fits as an anti-type for how Paul establishes his own policy of forsaking his right to accept their financial support (see 2 Thess 3:9; 1 Cor 9). Finally, we may have an early Christian warning along these lines that makes this sort of problem more explicit. The *Didache* offers this counsel:

> Act toward the apostles and prophets as the gospel decrees. Let every apostle who comes to you be welcomed as the Lord. But he should not remain more than a day. If he must, he may stay one more. But if he stays three days, he is a false prophet. When an apostles leaves, he should take nothing except bread, until he arrives at his night's lodging. If he asks for money, he is a false prophet (11:3–6)[16]

Reflecting on the situation in 2 Thessalonians, David deSilva wonders whether the *Didache* may be addressing a similar situation when it "offers regulations to cut down on the abuses of local church support by wandering spiritualists. They might have been the self-appointed spiritual directors of the community who gave up their mundane occupations to devote themselves full-time to regulating the lives (i.e., meddling, being busybodies) of their less spiritual brothers and sisters."[17]

Turning now to the text of 2 Thess 3:6–15, we can imagine how this third approach might work. Paul begins, in 3:6, by commanding the Thessalonians to put these idle troublemakers at a distance because they have

---

attach themselves to someone higher up on the ladder of success ("patrons") and request from them money and privileges. Some scholars hypothesize that failing to work and relying on patronage was a practice Paul frowned upon and it may have been a problem in Thessalonica; see Winter 1989: 303–15.

15. Shogren 2012: 335.

16. Translation from Powell 2009: 394. The *Didache* is an early Christian text that probably came into existence in the late first century or early second century AD.

17. deSilva mentions this as one possibility, but does not commit to this theory (see 2004: 549).

rejected Paul's teaching (especially about work). They are reminded of the value of imitating Paul, and especially his own habit of working to support his own needs specifically to avoid becoming a burden on any of them (3:7–9; cf. 1 Thess 2:9).

Interestingly, Paul then reminds them that he had taught them specifically that "Anyone unwilling to work should not eat" (3:10). Here, again, we ought to be reminded what Paul is *not* saying. As Judy Skeen aptly notes,

> Paul clarifies here that the issue is not *capability to work* but *desire to do one's part*. Paul does not mean that the community should not care for those who are not able to provide for themselves physically. Rather, he is warning against the rebellious attitude that holds oneself higher than those around one. The significance of the individual's actions and choices on the community is coming into view.[18]

Perhaps the best contextual clue for what motivated this non-working comes in 2 Thess 3:10, some were behaving as busybodies (*periergazomai*). Here Paul does not explain what it means to be a busybody, but we can appeal to 1 Tim 5:13, the only other New Testament text where we find this word: "they learn to be idle, gadding about from house to house; and they are not merely idle, but also gossips and busybodies, saying what they should not say."

Because Paul's language for "working" (*ergazomai*) is so similar to "being busybodies" (*periergazomai*), Gaventa offers this gloss: "They do not do their own work, but they busy themselves with the work of other people."[19] Such people lack integrity and care little for the strength and wholeness of the community. Centuries ago, Ambrosiaster offered this reflection on the vice of these busybodies.

> Those who want to be idle do this as often as they can and thereby make themselves welcome in the houses of the rich. They go about quietly collecting stories and opinions, knowing who wants to hear what about whom, so that they will be freely invited to dinner. The discipline of the Lord abhors that kind of thing. Their belly is the god of those who get what they need by disreputable means.[20]

---

18. Skeen 1999: 292.

19. Gaventa 1998: 129; Zwingli apparently translated this: "they do nothing and do too much"; as cited in Eadie 1877: 315.

20. See Bray 2009: 129.

The antidote to this meddlesome lifestyle is to work quietly and earn your own living (2:12; cf. 1 Thess 4:11). To work "quietly" (*meta ēsuxias*) does not refer literally to low decibels, but rather implies working for its own goodness and productivity rather than to attract attention; so Fee explains, it is about "not disturbing the *shalom* of the community by 'sponging' off other believers."[21]

Paul goes on to call the Thessalonians to do what is the right thing, to persevere even though it is hard to face challenges (3:13; cf. Gal 6:9). Even though Paul may be thinking in general terms (*always do what is right*), looking at the context of 2 Thess 3:6–15, one can't help but think that Paul is specifically addressing this problem with the idle troublemakers. What is "right" could be having that difficult talk with these troublemakers and show them they are disruptive. However, it could also be that "doing what is right" means having a tender and caring heart for them in spite of their unruliness. Howard Marshall writes, "This would be entirely in accord with the early Christian spirit of showing love to those who do not deserve it and do not return it. Paul thus deals with the situation of idleness in the church, not by telling the church to cut off supplies to the idlers but by admonishing the idlers to change their ways."[22]

Peace Benediction and Pauline Authentication (3:16–18)[23]

> **16**Now may the Lord of peace himself give you peace at all times in all ways. The Lord be with all of you. **17**I, Paul, write this greeting with my own hand. This is the mark in every letter of mine; it is the way I write. **18**The grace of our Lord Messiah Jesus be with all of you.

As with many of his letters, here Paul concludes with a reiteration of one of the key themes of the epistle: peace. The Thessalonians, due to *some* communication, were whipped up into a frenzy thinking that the wrath of God was imminent. Paul's word for them is peace, *shalom*. God is not a God who relishes in damnation or stirring up problems. Rather, he is the God who moves his sin-broken world towards harmony. At any given moment, life may not seem very peaceful, but there is much comfort in the presence

---

21. Fee 2009: 334–35.
22. Marshall 1984: 226.
23. On the question and concern in scholarship about whether this letter was written by Paul (in light of this authentication statement), see the Introduction, 30–37.

of the Lord through the Spirit (see 2 Cor 1:2–5). This reminds me of Jesus' words to his disciples in the Fourth Gospel: "Peace I leave with you; my peace I give to you. I do not give to you as the world gives. Do not let your hearts be troubled, and do not let them be afraid" (John 14:27).

In Romans, Paul also happens to mention the "God of peace." In his concern for those who "cause dissensions and offenses" in opposition to apostolic teaching, Paul calls the Romans to avoid troublemakers, for "such people do not serve our Lord Christ, but their own appetites, and by smooth talk and flattery they deceive the hearts of the simple-minded" (16:17–18). Paul exhorts them towards vigilance and shrewdness. The time is short because soon "the God of peace" will destroy the work of Satan (Rom 16:20). Again, the point is that, despite the afflictions of today, and even tomorrow, ultimately the God of peace wins over evil, and those who persevere to the end will find rest and *shalom*.

Fusing the Horizons: Leadership and Work

Recently I had a conversation with a pastor about the future of ministry in the United States. He is a church planter who also runs his own business. For many pastors, it is less than ideal to be a tent-maker (having a non-ministry-related income while also having a strong ministry vocation). Many desire to free themselves up to focus entirely on the growth of their church or ministry.

There is much to commend this thought and biblical support as well. According to Acts, apparently some widows were being neglected in the daily food distribution of the church. The twelve apostles, while concerned for these widows, thought it best to continue their primary work of teaching the Word of God and praying, and they selected a group of seven men to see that these widows received food (Acts 6:1–3). Paul himself mentions that the Lord Jesus, apparently during his earthly ministry, made the provision that those who preach the gospel should receive their living from this work (and not be forced into other work for income; see 1 Cor 9:14). And yet, in 1 Corinthians 9 Paul goes on to explain that he has chosen to offer the gospel and *not* to be dependent financially on his churches (9:18). Also, in his relationship with the Thessalonians, he wanted to serve as an example of one who "works for his own bread" and also make sure he is above reproach in how he handles money and wealth.

I admire Christian leaders in both contexts, those in full-time ministry *and* tent-makers. Sometimes, though, I am concerned with some in the former category because it can seem like the move to full-time ministry leadership lessens the value of mundane work and manual labor. Furthermore, when full-time pastors or Christian leaders see themselves as CEOs, they presume that they should be paid like CEOs rather than as those who labor simply and humbly for the sake of the gospel.

I am reminded of two stories. First, I had a mentor in college who was on staff with a Christian parachurch ministry. His income came from donors, but my memories of him are of someone who felt very comfortable working with his hands. I remember stopping by his house one day just to say hello and he invited me out back to talk in the yard—he grabbed two rakes and we raked leaves and chatted. Also, I remember another occasion where he invited several students from the ministry to come to his house for ice cream—and to pull up old carpet. We did not feel used because he got down on the ground cutting and tearing carpet with us, and we knew him to be a man who always lived humbly and simply.

Second story: this one comes from the sixth century BC. Lucius Quinctius Cincinnatus was a farmer in the Roman empire. In 458 BC, Rome appointed him dictator to rescue a consular army from the Aequi. He extinguished the threat in a day and stayed in power a mere sixteen days to restore stability. Then he relinquished his control and went back to the farm.

Sometimes, perhaps too often, positions of leadership can give us delusions of grandeur, plunge us into a competitive world where we begin to aspire to be recognized and rewarded. When Paul promotes eating one's own bread and living a quiet life, he is not condemning ambition, but rather a mindset of elitism and the denigration of simple labor. Living a quiet life means doing the work for the sake of its own productivity and return, rather than seeing freedom from mundane work as a sign of unique achievement and status.

Bibliography

Aasgaard, R. 2004. *My Beloved Brothers and Sisters! Christian Siblingship Language in Paul.* JSNTSup 265. London: T. & T. Clark.

Abbott, F. F. 1911. *The Common People of Ancient Rome: Studies of Roman Life and Literature.* New York: Scribner's.

Allison, D. C. 2007. "Day of the Lord." *NIDB* 2.46–47.

Ascough, R. S. 2000. "The Thessalonian Community as a Professional Voluntary Association." *JBL* 119.2: 311–28.

———. 2003. *Paul's Macedonia Associations: The Social Context of Philippians and 1 Thessalonians.* WUNT II/161. Tübingen: Mohr Siebeck.

———. 2004. "A Question of Death: Paul's Community-Building Language in 1 Thessalonians 4:13–18." *JBL* 123: 509–30.

———. 2010. "Of Memories and Meals: Greco-Roman Associations and the Early Jesus-Group in Thessalonikē." In *From Roman to Early Christian Thessalonikē*, edited by Nasrallah et al., 49–72. Cambridge, MA: Harvard University Press.

———. 2015. *1 and 2 Thessalonians: Encountering the Christ Group at Thessalonikē.* Sheffield: Sheffield Phoenix.

Aune, D. 1993. "Apocalypticism." *The Dictionary of Paul and His Letters,* edited by G. F. Hawthorne, R. P. Martin, and D. G. Reid, 25–35. Downers Grove, IL: InterVarsity.

Aus, R. D. 1973. "The Liturgical Background of the Necessity and Propriety of Giving Thanks according to 2 Thess. 1:3." *JBL* 92: 432–38.

Bailey, J. 1978–1979. "Who Wrote II Thessalonians?" *NTS* 25: 131–45.

Bammel, E. 1960. "Ein Beitrag zur paulinischen Staatsanschauung." *TLZ* 85: 837–40.

Banks, R. J. 1994. *Paul's Idea of Community.* Grand Rapids: Baker.

Barclay, J. M. G. 1987. "Mirror-Reading A Polemical Letter." *JSNT* 31: 73–93.

———. 1993. "Conflict in Thessalonica." *CBQ* 55: 512–30.

———. 2008. "Grace and the Transformation of Agency in Christ." In *Redefining First-Century Jewish and Christian Identities: Essays in Honor of Ed Parish Sanders,* edited by Fabian E. Udoh, S. Heschel, M. Chancey, and G. Tatum, 372–89. Notre Dame: University of Notre Dame Press.

———. 2015. *Paul and the Gift.* Grand Rapids: Eerdmans.

Bassler, J. 1991. "Peace in All Ways: Theology in the Thessalonian Letters. A Response to R. Jewett, E. Krentz, and E. Richard." In *Pauline Theology,* edited by J. M. Bassler, 71–85. Vol. 1. Minneapolis: Fortress.

Beale, G. K. 2003. *1–2 Thessalonians.* IVPNTC. Downers Grove, IL: InterVarsity.

Beale, G. K., and B. Gladd. 2014. *Hidden But Now Revealed.* Downers Grove, IL: InterVarsity.

Beattie, G. 2005. *Women and Marriage in Paul and His Early Interpreters.* London: T. & T. Clark.

Best, Ernest. 1986. *The First and Second Epistles to the Thessalonians.* BNTC. Peabody, MA: Hendrickson.

Black, D. A. 1984. *Paul, Apostle of Weakness. Astheneia and its Cognates in the Pauline Literature.* New York: Lang.
Bonhoeffer, D. 2005. *Life Together and Prayerbook of the Bible.* Minneapolis, MN: Fortress,.
Boring, M. E. 2012. *An Introduction to the New Testament: History, Literature, Theology.* Louisville: Westminster John Knox.
———. 2015. *1-2 Thessalonians.* NTL. Louisville: Westminster John Knox.
Boyd, G. A. 2001. *Satan and the Problem of Evil.* Downers Grove, IL: InterVarsity.
Bray, G., ed. 2009. *Commentaries on Galatians-Philemon.* ACCS. Downers Grove, IL: InterVarsity.
Bridges, L. M. 2008. *1 & 2 Thessalonians.* SHBC. Macon: Smyth & Helwys.
Brown, R. E. 1997. *An Introduction to the New Testament.* New York: Doubleday.
Bruce, F. F. 1982. *1 & 2 Thessalonians.* WBC 45. Waco, TX: Word.
———. 1990. *The Acts of the Apostles.* Grand Rapids: Eerdmans.
Burke, T. J. 2003. *Family Matters: A Socio-Historical Study of Kinship Metaphors in 1 Thessalonians.* LNTS. London: T. & T. Clark.
Byron, J. 2014. *1 and 2 Thessalonians.* SoGBC. Grand Rapids: Zondervan.
Cambell, W. S. 2006. *Paul and the Creation of Christian Identity.* London: T. & T. Clark.
Carter, C. 2010. "A Consideration of the Theme of Reputation in 1 and 2 Thessalonians." *AJPS* 13.2: 282–99.
Carter, W. 2006. *The Roman Empire and the New Testament: An Essential Guide.* Nashville, TN: Abingdon.
Cohen, S. J. D. 1999. *The Beginnings of Jewishness: Boundaries, Varieties, Uncertainties.* Berkeley, CA: University of California Press.
———. 2006. *From the Maccabees to the Mishnah.* 2nd ed. Louisville: Westminster John Knox.
Cohick, L. 2009. *Women in the World of the Earliest Christians. Illuminating Ancient Ways of Life.* Grand Rapids: Baker.
Collins, J. J. 1998. *The Apocalyptic Imagination: An Introduction to Jewish Apocalyptic Literature.* Grand Rapids: Eerdmans.
Collins, R. 1996. *Preaching the Epistles.* Mahweh, NJ: Paulist.
———. 2008. *The Power of Images in Paul.* Collegeville, MN: Liturgical.
Cook, S. L. 2003. *The Apocalyptic Literature.* Nashville, TN: Abingdon.
Cousar, C. B. 2001. *Reading Galatians, Philippians, and 1 Thessalonians: A Literary and Theological Commentary.* Macon, GA: Smyth & Helwys.
Cullmann, O. 1936 "Le caractère eschatologique du devoir missionnaire et de la conscience apostolique de S. Paul: étude sur le katéchon (-ōn) de 2 Thess. 2: 6–7." *RHPR* 16: 210–45.
Date, C. M., G. G. Stump, and J. W. Anderson, eds. 2014. *Rethinking Hell: Readings in Evangelical Conditionalism.* Eugene, OR: Cascade.
Dewey, A. J., et al., eds. 2010. *The Authentic Letters of Paul: A New Reading of Paul's Rhetoric and Meaning.* Salem, OR: Polebridge.
deSilva, D. A. 1996. "'Worthy of His Kingdom': Honor Discourse and Social Engineering in 1 Thessalonians." *JSNT:* 49–79.
———. 1999. *The Hope of Glory: Honor Discourse and New Testament Interpretation.* Collegeville, MN: Liturgical.
———. 2000. *Honor, Patronage, Kinship & Purity: Unlocking New Testament Culture.* Downers Grove, IL: InterVarsity.
———. 2001. *New Testament Themes.* St Louis: Chalice.

———. 2004. *An Introduction to the New Testament*. Downers Grove, IL: InterVarsity.
deVilliers, P. G. R. 2011. "The Future Existence of the Believers According to 2 Thessalonians." *HTS* 67.1: 1–9.
Diogenes, Laertius. 1853. *The Lives and Opinions of Eminent Philosophers*. Translated by C. D. Yonge. London: Bohn.
Donfried, K. 1985. "The Cults of Thessalonica and the Thessalonian Correspondence." *NTS* 31: 349–51.
———. 1997. "The Imperial Cults and Politic Conflict in 1 Thessalonians." In *Paul and Empire*, edited by R. A. Horsley, 215–23. Harrisburg, PA: Trinity.
———. 2002. *Paul, Thessalonica, and Early Christianity*. Grand Rapids: Eerdmans.
Donfried, K. and I. H. Marshall. *The Theology of the Shorter Pauline Letters*. NTT. Cambridge: Cambridge University Press, 1993.
Dunn, J. D. G. 1998. *The Theology of Paul the Apostle*. Grand Rapids: Eerdmans.
———. 2009. *Beginning from Jerusalem*. Christianity in the Making 2. Grand Rapids: Eerdmans.
Eadie, J. 1877. *Commentary on the Greek Text of the Epistles of Paul to the Thessalonians*. New York: Macmillan.
Elgvin, T. 1997. "'To Master His Own Vessel': 1 Thess 4:4 in Light of New Qumran Evidence." *NTS* 43: 604–19.
Elliott, N., and M. Reasoner, eds. 2011. *Documents and Images for the Study of Paul*. Minneapolis, MN: Fortress.
Esler, P. F. 2001. "1 Thessalonians." In *The Oxford Bible Commentary*, edited by J. Barton and J. Muddiman, 1199–1212. Oxford: Oxford University Press.
Fee, G. D. 2007. *Pauline Christology: An Exegetical-Theological Study*. Peabody, MA: Hendrickson.
———. 2009. *The First and Second Letters to the Thessalonians*. NICNT. Grand Rapids: Eerdmans.
Foster, P. 2012. "Who Wrote 2 Thessalonians? A Fresh Look at an Old Problem." *JSNT* 35: 150–75.
Frame, J. E. 1912. *The Epistles of St. Paul to the Thessalonians*. ICC. Edinburgh: T. & T. Clark.
Fredriksen, P. 2015. "The Question of Worship: Gods, Pagans, and the Redemption of Israel." In *Paul within Judaism: Restoring the First-Century Context to the Apostle*, edited by M. D. Nanos and M. Zetterholm, 175–202. Minneapolis: Fortress.
Furnish, V. P. 2007. *1 Thessalonians, 2 Thessalonians*. ANTC. Nashville: Abingdon.
Fugde, E., and R. A. Peterson. 2000. *Two Views of Hell: A Biblical and Theological Dialogue*. Downers Grove, IL: InterVarsity.
Garroway, J. D. 2012. *Paul's Gentile-Jews: Neither Jew nor Gentile, but Both*. New York: Palgrave Macmillan.
Gaventa, B. R. 1998. *First and Second Thessalonians*. Interpretation. Louisville: Westminster John Knox.
———. 2007. *Our Mother Saint Paul*. Louisville: Westminster John Knox.
Goheen, M. W. 2011. *A Light to the Nations: The Missional Church and the Biblical Story*. Grand Rapids: Baker.
Goodman, M. 2013. *The Roman World: 44 BC–AD 180*. London: Routledge.
Gorday, P., ed. 2000. *Colossians, 1–2 Thessalonians, 1–2 Timothy, Titus, Philemon*. ACCS. Downers Grove, IL: InterVarsity.
Gorman, M. J. 2004. *Apostle of the Crucified Lord*. Grand Rapids: Eerdmans.

———. 2011. *Reading Revelation Responsibly: Uncivil Worship and Witness, Following the Lamb into the New Creation.* Eugene, OR: Cascade.
———. 2015. *Becoming the Gospel: Paul, Participation, and Mission.* Grand Rapids: Eerdmans.
Green, G. L. 2002. *The Letters to the Thessalonians.* PNTC. Grand Rapids: Eerdmans.
Gundry, R. H. 1976. *SOMA in Biblical Theology.* SNTSMS. Cambridge: Cambridge University Press.
Gupta, N. K. 2008. "An Apocalyptic Reading of Psalm 78 in 2 Thessalonians 2." *JSNT* 31.2: 179–94.
———. 2009. "The Theo-Logic of Paul's Ethics in Recent Research." *CBR* 7: 336–61.
———. 2010. *Worship that Makes Sense to Paul.* BZNW. Berlin: Walter de Gruyter.
———. 2012. "Mirror-Reading Moral Issues in Paul's Letters." *JSNT* 34.4: 361–81.
———. 2014. "'They Are Not Gods!': Jewish and Christian Idol Polemic and Greco-Roman Use of Cult Statues." *CBQ* 76.4: 704–19.
Guthrie, G. H. 2015. *2 Corinthians.* BECNT. Grand Rapids: Baker.
Harrington, H. K. 2001. *Holiness: Rabbinic Judaism in the Graeco-Roman World.* New York: Routledge.
Harris, M. J. 1999. *Slave of Christ: A New Testament Metaphor for Total Devotion to Christ.* Downers Grove, IL: InterVarsity.
———. 2013. "The Thessalonian Correspondence." *All Things to All Cultures: Paul among Jews, Greeks, and Romans*, edited by M. Harding and A. Nobbs, 269–301. Grand Rapids: Eerdmans.
Harrison, J. R. 2011. *Paul and the Imperial Authorities at Thessalonica and Rome.* WUNT I/273. Tübingen: Mohr Siebeck.
Hays, R. B. 1996. *The Moral Vision of the New Testament: Community, Cross, New Creation.* San Francisco: HarperSanFrancisco.
———. 1997. *First Corinthians.* Interpretation. Louisville, KY: Westminster John Knox.
Heinemann, K. 1913. *Thanatos in Poesie und Kunst der Greichen.* Munich: Kastner and Callwey.
Hellerman, J. 2009. "Brothers and Friends in Philippi: Family Honor in the Roman World and in Paul's Letter to the Philippians." *BTB* 39.1: 15–25.
Hock, R. 1999. "God's Will at Thessalonica and Greco-Roman Asceticism." In *Asceticism and the New Testament*, edited by L. E. Vaage and V. L. Wimbush, 159–70. New York: Routledge.
Holmes, M. W. 1998. *1 and 2 Thessalonians.* NIVAC. Grand Rapids: Zondervan.
Holtz, T. 1986. *Der erste Brief an die Thessalonicher.* EKKNT 13. Zürich: Benziger.
Hooker, M. D. 2008. *Paul: A Beginner's Guide.* Oxford: Oneworld.
Horrell, D. 2001. "From *adelphoi* to *oikos theou*: Social Transformation in Pauline Christianity." *JBL* 120.2: 293–311.
———. 2005a. "Familiar Friend or Alien Stranger? On Translating the Bible." *ExpTim* 116.12: 402–8.
———. 2005b. *Solidarity and Difference: A Contemporary Reading of Paul's Ethics.* London: T. & T. Clark.
Horton, F. L. 2011. "Dualism in the New Testament: A Surprising Rhetoric and a Rhetoric of Surprise." In *Dualism in Ancient Mediterranean Religion and the Contemporary World*, edited by Armin Lange, et al., 186–208. Göttingen: Vandenhoeck & Ruprecht.
Hubbard, T. K., ed. 2014. *A Companion to Greek and Roman Sexualities.* Malden: Wiley-Blackwell.

Humphrey, E. 2013. *Scripture and Tradition: What the Bible Really Says*. Grand Rapids: Baker.
Jervis, L. A. 2007. *At the Heart of the Gospel: Suffering in the Earliest Christian Message*. Grand Rapids: Eerdmans.
Johnson, Andy. 2016. *1 and 2 Thessalonians*. Two Horizons New Testament Commentary. Grand Rapids: Eerdmans.
Johnson, E. E. 2012. "Paul's Reliance on Scripture in 1 Thessalonians." In *Paul and Scripture: Extending the Conversation*, edited by C. D. Stanley, 143–62. Atlanta: SBL.
Johnson, Luke Timothy. 1989. "The New Testament's Anti-Jewish Slander and the Conventions of Ancient Polemic." *JBL* 108.3: 419–41.
———. 1992. *The Acts of the Apostles*. Sacra Pagina. Collegeville: Liturgical.
———. 1999. *The Writings of the New Testament*. 2nd ed. Minneapolis, MN: Fortress.
Johnson-DeBaufre, M. 2010. "'Gazing Upon the Invisible': Archaeology, Historiography and the Elusive Women of 1 Thessalonians." In *From Roman to Early Christian Thessalonikē*, edited by L. Nasrallah et al., 109–32. Cambridge: Harvard University Press.
Just, A. A., ed. 2003. *Luke*. ACCS. Downers Grove, IL: InterVarsity.
Keener, C. S. 2009. *Revelation*. NIVAC. Grand Rapids: Zondervan.
———. 2012. *Acts: An Exegetical Commentary*. Vol. 1. Grand Rapids: Baker.
Keller, M. N. 2010. *Priscilla and Aquila: Paul's Coworkers in Christ Jesus*. Collegeville: Liturgical.
Koester, H. 1979. "1 Thessalonians—Experiment in Christian Writing." In *Continuity and Discontinuity in Church History*, edited by F. F. Church and T. George, 33–44. Leiden: Brill.
Krentz, E. 1991. "Through a Lens: Theology and Fidelity in 2 Thessalonians." In *Pauline Theology*, edited by J. Bassler, 52–62. Vol. 1. Minneapolis: Fortress.
———. 1992. "Thessalonians, First and Second Epistles." In *The Anchor Bible Dictionary*, edited by D. N. Freedman, 515–23. Vol. 6. New York: Doubleday.
———. 2003. "Paul, Games, and the Military." In *Paul in the Greco-Roman World: A Handbook*, edited by P. Sampley, 344–83. Harrisburg, PA: Trinity Press International.
———. 2009. "A Stone that Will Not Fit: The Non-Pauline Authorship of 2 Thessalonians." In *Pseudepigraphie und Verfasserfiktion in Frühchristlichen Briefen*, edited by J. Frey et al., 439–70. WUNT 246. Tübingen: Mohr Siebeck.
Kreinecker, C. M. 2013. "The Imitation Hypothesis: Pseudepigraphic Remarks on 2 Thessalonians with Help from Documentary Papyri." In *Paul and Pseudepigraphy*. edited by S. E. Porter and G. P. Fewster, 197–220. Boston: Brill.
Lange, A., et al., eds. 2011. *Light Against Darkness: Dualism in Ancient Mediterranean Religions and the Contemporary World*. Göttingen: Vandenhoeck & Ruprecht.
Lewis, C. S. 1996. *The Problem of Pain*. New York: HarperCollins.
Longenecker, R. N. 1995. *Acts*. EBC. Grand Rapids: Zondervan.
Louw, J. P., and E. Nida. 1988. *A Greek-English Lexicon of the New Testament Based on Semantic Domains*. 2nd ed. New York: UBS.
Lövestam, E. 1963. *Spiritual Wakefulness in the New Testament*. Lund: Gleerup.
Malherbe, A. J. 2000. *The Letters to the Thessalonians*. AB. New York: Doubleday.
Malina, B. 2003. *Social-Science Commentary on the Synoptic Gospels*. 2nd ed. Minneapolis: Fortress.
Marshall, I. H. 1984. *1 and 2 Thessalonians*. NCB. Grand Rapids: Eerdmans.
———. 2004. *New Testament Theology*. Downers Grove: IL: InterVarsity.

Marxsen, W. 1969. "Auslegung von 1 Thess 4,13–18." *ZTK*. 66: 21–37.
Matera, F. J. 1999. *New Testament Christology*. Louisville: Westminster John Knox.
———. 2007. *New Testament Theology*. Louisville: Westminster John Knox.
———. 2012. *God's Saving Grace: A Pauline Theology*. Grand Rapids: Eerdmans.
McNeel, J. H. 2014. *Paul as Infant and Nursing Mother: Metaphor, Rhetoric, and Identity in 1 Thessalonians 2:5–8*. Atlanta: SBL.
Menken, M. J. J. 1994. *2 Thessalonians*. NTR. New York: Routledge.
Meyers, E. M. 2011. "From Myth to Apocalyptic: Dualism in the Hebrew Bible." In *Dualism in Ancient Mediterranean Religion and the Contemporary World*, edited by Armin Lange, et al., 92–106. Göttingen: Vandenhoeck & Ruprecht.
Milligan, G. 1912. *Selections from the Greek Papyri*. Cambridge: Cambridge University Press.
Morgan, C. W., and R. A. Peterson, eds. 2004. *Hell Under Fire: Modern Scholarship Reinvents Eternal Punishment*. Grand Rapids: Zondervan.
Morris, Leon. 1975. *The First and Second Epistles to the Thessalonians*. Grand Rapids: Eerdmans.
Munck, J. 1959. *Paul and the Salvation of Mankind*. London: SCM.
Murphy, F. J. 2002. *Early Judaism from the Exile to the Time of Jesus*. Peabody, MA: Hendrickson.
Nasrallah, L., C. Bakirtzis, and S. J. Friesen, eds. 2010. *From Roman to Early Christian Thessalonikē*. Cambridge, MA: Harvard University Press.
Nestor, O. M. 2012. *The Practice of Hope: Ideology and Intention in First Thessalonians*. Minneapolis: Fortress.
Nicholl, C. R. 2004. *From Hope to Despair in Thessalonica*. Cambridge: Cambridge University Press.
Nigdelis, P. 2015. "The Age of the Macedonian Kingdom and the Period of Roman Rule." Museum of Byzantine Culture. Online: http://site.lpth.gr/en/texts/Nigdelis_en.pdf.
Nouwen, H. 1996. *Reaching Out*. London: Fount.
Oden, T. C. 2014. *A Change of Heart: A Personal and Theological Memoir*. Downers Grove, IL: InterVarsity.
Pearson, Birger A. 1971. "1 Thessalonians 2:14–16: A Deutero-Pauline Interpolation." *HTR* 64: 79–94.
Peterson, D. 2001. *Possessed by God: A New Testament Theology of Sanctification and Holiness*. New Studies in Biblical Theology. Downers Grove, IL: InterVarsity.
Pillar, E. 2013. *Resurrection as Anti-Imperial Gospel: 1 Thessalonians 1:9b–10 in Context*. Minneapolis: Fortress.
Pitts, A. W. 2013. "Style and Pseudonymity in Pauline Scholarship: A Register Based Configuration." In *Paul and Pseudepigraphy*, edited by S. E. Porter and G. P. Fewster, 113–52. PAST. Boston: Brill.
Plummer, A. 1918. *A Commentary on St. Paul's First Epistles to the Thessalonians*. London: Robert Scott.
Pobee, J. S. 1985. *Persecution and Martyrdom in the Theology of Paul*. JSNTSup 6. Sheffield: JSOT Press.
Powell, M. A. 2009. *Introducing the New Testament: A Historical, Literary, and Theological Survey*. Grand Rapids: Baker.
Richard, E. J. 1995. *First and Second Thessalonians*. SP. Collegeville, MN: Liturgical.
Richardson, P. 1969. *Israel in the Apostolic Age*. Cambridge: Cambridge University Press.
Ridderbos, H. 1975. *Paul: An Outline of His Theology*. Grand Rapids: Eerdmans.

Rigaux, B. 1956. *Saint Paul: les épîtres aux Thessaloniciens*. Paris: Gabalda.
Roose, H. 2006. "'A Letter as by Us': Intentional Ambiguity in 2 Thessalonians 2.2." *JSNT* 29: 107–24.
Rossing, B. R. 2004. *The Rapture Exposed: The Message of Hope in the Book of Revelation*. New York: Basic.
Runesson, A., D. D. Binder, and B. Olsson. 2008. *The Ancient Synagogue from its Origins to 200 C.E*. Leiden: Brill.
Sailors, T.B. 2000. "Wedding Textual and Rhetorical Criticism to Understanding the Text of 1 Thessalonians 2:7." *JSNT* 80: 81–98.
Shogren, G. 2012. *1 and 2 Thessalonians*. ZECNT. Grand Rapids: Zondervan.
Skeen, Judy. 1999. "Not as Enemies, But Kin: Discipline in the Family of God—2 Thessalonians 3:6–10." *Review & Expositor* 96.2: 287–94.
Smith, A. 2000. "The First Letter to the Thessalonians: Introduction, Commentary, and Reflections." *NIB* 11: 671–737.
———. 2004. "Unmasking the Powers: Toward a Postcolonial Analysis of 1 Thessalonians." In *Paul and the Roman Imperial Order*, edited by R. A. Horsley, 47–66. Harrisburg, PA: Trinity.
Smith, J. E. 2001. "1 Thessalonians 4:4: Breaking the Impasse." *BBR* 11: 65–105.
Spicq, C. 1994. *Theological Lexicon of the New Testament*. Peabody, MA: Hendrickson.
Still, T. D. 1999. *Conflict at Thessalonica: A Pauline Church and Its Neighbours*. JSNTSup 183. Sheffield: Sheffield Academic.
———. 2007. "Interpretive Ambiguities and Scholarly Proclivities in Pauline Studies: A Treatment of Three Texts from 1 Thessalonians 4 as a Test Case." *CBR* 5: 207–19.
———. 2011. "Paul and the Macedonian Believers." In *The Blackwell Companion to Paul*, edited by S. Westerholm, 30–45. Oxford: Wiley-Blackwell.
Stuckenbruck, L. T. 2011. "The Interiorization of Dualism within the Human Being in Second Temple Judaism: the Treatise of the Two Spirits (1QS III: 13-IV: 26) in its Tradition-Historical Context." In *Dualism in Ancient Mediterranean Religion and the Contemporary World*, edited by Armin Lange, et al., 145–68. Göttingen: Vandenhoeck & Ruprecht.
Swartley, W. 2006. *Covenant of Peace: The Missing Peace in New Testament Theology and Ethics*. Grand Rapids: Eerdmans.
Talbert, C. H. 1991. *Learning through Suffering: The Educational Value of Suffering in the New Testament and In Its Milieu*. Collegeville, MN: Liturgical.
Taylor, N. H. 2002. "Who Persecuted the Thessalonian Christians?" *HTS* 58.2: 784–801.
Thiselton, A. 2011. *1 and 2 Thessalonians through the Centuries*. Oxford: Wiley-Blackwell.
Thompson, J. W. 2006. *Pastoral Ministry according to Paul: A Biblical Vision*. Grand Rapids: Baker.
———. 2011. *Moral Formation according to Paul: The Context and Coherence of Pauline Ethics*. Grand Rapids: Baker.
Thurston, B. 1995. *Reading Colossians, Ephesians, and 2 Thessalonians: A Literary and Theological Commentary*. New York: Crossroad,
Tidball, D. 2010. *The Message of Holiness*. Downers Grove, IL: InterVarsity.
Trebilco, P. 2012. *Self-Designations and Group Identity in the New Testament*. Cambridge: Cambridge University Press.
———. 2013. "Early Christian Communities in the Greco-Roman City: Perspectives on Urban Ministry from the New Testament." *Ex Auditu*: 25–48.

Trozzo, L. M. 2012 "Thessalonian Women: The Key to the 4:4 Conundrum." *Perspectives in Religious Studies* 39: 39–52.
Twelftree, G. 2013. *Paul and the Miraculous*. Grand Rapids: Baker.
Van der Watt, J., ed. 2006. *Identity, Ethics, and Ethos in the New Testament*. Berlin: Walter de Gruyter.
Van Kooten, G. 2005. "'Wrath Will Drip in the Plains of Macedonia': Expectations of Nero's Return in the Egyptian *Sibylline Oracles* (Book 5), 2 Thessalonians, and Ancient Historical Writings." In *The Wisdom of Egypt: Jewish, Early Christian, and Gnostic Essays in Honour of Gerard P. Luttikhuizen*, edited by A. Hilhorst and G. H. van Kooten, 177–215. Leiden: Brill.
Wanamaker, C. A. 1990. *The Epistles to the Thessalonians*. NIGTC. Grand Rapids: Eerdmans.
Weima, J. 2014. *1-2 Thessalonians*. BECNT. Grand Rapids: Baker.
Weima, J. 1994. *Neglected Endings: The Significance of the Pauline Letter Closings*. JSNTSup 101. Sheffield: JSOT.
———. 2006. "The Slaying of Satan's Superman and the Sure Salvation of the Saints: Paul's Apocalyptic Word of Comfort (2 Thessalonians 2:1–17)." *CTJ* 41: 67–88.
———. 2012. "'Peace and Security' (1 Thess 5.3): Prophetic Warning or Political Propoganda?" *NTS* 58: 331–59.
Wengst, K. 1987. *Pax Romana and the Peace of Jesus Christ*. London: SCM.
Wenham, D. 1995. *Paul: Follower of Jesus or Founder of Christianity?* Grand Rapids: Eerdmans.
White, J. 2013 "'Peace and Security' (1 Thess 5:3): Is It Really a Roman Slogan?" *NTS* 59: 382–95.
Whitford, D. 2011. *Luther: A Guide for the Perplexed*. London: Bloomsbury.
Williams, C. A. 2014. "Sexual Themes in Greek and Latin Graffiti." In *A Companion to Greek and Roman Sexualities*, edited by T. K. Hubbard, 493–508. Malden: Wiley-Blackwell.
Williams, D. J. 1999. *Paul's Metaphors: Their Context and Character*. Peabody, MA: Hendrickson.
Winter, B. W. 1989. "'If a Man Does Not Wish to Work...': A Cultural and Historical Setting for 2 Thessalonians 3:6–16." *Tyndale Bulletin* 40.2: 303–15.
———. 1994. *Seeking the Welfare of the City*. Grand Rapids: Eerdmans.
Witherington, B. 2006. *1 and 2 Thessalonians: A Socio-Rhetorical Commentary*. Grand Rapids: Eerdmans.
———. 2008 "Homeland Security: The Spiritual Lust for An Escape Clause." *Ex Auditu* 24: 150–75.
Witmer, S. E. 2008. *Divine Instruction in Early Christianity*. WUNT II/246. Tübingen: Mohr Siebeck.
Wrede, W. 1903. *Die Echtheit des zweiten Thessalonicherbriefs*. Leipzig: Hinrichs.
Wright, N. T. 2004. *Paul For Everyone: Galatians and Thessalonians*. Louisville, KY: Westminster/John Knox.
———. 2013. *Paul and the Faithfulness of God*. Minneapolis, MN: Fortress.
Yarbrough, O. L. 1985. *Not Like the Gentiles: Marriage Rules in the Letters of Paul*. SBLDS 80. Atlanta: Scholars.
Yinger, K. L. 2009. "Reformation Redivivus: Synergism and the New Perspective." *JTI* 3.1: 89–106.

Subject Index

Aasgaard, Reidar, 84n17, 85
accountability, Christian leaders fostering, 60
Achaians, 47
"active waiting," for the Parousia, 20
Acts, historicity of, 5n11
adelphoi ("brothers"), as inclusive of women, 9
adelphos (brother), in 1 Thessalonians, 17n50
adultery, 79, 83
affirmation, of Gentiles, 13
afflicters, will be "repaid," 125
afflictions, 13, 124–25
Against Neaera oration, 79
agapē. *See* love (*agapē*)
agency, capable of, 127
agnostic view, towards identity of the restrainer, 136n25
Akiba, R., 123
Allison, Dale, 131
Ambrosiaster, 54n6, 141n36, 150
Andriscus, 3
Andronicus, 63n5
angel(s)
    opposing forces of the enemy, 137n30
    restrainer as, 136
anthropological language, Paul's, 115–16
Antichrist, in the Armenian language, 134n13
anticipatory imagination, Christian hope as, 23
anti-God figures, kinds of, 134
Anti-Law One, 133
Antiochus Epiphanes, 134
Antipater of Thessalonica, 4
anti-Semitic, Paul as, 62–63

apantēsis, translating as "meeting," 97
apocalyptic discourse, of Paul, 95
apocalyptic frenzy, 148n13
apocalyptic imagination, 93, 94
"apocalyptic" perspective/worldview, 94–95
apocalyptic signs, 26
apocalypticists, 35
apokalypsis, meaning "revelation" or "disclosure," 94
apostles, maintaining a cool distance, 57
apostolic team, "approved by God," 53
Aquila, 8n24
Aquinas, St. Thomas, 70n15
"archangel," 94, 94n12
Aristarchus, 6n12
Aristotle, 3, 54
armor
    of light, 20
    of loyalty, love, and hope, 20
    spiritual, 106
    Thessalonian believers wearing, 107
Ascough, Richard, 6n15–7n15, 8, 88, 89
"asleep," dead as, 91
Asmodeus (demon), 136n23
asphaleia (security/safety), as extremely common, 105
"aspiration" (*philoteimia*), 89, 90
Assyria, judgment of, 137
ataktōs ("in an idle/unruly way"), 147, 148n12
atakteō ("to be idle/unruly"), 144, 147
ataktoi (the idle troublemakers"), 15, 25
ataktoi Thessalonians, 148n12
"atheism," being charged with, 10

Subject Index

attention and interest, selection through persistent, 44
Augustine (Saint), 59, 86–87
Aus, Roger, 120–21
authenticity, 36, 36n102
authority, Paul not reinforcing, 38
authorship, of 2 Thessalonians, 36–37

Barclay, John, 26n70, 35
Barclay, John M. G., 127
Barnabas, 38, 128
Barth, Markus, 36
Battle as Day-People section, 106–7
Beale, G., 33n92
Beale, G. K., 81
"becoming," Christ's own, 46
behavior, God's expectations for, 78
being with the Lord, 98
Bel and the Dragon, 47
believers
    anticipation of Jesus' arrival, 103
    becoming less glorious in the eyes of the world, 46
    co-glorification of, 126
    concerns and questions, 96
    confidence in God's power over evil, 95
    devoting themselves exclusively to the one God, 10
    died due to persecution, 96
    engaged in a conflict, 108
    fate of those still alive, 101
    known from the beginning, 141n36
    physically injured in event that led to deaths, 112
    as "saints" or "holy people," 19
    secret snatching away from the earth, 96
    shaming and shunning reinforcing certain, 25
    suffering as, 129
    transforming into something better, 45
    "without defect or blemish," 19
"beloved by the Lord," Thessalonians as, 140

beloved children, admonishing as, 57
Ben Sira, on endurance, 41–42
bereavement, struggling with, 98
Beroea, Paul's successful ministry in, 6
Best, Ernest, 57n16, 102, 117, 131
Bible, violence and gruesomeness of, 107
biblical texts, folly of cutting out offensive, 62n3
blameless ministry, of Paul, 50–60
"blood-blind" Christians, 42
"boasting," Paul writing positively about, 68
body
    meaning of, 116
    as sacred, 81
bondage-breaking power, of God, 82
Bonhoeffer, Dietrich, 75–76
Boring, Eugene, 7, 36n101
both-and approach, to Paul's final instructions, 111n2
"bounden duty," to honor God, 120
Boyd, Gregory A., 67n3
breath of his mouth, 137
Bridges, Linda McKinnish, 8n22, 33
brothers and sisters (*adelphoi*), 111
    calling each other, 84
    kisses as a symbol and gesture of, 117
    Paul calling the Thessalonians, 17
    as Paul's central image in 1 Thessalonians, 42
    through the Messiah, 17
Brown, Raymond, 31n80, 136n25
Bruce, F. F., 35n99, 39n2, 62, 72, 79, 120, 129
Brutus, 4
burden (*katanarkoō*), 51
burdened (*katabareō*), 51, 52
burdening (*epibareō*), language of, 52
busybodies (*periergazomai*), 27, 144, 148, 149, 150

Cabirus, myth of, 4
Caesar, 4, 5
calling of God, 58, 78

Calvin, John, 85
Capitolina, 7
carnal passions and lusts, mastery over, 80
Cassander, 3
Cassius, 4
Catullus, 91
"caught up" (*harpazō*), 96
charis, translation of, 39n3
chastening, of the Lord, 123
Chicken Little, story of, 132
choice, to let Jesus rule, 82
Christian community. *See also* community
 "reversal of fortune" for, 98
 tragedy struck, 89
Christian dead, hopeful fate of, 91–100
Christian devotionals, extracting a snippet of, 110
Christian eschatology. *See* eschatology
Christian fellowship
 cherishing, 76
 as "life together," 75
Christian hope
 clinging to, 99
 defined, 23
Christian leaders. *See* leaders
Christian siblings
 adopted into a single family and household, 42
 Thessalonians as, 52
Christian spirit, showing love, 151
Christian unity, 74–75
Christians
 being called incestuous, 17
 living in hope, 3
 living in "waiting," 2–3
 meeting privately, 84n18
Chrysostom, John (saint), 67n6, 112
church
 desire to see a healthy, 144
 as family, 17
 of the Thessalonians, 6–7
church fellowship, Martin Luther on, 76n23

Cicero, 59
Cincinnatus, Lucius Quinctius, 153
civitas libera (free city), status of, 4
clandestine attack, hypothesizing, 14–15
classifications, living by, 64
1 Clement, language of "deep conviction," 44n9
Clement of Alexandria, 4
clients, attaching themselves to "patrons," 89, 148n14–49n14
Cohen, Shaye, 11
Collins, Raymond, 22, 97, 142
"color-blind" Christians, 42
Colossians, authenticity of, 36
combat imagery, in the New Testament, 108
comforting (*paramytheomai*), 58
coming of the Lord, 15, 67, 97
commitment to Jesus, recalling, 52
communal love, of the Thessalonians, 73
community. *See also* Christian community
 appreciation for, 99
 being a contributor to, 22
 hospitable for all people, 64–65
 importance to humans, 75–76
 relationship with God and Jesus the Messiah, 38
 of relationships, 74
 requiring consistency and self-discipline, 89
 unexpected death of members, 86, 86n25
community life, undermining, 27
community-orientation, detail regarding, 107
compatriots (*symphyletēs*), meaning of, 10, 10n34–11n34, 12
concern, of Paul for the Thessalonians, 66
concubine (*pallakē*), 79
consecration, 78, 142
console (*paramythia*), 58
contentment, coming from peace with God, 90

controlling one's body, 82
conversion, 8, 44, 52
co-participation, human and divine, 127
"copycat" nature, of 2 Thessalonians, 30–31, 33–34
Corinthians, letters Paul wrote to, 24
corrective teaching, of the leaders, 112
cosmic battle, as a contest for all believers, 108
cosmology, 94
counterfeit prophets, 105
courage, of Paul, 52–53
Cousar, Charles, 55, 56
Cowper, William, 100
crafty person (*panourgos*), 51
"crown of boasting," 68
cruciform love, 24
cult, as image in 1 Thessalonians, 18–19
Cyril of Alexandria, 92

damnation, 124, 125
darkness, choosing to live in, 83
day of grace, 132n7
Day of the Lord
  being taught about the arrival of, 26
  coming like a thief, 103
  coming of, 131
  as one public appearance, 97
  preparedness and perseverance, 101–9
  unexpected (wrath-bearing) nature of, 103
Day of the Messiah, 131, 131n5
  justice at, 122–25, 126
  weight of hope on, 93
"day of Yahweh," Old Testament's reference to, 131
Day-and Light-People section, 105–6
"day/light"- people, 102, 105
dead
  hopeful fate of Christian, 91–100
  in the Messiah, 14
  resurrection of, 75
  reunited with Thessalonians and the Lord Jesus, 91
death, 26, 46, 92
deceit (*dolos*), 51
defensive text, by Paul in 2 Corinthians, 51
defensive tone, in Paul's self-description, 16
defensiveness, of Paul, 50–51
delusion, God sending a powerful, 139
Demosthenes, 79
deSilva, David, 24, 25, 121, 149
"destruction" (*apōleia*)
  New Testament language of, 134n11
  opposites of, 134n11
  representing damnation, 125
"destructive opinions," 139
"devout Greeks," responded positively to Paul's preaching, 6
Didache ("The Teaching of the Twelve Apostles to the Gentiles"), 79, 149, 149n16
dignity and honor, as themes in 2 Thessalonians, 28–29
disobedience, warning against, 147–51
divination, 113
divine *orgē*, about God's anger, 21
divine sovereignty, language of, 95
divine will, guiding believers, 115
divine wrath, 20–21
dolos (deceit), 52
doxological prayer, offered by Paul, 73
drunkenness, as "metaphor for absorption in the affairs of the world," 106n16–7n16
dualism and conflict, of apocalyptic texts, 94
dualistic imagery, 105

earthen vessels (*skeuos*), as a person's own body, 81
Egyptian gods, 4

eirēnē (peace), as extremely common, 105
eis telos ("to the end"), 62
Elijah, feeling alone, 141
elitism, condemning a mindset of, 153
end of the world, presumptions about, 88
end-time ingathering, 131
endurance, 41, 61–65
"endurance of hope," 22
enemy, characterized by disobedience to God, 27
epibareō
    Paul's use of, 54
    root in Greek (*bar*), 52n2
ēpioi, swapped out by a textual scribe, 55
epiphaneia (appearance), 137
eschatological discourse, in Matthew 24, 27
eschatological emphasis, in 1 Thessalonians, 32–33
eschatological events
    Paul's main points about, 26–27
    Paul's teaching about, 21
    response to teaching on, 140
    revealing through a "word of the Lord," 95
    underscoring that Messiah Jesus will prevail, 130
eschatological horizon, 68n7
"eschatological matters," importance to Paul, 135n18
eschatological offering, preparing, 19
eschatological pressure, Paul ramping up, 103n8–4n8
eschatological timing, 102
eschatology
    in 2 Thessalonians, 25–27
    "apocalyptic" worldview and, 94
Esler, Philip, 10
eternal destruction, language of, 125–26
eternality, about finality, 125
ethical statement, about two kinds of people, 105

"ethics," compared to "theology," 78
events
    tying to ways that God might be leading us, 113
    yet to come, 132–40
"evidence" (*endeigma*)
    kinds of, 55
    of the right judgment of God, 123
evil, opposition against, 19
"evil and wicked people," posing a threat, 146n5
Evil One, testing people, 70
exhortation, 52, 107
exploitative dependence, Paul rejecting, 87
external evidence, 55, 55n9
Ezekiel, 104

face to face, talking with, 9
"faint-hearted" (*oligopsychos*), 112
faith
    anchoring, 2
    opposed to "work," 21
    referring to believers' commitment, 40n5–41n5
    representing reliance on an alternative reality, 2
    targeted, 1
"faith" language, in Galatians, 145
faithful endurance, thanksgiving for, 120–22
faithful Lord, hoping in, 144–46
faithfulness and integrity, in everyday work, 87
faith/love, statements about, 41
"false" (*pseudos*) "signs and wonders," 138–39
familial metaphors, of Paul, 57
family, 17, 66–67
family (*philadelphia* -"sibling love"), loving one another like, 24
family members, 117
Father
    collocation with "Lord Messiah Jesus," 39n2
    continuing to care for the Thessalonians, 143

Subject Index

Father (*continued*)
    God called, 17
    putting trust in, 144
    rescued us, 39
father (*pater*)
    encouraging his children, 18
    invested in seeing their children matured, 58
    treating his children with care and concern, 57
fear, 132, 143
Fee, Gordon, 33, 55n9, 56, 81, 126, 136n25, 148, 151
Felix, Minucius, 84–85
fellowship, 74, 99
    Christian, 75, 76
    church, 76n23
    with-each-other and for-each-other, 99
    New Covenant Community and, 64
final instruction, 110–18
final state, of the Thessalonians, 142
finality, eternality about, 125
financial support, of Paul, 54n6
first fruits, of field labors, 141
"first-fruits," of Thessalonica, 27
flatterers, Aristotle on, 54
"fog," of current concerns, 107
"forever" (*pantote*), meaning no going back, 95
formation, setting concern on, 115
fornication, not practicing, 79
Foster, Paul, 36n101
Frame, James, 88
fraud, rumors of Paul as, 51
Fredriksen, Paula, 11
Fronto, Marcus Cornelius, 84
fruits, knowing by, 87
full-time ministry, Christian leaders and, 153
Furnish, Victor, 96n16, 102
future, God's promises for, 2
future events, knowledge of significant, 94

Galatians, *adelphos* appearing only four times, 17n50
Gaventa, Beverly, 47–48, 81n15, 98, 124
Geertz, Clifford, 2
Gentile god-fearers, 6, 11
Gentiles
    being included in the unique adoption of Israel, 17
    common Jewish criticism of as "godless," 82
    drawing into the story and identity of Israel, 12–13
    harassed Paul and Barnabas at Iconium, 53
    some having chosen darkness, 83
    written into the story of Israel, 141
gentle (*ēpioi*), 54
ginomai, translated "to come" or "to become," 45
giveaways, 32
glorification (*doxazō*), 28, 58
"glorious kingdom," 58, 78
glorious transformation, 46
"glory," Thessalonians as Paul's own, 68
God
    allowing Thessalonians to face persecution, 124
    "beloved" truly known by, 43
    called Israel to be a holy nation, 18
    changing everything forever, 98
    chose Thessalonians to be "first fruits" for salvation, 141
    covenantal love of, 141
    displaying the true nature of, 18
    entrusting pagan rulers with authority, 135n20
    as in fact just (*dikaios*), 125
    fairness of, 29
    identity in as beloved and precious, 44
    impressing a delusion upon people, 139

intending to restore the Christian dead, 95
moving his sin-broken world towards harmony, 151
planning periods and events, 102
ultimate opponent of, 138
as witness, 51
"God of peace," destroying the work of Satan, 152
God the Father. *See* Father
God the Spirit, being taught by, 86
God-fearers, 11, 47n10
godly-behavior, Paul's concern with, 106
gods, denying the reality of, 10
"God's beloved," as a descriptor, 43
God's will, acting on behalf of, 118
"God-taught," having been, 85
good and evil, 94, 108
good news
    of Messiah Jesus, 48–49
    reception of the message of, 44
    Thessalonians initial reception of, 61
Goodman, Martin, 92n7
good-news message, "entrusted" to apostolic team, 53
Gorman, Michael, 29
grace, 75, 76
"grace and peace," Paul's wish for God's, 39
great rebellion, coming of, 133
Greco-Roman lifestyle, male sexuality and, 14
Greco-Roman world
    as fiercely competitive, 90
    sexual immorality in, 79–80
Greek deities, traditional, 4
Greeks
    adopted gods and practices of "barbarian" nations, 11
    belief in an afterlife, 92
    devout, 6
grief, with hope, 22–23
guilds, in Thessalonica, 8

hagiasmos, "consecration" ("sanctification"), 19
hands, working with, 88
happy news, of the Thessalonians' perseverance, 71
harlot (*pornē*), 79
harmony, as the ultimate hope, 29
Hays, Richard, 82n16, 89–90
heartbreak, felt by Paul, 18
hearts, God testing, 53n5
Hebrews, on Old Testament people of faith, 1
hell, 125, 126
Henny Penny, 132
Hermas Similitudes 9, 120–21
Herodion, 63n5
hindrances, as schemes of Satan, 67
historical implausibility, of 2 Thessalonians, 31–32, 34
historical reconstruction, methodology on, 9n30
holiness
    God's call to, 78–79, 80–84
    how Jews understood, 18
    Paul extending the sphere of, 19
    Paul's overall concern for, 83
    as true freedom in God, 82
    wish-prayer for, 114–16
holiness (*hagiosynē*), of the Thessalonians, 73
holiness ("religion," *hosios*), concern for proper, 83
Holmes, Michael, 16, 52, 148
holy God, idea of, 18
holy kiss, greeting and exchanging a, 116–17
Holy Spirit, 44, 87. *See also* Spirit
honor, social values of, 28
honor discourse, perspective of, 121
Hooker, Morna, 73n20
hope
    as a central theme for 1–2 Thessalonians, 22
    Christian, as not lazy, 3
    clinging to, 99
    exercising, 23
    found in Jesus alone, 13

hope (*continued*)
    grieving with, 92
    for Paul, 1
    pointing to a future, 29
    tenacious clinging to, 100
    Thessalonians as Paul's, 67
    as a worldview word, 2
hope and endurance, as themes in 1 Thessalonians, 22–23
hoping, 143, 144–46
Horace, 79
hospitality, 64
hostile rhetorical, 63
"how," of Christian living, 102
hucksters, Hellenistic concern with, 54
human agency, 127
human beings, importance of community to, 75–76
human lives, transforming and changing, 127
humiliation, patience in times of, 53n5
hybrizō ("mistreated"), 53
Hypnos (Sleep), 91
hypomonē, track record of "endurance," 41

idea, modifying in order to make it simpler, 56
identical salutations, in 1 Thess and 2 Thess, 30
"idle" (*aktateō*), not associating with or going the way of, 144, 147
"idle" or "disorderly" (*ataktoi*), emerging as a more evident problem, 15, 25
idle troublemakers
    Paul addressing, 27–28
    warning against, 147–51
idlers, asking support from the church, 88
idolatry, associated with sexual perversion and greed, 47
idols, 47–48
ignorance motif, 62

"the image of (God's) Son," reshaped into, 45
"images," dominating 1 Thessalonians, 16
impeccable character, of Paul, 57
in dubio pro reo, 36
individual attention (*hos hena hekaston hymōn*), emphasis Paul places on, 57
infant (*nēpioi*), like an, 54
infants, 56
"innocent until proven guilty," 36
insubordinates, causing trouble, 112–13
integrity
    living with, 87–88
    of Paul, 16, 53–54
"interim ethic," on moral expectations, 88
internal evidence, 55
intimacy, reinforced by the language of children, 56
Irene, facing reality that loved ones die, 98
Israel
    challenging cultural idolatry, 18n58
    crying out in pain, 93
    establishing memorials for God's faithful work, 40
    language of the adoption of, 140
    looking backward and forward, 18n58
    Lord's intimate love for, 43
    punished by God, 93
    suffering under foreign oppression in exile, 93
    Yahweh's care for, 44

Jason, 5–6, 63n5
Jesse, shoot from the stump of, 138
Jesus
    another king named, 6
    appearing in glory and vanquishing the Lawless One, 138
    becoming the firstborn, 42

being united with, 128
"coming" or "appearance"
  (*parousia*) of, 73
commanded the apostles to take
  gifts from believers, 21
derided and spat upon at his
  trial, 53
earthly words about love, 85
eschatological discourse in
  Matthew 24, 27
eschatological teaching in the
  Synoptics, 35n99
facing the shame of death on a
  cross, 46
miracles, wonders, and signs of,
  138
Paul's view of the nature of, 73
on peace, 39
as the Rescuer, 21
security in and through, 107
sharing the sufferings of, 128
slaying the Lawless One, 137
surrender and commitment to,
  46–47
waiting for the return of, 48
Jesus tradition, Paul drawing from,
  3n2
Jewish (non-Christian) prophets,
  predicted impending doom,
  102
Jewish cult, as image in 1
  Thessalonians, 18–19
Jewish hope, of the gathering together
  of the scattered exiles, 131
Jewish persecutors, "wrath of God"
  on non-Christian, 64
Jewish prophets, "predictions" of
  local, 105
Jewish texts, on suffering, 123
Jewish-Christian dialogue, sensitivity
  maintained in, 63
Jews
  attacking Jesus' followers, 133
  educated with stories reminding
    them that idols are not real
    gods, 47
  harassed Paul and Barnabas at
    Iconium, 53
  Paul's special bond with, 63n5
  Paul's statement and
    condemnation about, 62–63
  persecution from, 145
  role in the hostility against Paul's
    ministry, 10
  who persecuted believers-in-
    Jesus, 133n9
Jews and Gentiles, difference
  between, 83
Johnson, Luke Timothy, 63
Johnson-DeBraufre, M., 8
Joseph, Potiphar's wife and, 80, 83
Josephus, 58, 83
joy, of Paul at news of the
  Thessalonians, 67, 72
Judean believers, persecuted by
  Jewish neighbors, 10
judging-breath, of God, 137
judgment, Revelation's visions of, 29
"judgment" (*krisis*), Paul playing with
  the word, 124
judgment imagery, 73
Julius Caesar, 4
Junia, 63n5
justice and peace, as themes in 2
  Thessalonians, 29
justice-orientation, of God towards a
  rebellious world, 48
justification by faith, versus judgment
  according to deeds, 68n9

katabareō, root in Greek (*bar*), 52n2
kateuthynai, used in different
  contexts, 31
Keener, Craig, 134n13
"kingdom and glory," God calling
  them into, 58
kingdom of God, as a kind of
  invisible reality, 48
"kingdom of Israel," time of the
  restoration of, 102n3
"kiss of love," ecclesial holy kiss as,
  117
koimaomai, translations of, 92n4

koinōnia, meaning "commonness" or "share-ness," 74
Kreinecker, Christina, 31
Krentz, Edgar, 30, 32
ktaomai, use of, 81
kyrios, lord, Jesus referred to as, 97

labor, importance of, 87
labor and toil, of Paul, 57
lamb, "without defect or blemish," 19
last words, of Paul in 1 Thessalonians, 116–18
Lawless One, 27, 32, 108, 133, 135
    activity in "the temple of God," 134–35
    associated with the work of Satan, 138
    events surrounding the coming of, 138
    Paul not specifically identifying, 134
    persecutors of the Thessalonians as deceived followers of, 140n34
    restrainer holding back the full presence of, 137
    unveiling of, 137
lawless people, facing judgment, 140
lawlessness, 27, 136
leaders
    diligence, endurance, and reliability of, 112
    model Paul sets for Christian, 59–60
leadership
    exemption from labor for the sake of, 149
    positions of, giving us delusions of grandeur, 153
    proper respect for, 111
lectio difficilior principle, of textual criticism, 55
Left Behind books and movies, 96
letter, reading publicly in the church, 117–18
Lewis, C. S., 125–26
life, at work in you, 46

Life Together (Bonhoeffer), 75
lifestyle, 78, 82
light imagery, 105–6
living
    beyond fear, 143
    with integrity, 87–88
    quiet lives, 90, 153
load, carrying one's own, 88
logos kyriou, 96n16
Longenecker, Richard, 128–29
longing, of Paul to see the Thessalonians, 66–68, 74
longing (*epiptheō*), language of, 71
Lord
    coming of, 15
    standing against false prophets, 139n32
Lord Jesus
    "appearance of his presence," 137
    coming unexpectedly, 103
    destroying the Lawless One, 27
    Paul referring to the coming of, 131
    on provision of living for those teaching the gospel, 152
    return of, 73
Lord Messiah Jesus
    becoming one with, 127
    being brothers and sisters in, 42
    collocation with "God the Father," 39n2
    continuing to care for the Thessalonians, 143
    the dead in, 14
    defeating a great multitude of enemies, 138
    hope in, 140
    judgment of against Thessalonians persecutors, 142
    Paul extending his word of grace from, 118
    place in salvation history, 48
    as the prime model to care for the weak, 24
    putting trust in, 144
    as Son of God, 17

Louw, J.P., 70
love (*agapē*)
  as an active word, 41
  as the driving force sustaining the welfare of the church, 113
  increasing, 121
  marking communal life, 120
  Paul on, 122
  as a theme in 1 Thessalonians, 23–24
love (*philadelphia*, "sibling love"), 43, 84, 85–86
love for God, 146
"love" teachings, from the Old Testament, 85
"loved by God," as a descriptor, 43
loving sibling, safeguarding the well-being of the other, 24
"loyal endurance," of the Thessalonians, 122
loyalty (*pistis*), 21
  commending in 2 Thessalonians, 120
  concerned about the Thessalonians' *pistis*, 13
  growing, 121
  implying trust in Jesus or trust in the gospel, 145
  in an independent, unqualified way, 146
  marking the orientation of the will as an active word, 41
  meaning of, 13
  with the meaning of "pledge" or "bond," 41
  multi-faceted for Paul, 146
  not a characteristic of everyone, 146
  not belonging to everyone, 145
  Paul mentioning along with *hypomonē* (perseverance), 122
  reference to trust that goes against natural senses, 13n44
  taking on the meaning of "loyalty" or "trust," 40
  of the Thessalonians, 71

loyalty and work, as themes in 1 Thessalonians, 21–22
Lucius, 63n5
Luke, mentioning Thessalonian believers, 6n12
Luther, Martin, 3, 76n23, 134n13
Lydia, 5

Macedonia, conflict in, 43
Macedonians, 47
male genitalia, *skeuos* as a euphemism for, 81
Malherbe, Abraham, 34, 102, 112
Mark Anthony, 4
marriage, encouraging, 80–81
married woman, gratifying urges with, 84
Marshall, Howard, 9, 33, 48, 55, 131, 151
martyrs
  blessing and honor bestowed on, 121
  coming first in the resurrection, 96
  death of, 14
meddlesome lifestyle, antidote to, 151
"meeting" (*apantēsis*), 96
members of the church, death of some, 14
memories, catalyst for thanksgiving-prayer, 40
men, focus of the letters on, 8
Menken, Maarten, 132
Messiah Jesus. *See* Lord Messiah Jesus
messiahs, false, 139
"messianists," 63
metamorphosis, in 1 Thessalonians, 45–46
metaphors, mixing, 55
Metellus, 3–4
Michael (angel), 136
military analogy, portraying endurance, 41
military image, Paul's use of, 19–20
ministry, future of in the United States, 152

minority groups, powerless in the ancient world, 63
mission
 of the gospel, 20
 to seek to please God, 53
mistreatment, of the Thessalonians, 53
mistress (*hetaera*), 79
moral system, minimum-standard, 80
Morris, Leon, 33, 35, 145, 148
mortals, seeking the praise of, 59
mother, tenderly nourishing her beloved, 18
motherly image, of Paul in his letters, 18n53
mutuality, at the heart of Paul's concern, 107
mysterion, insofar as it is kept hidden, 136
mystery of lawlessness, 136

Nero *redivivus*, 32, 34
Nero *redivivus* theory, 134n13
New Covenant Community
 in action, 107–9
 grieving with hope, 99
 meant to be a fellowship for all people, 64
 as a people of prayer, 118
new covenant people, unique "way" of, 87
New Testament
 Christians preferring to read, 107
 combative language permeating, 108
NFFNSNC (*non fui, fui, non sum, non curo*), 92
Nida, Eugene, 70
night and darkness, symbolic relationships of, 105
"night/darkness" - people, 102
night-thief, language of, 103
non-ministry-related income, 152
nothing new under the sun, 59
Nouwen, Henri, 64
"nursing mother," metaphor of, 56

"objective genitive" reading, 146n6
Octavian, 4
Oden, Thomas, 119
opposition, being vigilant in the face of, 19
oppressors, punishment of, 125
oracle, consulting, 113
other-centeredness, at the heart of Paul's concern, 107
other-regard, ethic of, 112
"other-regarding morality," reinforcing, 85
ou mē, rare Greek negative construction, 95n14
Oxyrhynchus (Egypt), ancient letter found from, 98

paederasty, not commiting, 79
pagan worship, as a kind of ignorance and slavery, 47
Parable of the Prodigal Son, father kissed him, 117
parachurch ministry, mentor on staff with a Christian, 153
paramythia, related to *paramytheomai*, 58n19
Parousia, 95, 102, 106
parrēsiazomai, 53
pastors, 9, 59–60
patron-client system, 89
Paul
 addressing local issues, 111
 affection for the Thessalonians, 57
 as anti-Semitic, 62–63
 attentiveness to the Thessalonians in prayer, 72
 attuned to the reality of a cosmic war, 20
 becoming like an infant, 45
 calling the Thessalonians to persevere, 151
 choosing to not be dependent financially on his churches, 152
 combined general apostolic wisdom with concrete things, 111

concern for the Thessalonians, 66, 69
courage of, 52–53
defending himself, 16
as defensive, 50–51
embodying a kind, Moses-like encouragement, 58
encouraging Thessalonians left alive, 93
on eschatological events, 26–27
establishing a clear line dividing day-people from night-people, 106
examined and approved by God for his ministry, 51
facing Jewish opposition in Corinth, 145
final instructions and statements of, 110–18
fled from Thessalonica to Berea, 66
focus on bringing glory to the Mesiah, 54
gifts accepted, 54n6
having little or no interest in "hell," 126
having no need to copy himself, 31
on hope, 1, 3
hope in the Thessalonians, 22
humbly asking for prayer, 145
ignorance motif, 62
integrity of, 53–54
Jewish hostility against, 7
linking suffering with being worthy of the kingdom of God, 128
longing to see the Thessalonians, 66–68, 74
made his own living, 21
maintaining confidence in the Messiah, 73n20
as master-builder, 2
metaphors and images in 1 Thessalonians, 16
ministry of, 50–60

minor matters addressed in 1 Thessalonians, 15
not condemning all Jews of all time, 63
not quoting Old Testament (LXX) in 1 Thessalonians, 12
offering his prayer-wish both to God the Father and Jesus, 73
offering peace, 39
opened himself up to sharing life together with the Thessalonians, 76
performed signs and wonders, 138
pointing out his own habit of working for a living, 27–28
prayer-wishes of, 72–74
preached about Messiah Jesus, 5
premature separation from the Thessalonians, 51
reasons for writing 1 Thessalonians, 9–12, 13–14, 15–16
referring to fellow Jesus-believers, 63n5
referring to working with hands, 8
reminding Thessalonians that the Lord is faithful, 146
requesting prayer for apostolic work, 145
responsible for the offering of the Gentiles, 19
as restrainer, 135–36
sensitive to suffering and shame of Thessalonians, 121
serving as an example of one who "works for his own bread," 152
setting converts' eyes on hope beyond the grave, 95
style of undisputed letters, 31
sudden disappearance from Thessalonica, 16
tender care of, 54, 56–59
as their brother through Jesus, 18
in Thessalonica, 5–6

Paul (continued)
  undergoing a change for the sake of the Thessalonians, 46
  understanding of "hell," 125
  vision of a "man of Macedonia," 5
  vulnerability of, 67n2
  wanted to be with the Thessalonians, 72
  warned disciples about persecutions, 128
  on work, 3
  worked to stay above reproach regarding money, 21–22
  on wrath (*orgē*), 20–21
  writing 1 Thessalonians as a form of subversive rhetoric, 13
  writing 1 Thessalonians to a community losing its faith, 2
Pauline apostolic team, 50n1
Pauline authentication, 151–52
Pauline authorship, of 2 Thessalonians, 30–35
peace
  offered by whom, 104
  Paul conveying words of, 39
peace (*eirēnē*)
  Paul preaching, 112
  Paul's ultimate interest in, 29
peace (*shalom*), 151
"peace and security," as a slogan in support of Roman power and protection, 104–5
peace benediction, 151–52
peculiarities, of Paul's letters, 34
penultimate (next-to-last) activity, 29
peri de construction, 101
Peri Philadelphia/ De fraterno amore - "On brotherly love" (Plutarch), 85
persecution
  experienced by the Thessalonians, 10
  injustices of will be overturned, 139–40
  as the lot of Christians, 128–29
  Paul including himself as enduring, 125
  positive feature of, 128
  praiseworthy endurance amidst, 61–65
  struggling with ongoing, 98
  as a theme in 2 Thessalonians, 25
  Thessalonians faced bitter, 46–49
  true followers of Jesus bound to face, 69–70
persecutors, inevitable judgment upon, 25
perseverance
  encouraging, 131–32
  of Messiah Jesus, 146
  Paul inspiring, 142
  Thessalonians' good news of, 69–72
persons, tripartite view of, 115
philadelphia (sibling-love), matter of, 17
Philip II, 3
Philip V, 3
Philippi, Paul and Silas beaten and imprisoned, 5
Philippian church, Paul identifying, 12n41
Philo, 83, 120
Phoebe, 7
pistis. *See* loyalty (*pistis*)
Pitts, Andrew, 34, 34n95
pleasing message, of the Thessalonians' perseverance, 71
pledges of loyalty, within a covenantal relationship, 13
Plutarch, 85
polemic, primarily for internal consumption, 63
politarchs, 5
Pompeii, graffiti, 80
Pompey, profaned the Jerusalem temple, 134
Pope, as the "man of sin" and "son of perdition," 134n13
porneia (sexual immorality), 79
positive value, of the language of holiness, 78
Potiphar, respect for, 83

powerless, Thessalonians not, 145
praise, sacrifice of, 120
praise-worthy trust, thanksgiving for
    the Thessalonians,' 39–42,
    43–45, 46–49
"pray without ceasing," 118
prayer
    for the apostolic mission and
        worldwide glorification of the
        gospel, 144
    becoming a term associated with
        a believing will, 118
    explanation of in 2 Thessalonians,
        116n18
    in the name of Jesus, 145
    for Paul and his co-workers, 116
prayerful disposition, 114, 118
prayer-life, constancy and passion of
    Paul's, 40
prayer-wishes, of Paul, 66, 72–74
praying, with no beginning or end,
    118
preciousness, in God's eyes, 43–44
"predestination," 43
prescript
    to 1 Thessalonians, 38–39
    to 2 Thessalonians, 119
"pride," noble kind of, 68
priority, of dead believers in the
    Messiah, 96
Priscilla, 8n24
privilege, of believing in Christ and of
    suffering for him as well, 129
problems, working through, 71
prophecies
    false, 15
    judging, 114
prophets
    false, 139
    local pagan or Jewish, 114n9
pseudonymity, 33–35
pseudonymous "tells," in 2
    Thessalonians, 32, 34–35
psychē
    interpreting as "the seat of
        affection and will," 57n16

    translated as "souls" but not a
        spiritual self, 57
punishment, of eternal destruction,
    125
purity (*amemptos*), 73, 79

quiet lives, 90, 153
"quietness," 88

radical transformation, sense of, 95
Rahab, 47
Raphael (angel), 136n23
"rapture" theology, 96, 97n19
Ready for the Night Thief section,
    102–3
reality, social nature of
    understanding, 2
rebellion
    among those claiming to know
        God, 26
    human participants in, 133
rebellious attitude, Paul warning
    against, 150
"rebellious idle," 112
refusing, to work, 144
"register," defined, 34n95
"register influences," 34
religion
    in Roman Thessalonica, 4–5
    strengthened the existing social
        order, 10
religious life, lived at all times, 78
resistance to God, supercharged by
    God, 139
response to afflictions, as proof of
    God's right judgment, 124
restoration, emphasis on, 98
restrainer
    holding back the Lawless One,
        27, 137
    as Paul, 135–36
    as the principle of law and order,
        135
    as spiritual power, 136
resurrection
    of the dead, 75
    of "the dead in the Messiah," 94

resurrection (*continued*)
  waiting just as morning waits for the sleepers, 92
revelation, "apocalyptic: worldview and, 94
Revelation (book of)
  encouraging Smyrnians to endure, 70
  judgment language in, 29
reward, great in heaven, 128
Richard, Earl, 36n101, 135n20
right judgment of God, "evidence" (*endeigma*) of, 123
righteous, God dealing strictly with the, 123
righteousness, signposts of, 103
role models, leaders serving as, 112
Roma, cult in honor of the goddess, 5
Roman Empire, as restrainer of the Lawless One, 135
"Roman slogan," 104–5
Roman society, sexual license in, 79
Roman soldiers, characteristics of, 20
Romans
  adopted gods and practices of "barbarian" nations, 11
  belief in an afterlife, 92
"ruffians," incited to turn the city against Paul and Silas, 5

salvation
  "first fruits" for, 141
  God destined the Thessalonians for, 107
Satan
  as the arch-tempter and deceiver, 138
  blocking the way, 67
  empowering the Lawless One, 138
  God's adversary, 67
  grandiose rebel in league with, 134
  no power to control human will, 70
  as presently active, 137
Schmidt, J. E. C., 30n76

school shootings, on the campus of a Christian college, 99
seasons (*kairos*), meaning of, 102n2
Seattle Pacific University (SPU), shooting at, 99–100
Second Advent, epoch of, 132n7
Secundus, 6n12
security, offered by whom, 104
"seer," 94
self, transformation of, 127
self-control, repeated teaching about, 79
self-preservation, natural focus on, 112
self-sustaining community, believers living in, 88
sender-recipient-greeting, in ancient letters, 38
separated (*aporphanizō*), image of, 66
Serapeion temple, 4
service, as life-giving, 48
"serving a new master" (*douleuō*), 48
sexual immorality, in the Greco-Roman world, 79–80
sexual passions, in the Greco-Roman world, 78–79
sexual purity
  addressed by Paul in 1 Thessalonians, 14
  Paul's overall concern for, 83
sexual vices, choice to indulge in, 82
"shaken," *sainomai*, defined, 70
shalom - benediction, 144
shame, 28, 142
"shared-ness," associated with *koinōnia*, 74
Shogren, Gary, 149
"sibling love" (*philadelphia*), 84–85
sibling relationship
  in the Roman world, 17n51
  superior to one of friendship, 85
siblings
  Christian, 42, 52
  in the Greco-Roman world, 42
siblingship
  distinctive (and strange) early Christian use of, 84

linking perfect strangers by the bond of, 42–43
"signs and wonders" (miracles), manifestation of, 44
"signs and wonders" (*sēmeiois kai terasin*), false, 138
Silas, 5, 45, 66, 145
Silvanus, 38, 52–53, 130
"silver lining," of death, 93
sin, as a battle for control, 81
sinful hostility, meet divine reckoning, 62
Sirach apocryphal text, 41
Sitz im Leben (life setting), 36n102
Skeen, Judy, 150
slaughtered lamb, image of, 108
slave of Yahweh, becoming, 48
slavery, sexual immorality and, 79
sleep, "metaphor for absorption in the affairs of the world," 106n16–7n16
Smyrnian church, 70
social club, kind of, 88–89
social gatherings, fellowship referring to, 74
social problems, relating issue of idleness with, 88–89
socio-cultural dimensions, of kissing in Paul's world, 117
socio-economic problem, of leeching off wealthier church members, 148
soldiers, characteristics of model, 109
"the Son of Destruction," 133
"sons of darkness," in the Dead Sea scrolls texts, 106n15
"sons of light," in the Dead Sea scrolls texts, 106n15
Sosipater, 63n5
"soul," meaning of, 116
Spicq, Ceslas, 148n12
Spirit. *See also* Holy Spirit
    inward, transformative work of, 85
    living according to, 82
    not suppressing, 114
    presence of the Lord through, 151–52
    walking by, 142
"spirit," meaning of, 116
"spirit, soul, and body," preserving at the Parousia, 115
Spirit-empowered mission, taking priority over eschatological knowledge, 102n3
spiritual ancestors, story of, 82n16
spiritual battle, believers taught to engage in, 108–9
spiritual leaders, local leaders "dubbing" themselves, 27
spiritual power, as the restrainer, 136
standing with God, measuring by misfortunes, 124
Steele, Richard, 99–100
Still, Todd, 7, 69n11, 122
stubbornness, of Paul, 53
style, of 2 Thessalonians, 31, 34
"subjective genitive" reading, 146n6
subversive rhetoric, form of, 13
suffering
    bringing out weakness, 121
    everyone will face, 129
    inevitability of Christian, 70
    for the kingdom as blessing, 127–29
    not a sign of shame, 28
    not the last word, 142
    theological reflection on the meaning of, 123
suffering and wrath, as penultimate things, 29
suffering or perseverance, God's fairness and, 123
sure salvation, hope of, 21
sword, striking down the nations, 108
symphyletēs, meaning of, 10, 10n34–11n34, 12
synagogue population, of interested outsiders, 11n37
synergism, 127

Tacitus, 26n70
takt, meaning "order," 147

Subject Index

"teaching," infused with an ineffable sweetness, 86
team, Paul, Silvanus, and Timothy as, 38
temple, Lawless One setting himself up in, 34
temple service and sacrifice, holiness of, 18
temptation
 defined, 70n15
 to exploit the kindness of others, 87
"Tempter," as Satan, 70
tender care, of Paul, 54, 56–59
tent-makers
 being, 152
 Christian leaders as, 153
testimony, idea of public, confident, 53
testing, preparing for, 53n5
Thanatos (Death), 91
thanksgiving
 expressing to God, 140
 for faithful endurance, 120–22
 following an opening greeting, 40
 for the Thessalonians' praise-worthy trust, 39–42, 43–45, 46–49
thanksgiving and joy, 23
themes
 in 1 Thessalonians, 20–24
 in 2 Thessalonians, 28–29
Theocritus, 92
theodicy, 29
theodicy issue, Paul addressing, 61
theodidaktoi ("God-taught" or "taught by God"), 85n22
Theodora, Junia, 7n17
Theodore of Mopsuestia, 126n18
theologian, being a successful, 119
theological differences
 in 2 Thessalonians, 32–33
 not a serious obstacle in view of authenticity, 35
"theology," compared to "ethics," 78
theories, devised to determine an original word, 55

Thessalonian church, Paul's attachment to, 74
Thessalonian Jewish synagogue, 5
Thessalonians
 believing that the "Day of the Lord" had arrived, 25–26
 called to share in the glory of Messiah Jesus, 142
 church of, 6–9
 clandestine attack by opponents, 14–15
 confused by the predictions of local prophets, 102
 consulting oracles, 113
 doubting their sense of worth and dignity, 28
 enjoined to remember their own record of trust, 40
 facing many burdens, worries, and afflictions, 39
 God's own relationship and attitude towards them, 43
 as mostly Gentile believers, 7n15, 47
 not failing in their obedience to God, 78
 not in darkness, 83
 pattern shared with believers in Judea, 61
 Paul's relationship with, 67
 persecuted by Gentile Thessalonians, 10
 as safe and secure in Messiah Jesus, 26
 struggled with pressures from those around them, 28
 things not getting better after Paul's first letter, 24–25
1 Thessalonians
 images and themes in, 16–24
 Paul's reasons for writing, 9–12, 13–14, 15–16
 prescript, 38–39
 saturated with Old Testament imagery, 12
 written before Mark, 3n2

Subject Index 181

written for the sake of the Thessalonians, 52
2 Thessalonians
   author's preference for longer and more complex sentences, 31
   authorship of, 24n65, 30–35
   conclusion on authorship, 36–37
   copying or a conscious dependence on 1 Thessalonians, 31
   defending Pauline authorship of, 33–35
   including vocabulary unusual for Paul, 30n77
   not offering a point-by-point timeline of eschatological events, 26
   prescript, 119
   relationship to 1 Thessalonians, 24
   similarity to 1 Thessalonians, 30
   the story continues, 24–37
   themes of, 28–29
   timing of the writing of, 24n66–25n66
Thessalonica
   city of, 3–4
   Paul in, 5–6
   political moves by, 3–4
   religion in, 4–5
Thomson, James, 19
"thorn in the flash," as a messenger from Satan, 67
Thurston, Bonnie, 36n102
timeline, phases in, 102
times (chronos), meaning of, 102n2
"times and seasons," 101, 102
Timothy, 52–53
   dispatched to see about *pistis*, 13
   "good news" of ongoing allegiance to the Messiah, 21
   in prescript of 1 Thessalonians, 38
   report of "trust and love," 41
   requesting prayer for apostolic work, 145
   returned with news that the Thessalonians were enduring, 71
   sent to check in on the Thessalonians, 69
   unknown by non-Christian opposition, 69n11
Titus, not taking advantage of the Thessalonians, 51
tone, of 2 Thessalonians, 32, 34
Torah (the Law of Moses), 145
tradition
   appeals to, 31–32, 34
   holding firmly to, 131, 142
   language of in the New Testament, 142n39
trials, faith of believers strengthened by, 71
"trichotomist," 115
troublemakers
   avoiding, 152
   in a crisis, 113
   establishing as deviants, 147
   sowed the seed of fear, 132
Trozzo, Lindsey, 8
trust, in the truth, 142
trust, hope, and love, Paul's triad of, 40
"truth" of the world, living contrary to, 142

ultimate (final) activity, 29
"unalterable togetherness," 95
unbelievers, in Judea, 145n3
unjust suffering, of the Thessalonians, 61–62

vengefulness, not giving vent to, 99
"vessel" (*skeuos*), 80–81, 81n12
Via Egnatia, 4
vigilance
   Christian, 102
   required, 137
vindication, Thessalonians will experience, 126
virtues, Pauline triad of, 107
vocabulary, of 2 Thessalonians, 30n77

"voluntary association," Thessalonian church as, 88–89
vulnerability, of Paul, 67n2

"wait" (*anamenō*), as in "to stay put," 48
"walking" (*peripateō*), idea behind, 78
Wanamaker, Charles, 57
wandering spiritualists, 149
war metaphors, used by Paul, 19–20
"warfare," not characterized by violence, 20
warriors, people of God as, 108
way of the world, not copying, 90
weak, dedicating yourself to caring for, 24
"weak" (*asthenēs*), mentioned by Paul, 112
"webs of significance," sustaining a larger world, 2
weight (*baros*), Paul's use of, 54
Weima, Jeffrey, 51, 132
Wesley, John, 135n19
White, Joel, 105
wicked
    granting ease to, 123
    punishment of, 126n18
"wicked and evil people," impeding Paul's ministry, 145
the wicked and the righteous, dividing line between, 135
widows, neglected in the daily food distribution, 152
wife, function of, 79
will of God, 78, 113–14
Winter, Bruce, 89
wise decision-making, judgment as, 124
wish-prayers
    in 1 Thessalonians, 19
    giving attention to calling and faith and sure hope in Jesus, 126
for holiness, 114–16
for strength and comfort, 143
that the Lord might direct hearts, 146
with-each-other and for-each-other fellowship, 99
Witherington, Ben, 89, 114, 117
wives, restricting sexual activity to, 81
women, of wealth and influence, 6, 7
"word of God," initial reception of, 61
"word of the Lord"
    meaning of Paul's phrase, 95n16–96n16
    Paul's appeal to, 94
    as uniquely powerful, 137
"word of the Lord" (*ho logos tou kuriou*), 145
word pictures, 16
work
    focus on those refusing to, 28
    importance of, 21, 22, 87
    Paul using the language of, 3
    underscoring the value of good, honest, 28
    as a virtue, 111
"working" (*ergazomai*), Paul's language for, 150
working "quietly" (*meta ēsuxias*), 151
work/labor, statements about, 41
work-policy, Paul's, 45
world, defying leading to afflictions, 129
world-structure, threats and challenges to, 2
"wrath" and salvation, as themes in 1 Thessalonians, 20–21
wrath of fire, blamed on fire, 15
wrath of God, 13, 48, 62
Wrede, W., 30n76
Wright, N. T., 68, 115–16
writing by hand, Paul mentioning, 35n98

Yahweh, 44, 82

Scripture Index

ANCIENT NEAR EASTERN DOCUMENTS

Genesis Rabbah
33.1	124

Jewish Antiquities
2.	83
2.42	83

OLD TESTAMENT

LXX
	12

Genesis
1.	22
39:12	80
49	83

Exodus
19:6	18

Leviticus
1–9	19
10:10	18

Numbers
28–29	19

Deuteronomy
6:4–12	78
7:7–10	141–142
7:18	40
13:1–3	139
13:12	105n11
16:1–16	142

Joshua
2:9–11	47
4:7	40

Ruth
4:10	80

1 Kings
19:10	142
19:14	142

1 Chronicles
29:25	58

Nehemiah
10:1	13n43
10:37	142

Job
12:22	106
29:3	106

Psalms

13:10–1 ??	124
18:28	106
33:6	138
42:1	71
51:7 LXX	62n1
52:5	62n1
77	18n57
81:12	140
139:11–12	106

Proverbs

17:3	53n5
30:27	148n9

Ecclesiastes

1:9	59
2:13	106
4:1	103

Isaiah

5:1	43
5:20	106
11:1–2	139
11:4	139
30:33	138
40:7	138
44	44
44:1–2	44
53:4	24
57:8	43
63	94
63:17	94
64:1	94

Jeremiah

6:14	105
12:7	43

Ezekiel

13:9	140n32
13:10	105, 106
13:10a	105
13:16	105

Daniel

2:21	103
2:22	106
12:1	137

Hosea

6:1–3	22–23
11:1	43

Amos

5:18	106, 132
5:20	132

Jonah

1:6	114

Malachi

1:2	43

APOCRYPHA

3 Maccabees

5:51	138n30
6:18–19	138n30

4 Ezra

	139
13:9–10	139

Apocalypse of Sedrach

11.2	81n12
11.6	81n12

Bel and the Dragon

1:5	47

Judith

7.12	48

Psalms of Solomon

13:10–12	124
17:11–15	135

Sirach

2:1–5	53n5
2:14	41
17:24	42
36.29	80

On the Special Laws

1.224	121

Testament of Naphtali

2.2	81n12

Tobit

8:3	137

Wisdom

8:1–8	103

Wisdom of Solomon

6.1–4	136n20

NEW TESTAMENT

Matthew

4:8	58
7:13–14	135n11
7:15	140
7:20	87
8:17 NET	24
9:24	93
10:34	109
24	27
24:3	73
24:4–5	27
24:6–8	27
24:9	27
24:10	27
24:11	27, 140
24:13	27
24:14	146
24:24	140
24:27	73
24:30–31	97n16
24:36–44	104
24:37	73
24:39	73
24:43–44	104

Mark

5:39	93
13:7	105n11
13:22	140
13:34–37	3n2
16:15	146

Luke

6:22–23	129
8:52	93
12:38–40	104
12:41–48	15
13:4–5	114
18:32	53
21:9	105n11

John

1:11	46
11:19	58
11:31	58
14:27	39, 153
16:2	134n9
16:2–3	62
16:33	129
19:29	80
21:25	97n16

Acts

	153
1:6–7	103n3
2:22	139
5:41	125, 129
6:1–3	153
9:16	125
14	129
14:5	53
14:15	47
14:22	129
15:12	139
16:9	5
16–17	9

Acts (continued)

17	6, 6n15, 10, 12
17:1–2	5
17:1–10a	10, 11
17:4	5, 6, 7, 12
17:5–6	5
17:6–7	6
17:8–10	66
17:10	6
17:10a	16
17:11	6
17:13	6
17:14	51
18:5–17	146
20	25
20:4	6n12
27:2	6n12

Romans 31, 35n98

1:7	57
1:9	40, 51
1:11	72
1:12	72
1:18–32	82, 83, 140
1:21	83
2:6	74
2:22	47
5:3–4	71
5:3–5	23
6:12	82
6:17	34
6:19	81
8:17	69, 129
8:29	17, 42, 45
8:30	58
8:31	142
8:38–39	43
9:4	17
11:17	82
12:12 NET	46
12:19–20	63
13:11–14	107
13:12	19, 20, 83
13:14	82
15:3	24
15:13	44
15:16	19, 68
15:19	44, 139
15:30–31	146n3
16:7	63n5
16:11	63n5
16:16	118n22
16:17	34
16:17–18	153
16:20	67, 95, 119n23, 139, 153
16:21	63n5

1 Corinthians 21, 35, 82n16

1:1–2	19
4:5	67, 107
4:12	87
4:13	46
4:14	57
5:9–10	90
5:10–11	47
6:9	47
6:13	81
6:18	81
7:5	70, 139
7:17	102
8:1	102
9.	150
9:6–7	21
9:14	153
9:18	153
10:1 NRSV	82n16
10:11	96
10:14	57
11:2	34
12:1	102
13:13	40
15:23	94
15:31	68
15:52	99
15:57	99
16:1	102
16:20	118n22
16:21	34–35, 35n98
16:23	119n23

2 Corinthians 35n98, 51

1:2–5	153

1:19	38
1:23	51
2:11	67, 95, 139
3:18	45
4:8–9	99
4:12	46
5:7	3, 13n44, 143
5:17	96
6:7	19
6:14–16	107
7:4	68
10:3–6	109
10:4	19
10:17	68
11:14	139
12:7	139
12:7–8	67, 67n4
12:11–19	51
12:12	139
12:14–19	52
12:14–19 NET	51
12:16	52
12:21	81
13:12	118n22
13:13	119n23

1–2 Corinthians
31

Galatians
	31
1:9	143n39
1:23	146
2:9	38
2:14	149n12
3:28	64
4:5	17
5:11	17n50
5:13	17n50
5:16	82
5:20	47
5:24	82
6:1	17n50
6:2	88
6:4	68
6:6	88
6:9	152

6:11	35n98
6:18	17n50, 119n23
6:21	17n50
6:23	17n50

Ephesians
	33
1:5	17
5:27	19
6:11	95
6:11–17	19
6:12	109
6:16	67

Philippians
	31
1:8	51
1:10	94, 132
1:23	94
1:27	58, 75
1:28	135n11
2:2	75
2:5–11	46, 58
2:8	46
2:12	57
2:16	68, 94, 132
4:11–12	23
4:15	54n6
4:23	119n23

Colossians
	33, 36
1:13	17
1:13 AT	39
2:6	143n39
3:5	47
4:3	117n18
4:3–4	117n18
4:10–11	63n5
4:18	35n98

1 Thessalonians
1, 2, 3n2, 6n15, 9, 11, 12, 13, 14, 16, 16–18, 17, 18, 19, 20, 21, 21n62, 24, 25, 28, 31, 32

Scripture Index

1 Thessalonians

	32–33, 33, 35n98, 36, 42, 45, 52, 61, 62n3, 74, 77, 88, 120, 121
1:1	12, 17, 30, 38, 39, 42, 69
1:1–2	120
1:1–10	38–49
1:2	40, 119
1:2–3	23
1:2–10	39–42, 42, 43–45, 46–49
1:3	1, 3, 13, 17, 21, 24, 41, 42, 67, 87, 108, 112, 122, 122n7
1:4	12, 17n50, 43, 58, 108, 141
1:5	12, 44, 45, 61
1:5–7	45
1:6	10, 23, 45, 46
1:7	45
1:7–8	47
1:8	12, 13, 21, 122
1:9	8, 11n36, 47, 67n2
1:9–10	6, 11, 83, 136n18
1:10	2, 12, 21, 42, 48, 138
1:10b	48
1:29	69
2:1	17n50
2:1–2	52–53
2:1–7b	56
2:1–12	16, 45, 50, 50–60, 51, 52, 54n6, 66, 67
2:3	52, 53
2:3–7a	52, 53
2:4	51, 59
2:4a	53
2:4b	54
2:5	51, 54, 57
2:6	54
2:7	9, 18, 18n53, 45, 46, 54, 55
2:7–3:13	74
2:7b	54, 55–56, 56
2:7b–12	52, 54, 56–59
2:7c	56
2:7c–8	56
2:8	57, 76
2:9	3, 7, 17n50, 45, 51, 52, 57, 87, 112, 151
2:9–12	52
2:9b	54
2:10	45, 51, 57
2:11–12	18, 57
2:12	56, 58, 58n19, 78
2:13	23, 30, 61, 143n39
2:13–16	61–65, 62
2:14	10, 17n50, 45
2:14–15	46
2:14–16	10–11, 12, 62–63, 63, 64, 134n9, 146
2:15	7, 10, 13
2:16	61, 62
2:17	9, 17n50, 18, 51, 66, 74
2:17–3:10	66
2:17–3:13	66–76
2:17–20	66–68
2:17a NRSV	66n1
2:18	38, 67, 139
2:19	1, 22, 67n6, 73
2:19–20	74
3.	13
3:1–6	13
3:1–10	69–72
3:1–12	69
3:2	13, 17n50, 38, 69, 122
3:3	70
3:3–4	70
3:3b	69
3:4	34
3:5	3, 13, 38, 74, 87, 112, 122
3:5–7	13
3:5b	70
3:6	16, 21, 41, 71, 122
3:6b	71
3:7	17n50, 71, 122
3:8	71, 74
3:9	23, 72
3:10	9, 13, 41, 72, 122

Scripture Index 189

3:11	17, 31, 73	5:3	15, 39, 104, 105–106, 106
3:11–13	66, 72–74, 73		
3:12	24, 73, 122	5:4	17n50, 83
3:13	17, 19, 73	5:4–7	103, 106–107
3:13–14	115	5:4–11	107
4:1	12, 17n50, 71, 78	5:5	12
4:1–2	78	5:6	87
4:1–3	73	5:8	1, 3, 13, 19, 21, 40, 83, 87, 122
4:1–8	78–79, 80–84		
4:1–12	77–90	5:8–11	103, 107–108, 109
4:3	12, 19, 80, 114	5:9	12, 15, 21
4:3–4	14	5:9–10	108
4:3–5	83	5:11	42, 108
4:4	8, 80, 82	5:12	17n50
4:4–5	80	5:12–13	87
4:5	12, 78, 82	5:12–15	15, 112–114
4–5	93n3	5:12–22	108
4:6	14, 17n50, 63, 83	5:12–28	111–119
4:6b	84	5:13	3, 122
4:7	12, 78, 84	5:14	7, 15, 17n50, 24, 25, 27, 28, 87, 113, 148
4:8	84, 87		
4:9	17, 42, 43, 85, 122	5:15	42, 113
4:9–10	24, 78, 84, 85–86	5:16–18	114
4:9–11	15	5:16–22	114–115
4:9–12	88	5:17	40, 111, 119
4:10	17n50, 73, 122	5:18	23, 114
4:11	3, 7, 8, 23, 88, 89, 90, 152	5:20–21	15
		5:23	19, 73, 116
4:11–12	22, 78, 80, 87–88, 149n12	5:23–24	30, 59, 115–117
		5:24	59, 96
4:12	88	5:25–27	17n50
4:13	1, 17n50, 22	5:25–28	117–119
4:13–18	14, 92–101, 102	5:27	38, 118
4:15	14, 51, 73, 92, 95, 96		

1–2 Thessalonians

13n44, 22

4:15–17	94, 95, 96, 97n16
4:16	95, 97, 138
4:16–17	98

2 Thessalonians

15, 24, 24n65, 26, 28–29, 29, 30, 31, 32, 33, 34, 35, 36, 36n101, 36n102, 37n103, 114n6, 117n18, 120, 121, 133, 135, 135n13, 142

4:17	2, 96, 97, 132
4:18	42, 99
5:1	17n50, 103n2
5:1–2	34
5:1–3	103–104
5:1–11	15, 25, 88, 102, 102–110, 105
5:2	26, 132
5:2–3	15
1.	124

Reference	Pages
1:1	30, 120n2
1:1–2	120
1:1–3	131
1:1–12	120–130
1:2	120n2
1:3	28, 122, 122n7, 141
1:3–4	121–123
1:3–5	129
1:4	28, 123, 131
1:5	28, 124, 125
1:5–10	123–126, 127, 131, 143
1:6	126
1:7	126, 143
1:8	126
1:8–9	95n13, 143
1:9	126–127
1:10	127
1:11–12	127–128, 131
1:12	28
1:24	140
1:26	140
1:28	140
1:29	130
2.	25, 125, 144
2:1	73, 132
2:1–2	26, 132–133
2:1–12	26, 30n76, 32, 131
2:1–17	131–144
2:2	25, 132, 132n5
2:3	26, 134
2:3–4	27
2:3–11	135n11
2:3–12	133–141, 136, 138
2:4	34
2:5	136
2:6	136
2:6–8	27
2:7	137
2:8	27, 73, 94, 95n13, 109, 138, 139, 143
2:9	135
2:9–10	27
2:9–11	139
2:10	140
2:12	141, 152
2:13	30
2:13–14	143
2:13–15	27, 141–143
2:14	28
2:15	31, 132
2:16	1
2:16–17	144
2:20	146
3:1	117n18, 146
3:1–2	145
3:1–5	145–147
3:1–18	145–154
3:2	147
3:2b	146
3:2c	146
3:3–5	145, 147
3:4	147
3:5	147
3:6	31, 148, 149n12, 150
3:6–7	145
3:6–12	27, 148, 148–152
3:6–15	25, 150, 152
3:7	148
3:7–9	151
3:8	149
3:9	28, 150
3:10	145, 149, 151
3:10 NLT	28
3:11	27, 145, 148, 149
3:13	152
3:13–15	148–152
3:14	28
3:14–15	25
3:15	28, 145
3:16	31, 145
3:16–18	152–153
3:17	32, 34, 35
3:18	119n23
3:23	146
3:25	146
6:10	146

1 Timothy

5:13	151
5:15	67, 139
6:6	59

6:21	119n23

2 Timothy
4:22	119n23
1–2 Timothy	33

Titus
	33
3:15	119n23

Philemon
	31
1:19	35n98
1:25	119n23

Hebrews
9:14	47
11:13	1
12:1	41

James
5:7–8	73

1 Peter
	130
1:8	127
1:18	19
2:11	82
3:7	81n11
4:3	47
5:8	67
5:10	130
5:14	118

2 Peter
1:16	73
2:1	140
3:4	73
3:10	74, 104
3:11–13	104
3:12	73
3:12–13	94

1 John
2:28	73
4:1	140

2 John
1:12	9

Jude
9	95n12, 137

Revelation
2:2–3	42
2:10	70
7:17	99
12:7	137
16:15	104n7
19:15	109
19:20	140
19:20a	140
21:4	99

DEAD SEA SCROLLS

1QM (War Scroll)
	107n15

1QS (Rule of the Congregation)
	107n15

GRECO-ROMAN WRITINGS

Dem
23.141	103n2

Eth. Nic.
4.6.9	54

Xenophon, *Conviv*
2.10	80–81

EARLY CHRISTIAN WRITING

Aquinas, Thomas
Summa Theologiae
    70n15

Chrysostom, John
Homilies on 1 Thessalonians III.335
    67n6

Homily 4   142n36

Didache   150n16
1:4	79
2:2	79
3:3	79
5:1	79
11:3–6	150

1 Clement
42.3	44n9

Hermas Similitudes
9	121
9.28.3	122
9.28.4	122
9.28.5	122

www.ingramcontent.com/pod-product-compliance
Lightning Source LLC
Chambersburg PA
CBHW030855170426
43193CB00009BA/619